RABI

THIS BOOK IS PUBLISHED AS PART

OF AN ALFRED P. SLOAN FOUNDATION PROGRAM

RABI

Scientist and Citizen

JOHN S. RIGDEN

Basic Books, Inc., Publishers

NEW YORK

Library of Congress Cataloging-in-Publication Data

Rigden, John S.
    Rabi, Citizen and Scientist

    (Alfred P. Sloan Foundation series)
    Bibliographic Notes: p. 264
    Includes index.
    1. Rabi, I. I. (Isidor Isaac), 1898–   . 2. Physics—
United States—History.   3. Physicists—United States—
Biography.   I. Title.   II. Series.
QC16.R2R54   1987   530′.92′4   [B]   86–47736
ISBN   0–465–06792–1

CONTENTS

Contents

PREFACE TO THE SERIES

FOR many years the Alfred P. Sloan Foundation has had an interest in encouraging public understanding of science. Science in this century has become a complex endeavor. Scientific statements may reflect as many as four centuries of experimentation and theory, and are likely to be expressed in the language of advanced mathematics or in highly technical terms. As scientific knowledge expands, the goal of general public understanding of science becomes increasingly difficult to reach.

Yet an understanding of the scientific enterprise, as distinct from data, concepts, and theories, is certainly within the grasp of us all. It is an enterprise conducted by men and women who are stimulated by hopes and purposes that are universal, rewarded by occasional successes, and distressed by setbacks. Science is an enterprise with its own rules and customs, but an understanding of that enterprise is accessible, for it is quintessentially human. And an understanding of the enterprise inevitably brings with it insights into the nature of its products.

Accordingly, the Sloan Foundation has encouraged some outstanding and articulate scientists to set down personal accounts of their lives in science. The form these accounts take has been left to each author: an autobiographical approach, a series of essays, a description of a particular scientific community. The word *science* has not been construed narrowly, but includes technology, engineering, and economics as well as physics, chemistry, biology, and mathematics.

The Sloan Foundation expresses its appreciation of the great contribution made to the program by its advisory committee. The committee has been chaired since the program's inception by Robert Sinsheimer, Chancellor of the University of California, Santa Cruz. Present members of the committee are Simon Michael Bessie, Co-Publisher, Cornelia and Michael Bessie Books; Howard Hiatt, Professor, School of Medicine, Harvard University; Eric R. Kandel, University Professor, Columbia University College of Physicians and Surgeons and Senior Investigator, Howard Hughes Medical Institute; Daniel Kevles, Professor of History, California Institute of Technology; Robert Merton, University Professor Emeritus, Columbia University; Paul Samuelson, Institute Professor of

Economics, Massachusetts Institute of Technology; and Stephen White, former Vice President of the Alfred P. Sloan Foundation. Previous members of the committee were Daniel McFadden, Professor of Economics, and Philip Morrison, Professor of Physics, both of the Massachusetts Institute of Technology; Mark Kac (deceased), formerly Professor of Mathematics, University of Southern California; and Frederick E. Terman, Provost Emeritus, Stanford University. The Sloan Foundation has been represented by Arthur L. Singer, Jr., Eric Wanner, and Sandra Panem. The first publisher of the program, Harper & Row, has been represented by Edward L. Burlingame and Sallie Coolidge. This volume is the first edition to be published by Basic Books, represented by Martin Kessler and Richard Liebmann-Smith.

—ALBERT REES
President
Alfred P. Sloan Foundation

PREFACE

THE final five years of the nineteenth century were crowded with events momentous for the subject of physics: X rays, radioactivity, and the electron were discovered; Isidor Isaac Rabi was born. As a portent of things to come, Rabi and modern physics arrived together. The twentieth-century advances in physics and their consequences for modern culture have been, for I. I. Rabi, an agenda for life.

Two great theories of physics, each unique in the profundity and pervasiveness of its implications, were created during the early years of the twentieth century. The first, the special theory of relativity, is concerned with the spatial and temporal relationships between events that occur in nature. From the theory of relativity it was clear that the most basic concepts of physics had to be reassessed and, when the reformulation that followed was complete, physicists had conceptually restructured the space-time stage on which all the processes of nature play out their specific roles. For the discipline of physics, the effect of this restructuring was ubiquitous.

The second great theory is quantum mechanics. With the discovery of the electron, physicists recognized that the atom itself was not an irreducible entity; rather, the atom has inner parts; the atom has structure. Quantum mechanics is a theory of atomic structure; but, more, it is a comprehensive theory of matter. The influence of quantum mechanics on physical and philosophical thought has been so far-reaching and profound that today, sixty years after its creation, quantum mechanics is a subject of diverse interpretations.

If the creation of relativity by Albert Einstein is likened to an aria by a world-class tenor, then the development of quantum mechanics by Niels Bohr, Max Born, Paul Dirac, Werner Heisenberg, Wolfgang Pauli, and Erwin Schrödinger must be compared to a performance by a superb musical ensemble. In both cases, however, the principal artists performed in Europe. In America, it was Edison who attracted attention, not Einstein; it was light bulbs and telephones that were developed, not intellectual systems of physics.

The intellectual system that dominated Rabi's early life was not physics; it was religion. But, Orthodox Judaism is more than a religion; it is a design for disciplined living, a generalized system for thinking. It encouraged a style of thought that readied Rabi for physics. When Rabi discovered the sun-centered solar system of Copernicus, he found it easy to substitute the principles that provide a *physical* explanation of the moon's motion for those that invoke a *supernatural* cause. Yet, while Rabi substituted scientific for religious explanation and abandoned the practices of Judaism, the religious influences of his early environment remained a vital part of him: God is for Rabi a standard by which ideas and actions are judged.

Rabi's boyhood environment enhanced his sense of belonging to America, his sense of being American. When he was in Europe during the mid-1920s learning quantum mechanics, Rabi, with other American physics students, determined to make American physics the best. Throughout the 1930s, experimental results of seminal significance emanated from Rabi's laboratory and were published in America's principal journal of physics, *Physical Review*. By the end of the 1930s, Rabi's desire had been fulfilled: American physics was the best of the best.

The quality of American physics and the American educational system were amply demonstrated during the years of the Second World War . . . the physicists' war. Rabi was the associate director of the Radiation Laboratory at the Massachusetts Institute of Technology (MIT) where, starting in November 1940, physicists developed the microwave radar systems that came to be used in every theater of the war. Rabi was also one of two senior advisors (the other was Niels Bohr) to J. Robert Oppenheimer, who directed the physicists who built the atomic bomb; and Rabi was there when the first nuclear bomb was exploded over the sands of Alamogordo.

When the war ended, Rabi returned to his laboratory at Columbia University, but he was never able to recapture the single-minded focus in physics that he enjoyed before the war. He had, after all, won the Nobel Prize for physics in 1944 and he had been one of the principal policy makers at the MIT Radiation Laboratory. At the war's end, Rabi was a celebrity of physics with broad experiences and established powers. Most of all, however, Rabi could not bring his attention to a focus on physics because he recognized the global implications of the new energy found in the atomic nucleus.

Rabi never became a public figure in the postwar era as did Oppenheimer, but Rabi's influence was the more pervasive. For Rabi, science became the means for bringing the peoples of the world together. Since the culture of science transcends national boundaries and ideological commitments, science provides a common base for people even when their political and ideological passions pull in conflicting directions. In the United States, in Europe, through the United Nations, through NATO, and through UNESCO, Rabi used science as a means to develop and to implement the policies needed in a nuclear world.

In 1968, Rabi retired from Columbia University where he had been the first faculty member to hold the prestigious rank of University Professor. Today, Rabi is the elder statesman of physics, a survivor from an age of heroes. Through his own seminal contributions to physics and through his extraordinary students and associates who worked in his laboratory, Rabi is one of the stars of American physics. He is a statesman from an era when world leaders, recognizing the impact of science on world affairs, listened to scientists like Rabi and acted on their advice. Today, Rabi carries the aura of a man who has participated in the most momentous events of a most incredible century. This aura was apparent on May 14, 1986, when Rabi received the Vannevar Bush Award. The citation read:

For Pioneering with Vision, Boldness and Drive, the Discovery, Exploration, and Settlement of the New Frontiers in Science, Public Service and International Understanding.

Interpreter of the new physics to the new world, translator of quantum abstractions into visible spatial dimensions, trusted advisor to presidents and world leaders, founder of institutions that have contributed to the security of his country, nurtured Nobel laureates and stimulated international cooperation, his life attests to the profound humanism inherent in his conviction that "the proper study of mankind is science." A dedicated man whose stern demand for excellence has always been leavened by an original wit and deep respect for history, he bears with grace his well deserved distinction as the world's senior scientist-statesman.

Rabi, man of the twentieth century, wears the mantle of wisdom.

The seeds of this book were planted when I was a graduate student at the Johns Hopkins University. A simple line drawing in the textbook for my electricity and magnetism course illustrated Rabi's magnetic resonance method—it made a deep impression on me. A few years later, I met V. W. Cohen, Rabi's first graduate student. Bill and I became friends and every time our paths came together, we invariably talked about the early days in the Rabi laboratory.

About the same time, I became interested in the history of science and began to think about science in historical, philosophical, and humanistic terms. This interest drew me closer to Rabi who, through his writings, views physics in the broadest cultural terms. Then, in 1968, I met Rabi. It was disappointing. Through my reading I had come to know him and somehow I expected him to know me; but, at this first meeting, I was, to him, a total stranger and he treated me accordingly.

In January 1981, I had a casual conversation with Norman F. Ramsey, who was then chairman of the American Institute of Physics Governing Board and Higgins Professor of Physics at Harvard University. I suggested that, for historical purposes, someone ought to get access to Rabi's papers. Ramsey agreed emphatically. At that time I had no thought of approaching Rabi myself, but a few months later I became intrigued with the idea of examining Rabi's work. After some thought, I wrote two letters: one to Rabi, one to Ramsey. Within two weeks my telephone rang. A voice said, "This is Rabi. You really want to do this thing?" A few weeks later, Stephen White, from the Sloan Foundation, suggested I write a book. In the meantime, Norman Ramsey had arranged for me to spend a year at Harvard.

During the 1982–83 academic year, Norman Ramsey was on leave from Harvard and I occupied his office in Lyman Laboratory, where I wrote much of the first draft of this book. It was an appropriate environment as Ramsey is one of Rabi's most illustrious students.

For me, writing this book has been pure joy. Many busy people graciously spent time talking with me about Rabi and his activities. For their help and insights, I thank Luis W. Alvarez, Robert F. Bacher, Hans Bethe, Felix Bloch (deceased), Lee A. DuBridge, Henry Foley (deceased), Wendell Furry (deceased), Gerald Holton, Polykarp Kusch, Edwin M. McMillan, Sidney Millman, Philip Morrison, William Nierenberg, Frank Oppenheimer (deceased), Melba Phillips, Emanuel Piore, Robert V. Pound, Edward M. Purcell, Shirley Quimby (deceased), Gertrude Rabi, Norman F. Ramsey, Julian Schwinger, Glenn T. Seaborg, Emilio Segrè, Stephen White, Herbert York, and Jerrold Zacharias (deceased).

I especially want to acknowledge two of the men mentioned above. Norman Ramsey was my host at Harvard. Even though he was on leave, he was always available, by either telephone or letter, and, better yet, he came back to Harvard many times through the year. Ramsey is a fount of knowledge and information. During my year at Harvard, I used

Ramsey's office which, to my good fortune, was next door to Edward Purcell's. Purcell had worked with Rabi at the MIT Radiation Laboratory and later served with him on the President's Science Advisory Committee during the Eisenhower administration. Purcell and I had conversations almost every day, on many different subjects. He is a wise and kind man who made me feel at home.

Of course, I am grateful to the Sloan Foundation for providing the support that enabled me to spend full time for one year working on this book. Stephen White, before he retired, was helpful in many ways. He knew, firsthand, many of the people mentioned in the pages that follow and supplied helpful information. Eric Wanner, who succeeded White at the Sloan, has always known when to dispense encouragement. I thank them both.

I have had both an informal and a formal editor. Diana E. Wyllie has been my most valuable aide and advisor throughout the writing of this book. Richard Liebmann-Smith, my editor at Basic Books, came later and has indulged and guided me through the many steps that brought the project to a conclusion.

Finally, and most of all, I must acknowledge my debt to Rabi and Helen. The Sloan series of books is autobiographical; consequently, I have worked closely with Rabi in writing this book. I have spent many days with Rabi and Helen in their home talking for hours on end. They have responded to my every request. And they have been gracious. They knew virtually nothing about me when I walked into their home the first time. Both Rabi and Helen (especially Rabi) were wary of me and remained so for some time. But the wariness eventually vanished, and the hours we spent together were relaxed, informative, and stimulating. I am grateful that writing this book provided me the opportunity to get to know both of them. Looking back, I am amazed that Rabi and Helen put so much confidence in me, a stranger. I hope their confidence is justified.

RABI

INTRODUCTION

American Physics Becomes Pre-eminent

> It's true that America was backward in physics
> —really underdeveloped—but Condon and I
> and some others promised ourselves that we
> would end this. And we did.
>
> —I. I. RABI

WHEN Isidor Isaac Rabi retired from Columbia University in 1968, he embodied the spirit of American physics. True to that spirit, Rabi did not regard retirement as an end, but as a new beginning. After all, the promises he had made forty years earlier, to himself and others, had been fulfilled: a tradition for great physics had become a vital part of American culture and, in 1968, American physics was, by any measure, the best. This was not the case when Rabi began his physics career in the mid-1920s.

Throughout the early decades of this century, the frontier of physics was largely populated by physicists from England and Europe. Quantum mechanics, for example, was almost exclusively a product of intellects from England and the Continent. Since the excitement in physics during the 1920s was in Europe, approximately fifty of America's brightest young men were there as well: among them were Gregory Breit, E. U. Condon, E. C. Kemble, Robert Mulliken, J. Robert Oppenheimer, Linus

3

Pauling, John Slater, J. A. Stratton, and J. H. Van Vleck. All were there to learn the new physics from its creators—as was I. I. Rabi.

Rabi loves to tell a story dating from this period: When he arrived at Hamburg University toward the end of 1927, he did what any newcomer to a place does: he looked around. In the physics library he was surprised to discover that the current issues of *Physical Review* were not on the shelf; moreover, the library did not receive *Physical Review* issue by issue, but, in order to save money, a year's worth of issues was received in one big package once each year. A revolution was under way in physics; yet American physics and its principal organ, *Physical Review,* were held in such low esteem that it was not judged worthy of the extra postage money to receive the journal on a monthly basis. Rabi ends the story in triumph: "Ten years later, *Physical Review* was the leading physics journal in the world."

While there is no clear or single reason that explains the rise of American physics, several factors that contributed to the rise can be proposed.

Long before American physics became the measure for the world, it had a character of its own; it had elements of greatness. Its character can be seen as a consequence of the American environment: a land to explore and a nation to build. The ingenious practicality that infused the pioneer spirit also influenced the attitudes and conduct of physicists. American physicists tended toward the practical rather than the abstract; they were typically engaged in applied rather than basic research; the American physicist performed experiments rather than created new theoretical ideas.

Among the few physicists in the United States before 1920 were some of world-class stature. Henry A. Rowland, during the 1880s, developed a ruled grating that was like no other. Rowland's grating spread light into its fullest spectrum so that the wavelength composition of a beam of light could be determined with great accuracy. Every laboratory in the world where spectroscopy was being done had to have one of Rowland's gratings in order to produce first-rate results. Albert A. Michelson, also during the 1880s, became fascinated with the challenge of measuring the earth's movement through the ether—the universal medium that was assumed necessary to propagate light from star to star. For this purpose, he designed the interferometer which itself became a necessity in laboratories where delicate optical experiments were carried on. Robert A. Millikan, during the second decade of the twentieth century, designed a device that enabled him to measure the charge carried by the electron. Then there was Josiah Willard Gibbs, a nineteenth-century theoretician, whose work in thermodynamics and statistical mechanics commanded the attention of none other than James Clerk Maxwell. But Gibbs, as a theoretician, was quite an exception within American physics; thus, any claim of greatness for physics in the United States had to be based on its experimentalists.

The First World War brought changes in American physics. Under the leadership of Millikan, physicists became organized and mobilized more effectively than ever before. Whether it was submarine-detection research or range-finding devices to locate enemy artillery emplacements, the physicists proved to be most resourceful. As a result, industrial and military leaders alike came out of the war recognizing more clearly than ever before that both technological and commercial advances sometimes required basic physics as a starting point. With their new importance, physicists could look for employment not only to the campus but also to the industrial laboratory.

The enhanced regard given to physics after the First World War would in itself have raised the activity level within the discipline. In addition, however, were the activities of philanthropic foundations—especially the Rockefeller Foundation. An unprecedented amount of money became available for postdoctoral fellowships. A large fraction of those individuals who received a Ph.D. in physics during the 1920s were awarded a National Research Council Fellowship, compliments of the Rockefeller Foundation.

These factors—postwar acclaim and postwar fellowship money—contributed to the sharp increase in the number of Ph.D.'s in physics who were graduated each year throughout the decade of the 1920s. That number rose steadily from approximately twenty in 1920 to about one hundred in 1930.[1]

It can be argued that both the new regard given to physics and the dramatic increase in the size of the physics community were necessary precursors for American greatness in physics. At the same time, however, these factors, taken together, are not sufficient to explain the way American physics surged to the forefront during the late 1920s and early 1930s. For a variety of reasons, it was the theory of quantum mechanics that lifted American physics to the rank of world class.

First of all, the creation of quantum mechanics was entirely an affair of the Europeans. During the intense three years of 1925 through 1927, the new theory of matter took form—"a heroic time," in Oppenheimer's words.[2] In order to learn the new theoretical ideas, young American physicists found it necessary to go to the great European centers of physics and work under the direction of foreign physicists. Never before had there been such a concentration of American physicists studying in Europe. There were typically several Americans at each of the major centers at any one time. Fellow countrymen can, under such circumstances—foreign environment, common language, common interests—quickly establish close relationships. They talked to each other about home and, at least in some cases, about American physics.

Aware that American physics was regarded poorly by many European physicists, some of those visiting Americans resolved to make American physics the equal to the best they saw in Europe. In Munich, for example, Sommerfeld's condescending attitude toward American physics had irked Rabi (see page 63); and later, in Leipzig, Rabi and Oppenheimer discussed the same subject and shared their determination to bring greatness to American physics. Many of those physicists who came home in 1927, 1928, and 1929, after learning the new quantum mechanics, carried this determination with them. They returned full of self-confidence. Not only had they watched the best physicists in the world argue with each other and discuss the subtleties of the new theory, but—even more important—they had joined in those arguments and discussions. They had, moreover, added to their knowledge a crucial ingredient. Oppenheimer has recounted how the physicists in Göttingen had given him "some sense and perhaps more gradually, some taste in physics."[3] Rabi expressed the same idea when he said that he went to Europe knowing the libretto, but returned knowing the music as well. In Europe, a generation of leaders was born.

The American physicists came back to the United States prepared to be leaders and found many young physicists ready to be led. Rabi likes to refer to the time bomb that was ticking away in America: that is, the scores of bright young students in colleges throughout the land who were majoring in physics, who were doing graduate work in physics, who were ready to accept postdoctoral appointments, and who themselves were poised to bring a style to their own physics, to add a melody to words they knew very well.

The creation of quantum mechanics had another effect: when Breit and Condon, Oppenheimer and Pauling, Van Vleck and Rabi came home from their sojourn in Europe, all physicists everywhere were, in a sense, starting from the same position. Quantum mechanics was revolutionary and wiped the board clean. The ideas were new to everyone, the formalism was new to everyone, the questions needing answers were available to everyone. It did not matter so much what had happened ten or twenty years earlier; in 1927, a brand-new theory was in place.

It was a theory, moreover, made to order for the American physicist. Even today, sixty years after its founding, the formalism of quantum mechanics is abstract, complex, and difficult. In 1927, it was formidable. It was couched in a strange mathematics; it required new concepts; it rested on a different epistemological foundation. Many of the older physicists, in letters and in conversations, admitted their difficulties in coming to grips with the new physics. The younger physicists, however, were eager to explore its intricacies and to learn its new language.

The American physicist possessed a quality of mind that facilitated the exploitation of quantum mechanics. Since the days of Rowland, Michelson, and Millikan, the hallmark of American physics had been its practical ingenuity. That practicality of mind showed itself in two ways in the years immediately following the creation of quantum mechanics and throughout the 1930s.

First, there was the practicality of the theorists. It is certainly true that theoretical physics was advanced in the United States by the corps of physicists who returned from Europe in the late 1920s. But they were American theorists and, as a rule, worked in closer collaboration with experimentalists than did the European theorists. Oppenheimer, for example, was a walking encyclopedia of experimental data. His early theory, carried out with such students as Melba Phillips and Robert Serber, was theory that experimentalists could draw on easily. This was true generally: Condon's, Mulliken's, and Slater's (as well as others') work applied directly to atomic and molecular spectroscopy; Mulliken's and Pauling's work on valence applied directly to a whole host of chemical problems; Van Vleck's work on electric and magnetic susceptibilities had a strong basis in experimental work.

Second, there were the experimentalists. In order to exploit the new quantum mechanics, an experimentalist had to know a lot of theory. American experimentalists excelled in this regard. Rabi is an archetypical example. Not a theorist as Oppenheimer was, Rabi developed the theory needed to advance his molecular-beam experiments. In fact, the physics done in his laboratory throughout the 1930s provides a wonderful example of the interplay between theory and data. When needed, he could do respectable theoretical work, as the Breit-Rabi theory and Rabi's papers in 1936 and 1937 exemplify. On the other hand, he could develop experimental methods to make his beam particles divulge their secrets.

The inbred practicality of the theorists and the theoretical astuteness of the experimentalists were enhanced by the close relationship that existed between theorists and experimentalists in the United States. Even more, the distinction between "theorist" and "experimentalist," as seen in the work a day world of the American physicist, was often blurred and indistinct. Rabi, when asked whether he was a theorist or an experimentalist, would respond, "I'm just a physicist."

European physicists visiting this country were often surprised by the grasp that American experimentalists had on theory. Paul S. Epstein, who came to the California Institute of Technology from Europe in 1921, recognized that "the relations of the theoretical physics to the experimental . . . differed from Europe's in . . . that the experimentalists knew a lot more theory than they did there." In Europe, "they left the theory to me . . . here they meddle the whole time themselves."[4] Later, when Felix Bloch, the Swiss physicist, came to Stanford University, he was surprised by how much theory David L. Webster knew: "The distinction, the division, between experimental and theoretical physics was much sharper [in Europe] than it was here. . . . Experimentalists here, by need or by desire, indeed were theoretically much better equipped than the experimentalists in Europe. This I found out."[5] Bloch himself was influenced by the American environment as he, a theorist in Europe, initiated important experiments after coming to this country. Heisenberg was struck by the willingness of American physicists, in contrast to his European colleagues, to accept the novel approach of quantum mechanics without "too many reservations."[6]

Quantum mechanics was the ideal challenge for American physicists: their heritage, their talents, and their attitudes enabled them to use the new theory as a springboard to national greatness. Pre-eminence followed quickly.

The year 1932 was more than a banner year for physics; it has been called a miraculous year.[7] In that year, Carl D. Anderson discovered the positron—the electron's antiparticle—which brought to completion Dirac's theory of the electron; James Chadwick discovered the neutron —an elementary particle that is one of the two basic constituents of the atomic nucleus; John D. Cockroft and Ernest T. S. Walton built a modest particle accelerator that enabled them to demonstrate that light nuclei can be disintegrated by a beam of low-energy protons; Ernest O. Lawrence and M. Stanley Livingston accelerated particles in their 11-inch cyclotron and reached their goal of 1,000,000 volts of energy; Harold Urey, F. W. Brickwedde, and G. M. Murphy discovered the isotope of hydrogen which came to be known as "deuterium." All five of these events were of first-rank importance for physics; and three of them—the positron and deuterium discoveries and the cyclotron result—were the products of American physicists working in American laboratories.

By 1932, Rabi's molecular beam laboratory was formed; and by 1935, first-rate papers were coming from it and being published in *Physical Review*. Likewise, papers were coming from Oppenheimer's groups at Berkeley and Pasadena and from research groups working at Harvard, the Massachusetts Institute of Technology, the University of Michigan, Princeton, the University of Wisconsin, the University of Chicago, Johns Hopkins University, the University of Illinois, and others. The quality of these papers was such that the French Nobel physicist, Louis de Broglie, was prompted to comment (in 1935) as follows: "Today scientific publications from the United States are awaited with an impatience and curiosity inspired by those from no other country."[8]

From 1933 to the beginning of the Second World War, refugee physicists came to the United States from Europe. They took their places within a physics community that, taken collectively, had already achieved the status of excellence, the rank of world leader. Of course, some departments lagged behind. Hans Bethe has described his arrival at Cornell in 1935: "I found . . . a department full of ambition. . . . The year before, it had been decided to build a cyclotron—the first one to be built outside of Berkeley. . . . I found my colleagues terribly eager to learn, but not very knowledgeable."[9] These immigrant physicists added additional strength—particularly in theory; certain ones, such as Bethe at Cornell and Bloch at Stanford, enabled their departments to join the élite group of top-flight departments.

On May 23, 1967, there was a gathering at Columbia University to pay tribute to Rabi on the occasion of his retirement as a University Professor of Physics. Among those participating was Lee A. DuBridge, who described Rabi's work in the context of American physics: "I would say that since the 1920's Rabi has been a key figure in lifting American physics and other areas of American science from the primitive role they occupied during his student days to the position of international leadership which American science occupies today."[10] Later the same day, Jerrold Zacharias, Rabi's associate throughout much of the 1930s, spoke, showing why Rabi is a "key figure" in the rise of American physics. Zacharias displayed the "Rabi Tree."

In 1958, the Office of Naval Research desired a compelling means to illustrate the importance of basic research—specifically, the importance of the ONR's maintaining programs of support for basic research. To this end, the ONR engaged the services of the Arthur D. Little Company, which was charged, as a part of their report, to find a professional scientist and build around that scientist and that scientist's work the case for supporting basic research. The scientist selected was I. I. Rabi.

A schematic model was adopted to show the impact of Rabi's research (see pages 12–13). The model was a tree with strong roots—a tree growing vigorously, with branches expanding out and reaching upward. The roots of the tree are the experiments carried out by the European pioneers of the molecular-beam method: L. Dunoyer, a French physicist whose earlier work—before molecular beams—was done in the laboratory of Marie Curie, and Otto Stern. The lower part of the main trunk is primarily formed by the basic work of Rabi and his co-workers at Columbia University during the 1930s: the Breit-Rabi theory of 1931; the Cohen-Rabi paper of 1934; the Kellogg, Rabi, and Zacharias paper of 1936; the Rabi and Schwinger papers of 1936; the Rabi paper of 1937; the first magnetic resonance paper of 1939 with Rabi, Millman, Kusch, and Zacharias; and the 1940 papers with various collaborators.

From the trunk of the tree come the branches, which are made up by the research inspired, directly or indirectly, by Rabi's basic papers. Thus, there are main branches growing directly out of the main trunk; while other branches originate from these. Many of the branches are made up by physicists who were once the students or associates of Rabi. Nested within the branches of the Rabi Tree are the names of twenty Nobel laureates. Ten of the laureates are American; the work of four others was done in America.

The Rabi Tree gives a graphic indication of the pervasive influence of Rabi on physics in general and on American physics in particular. Also, the branches of the tree fanning out from the trunk show the profound versatility of quantum mechanics. Since Rabi's work was based on the theory of quantum mechanics, the work it inspired represents further applications of the theory.

Drawn in the late 1950s, the Rabi Tree is far from complete; yet the tree still lives. Nourishment still flows freely and vigorously from the trunk through the major branches. New branches continue to sprout, and the tree grows outward and upward.

KEY TO RABI'S TREE

1911. Dunoyer. Verification of straight-line motion of gas molecules
1920. Stern. Verification of Maxwell distribution of molecular velocities by means of molecular beams

1924. Stern and Gerlach. Direct demonstration of space quantization

1928. Darwin. First suggested observation of non-adiabatic transitions
        T. Johnson. Reflection of atomic hydrogen from crystals

1929. Rabi. Effect of magnetic field on motion of molecular moment through magnetic field
        J. B. Taylor. Surface ionization detector

1931. Breit and Rabi. Coupled nuclear and electron moments in magnetic field
        Güttinger. Non-adiabatic transitions analyzed
        Phipps and Stern. Experiments involving non-adiabatic transitions

1933. Frisch and Segrè. Experiments involving non-adiabatic transitions
        Majorana. Theory of atomic moments interacting with oscillating fields
        Meissner. Atomic beam light source

1934. Cohen and Rabi. Magnetic deflection experiments
        Cleeton and Williams. First direct observation of ammonia inversion line

1935. Schuler. Hollow cathode discharge tube; interval rule variation in hyperfine structure

1936. Casimer. Theory of electric quadrupole moments
        Gorter. Unsuccessful experiment on nuclear magnetic resonance
        Kellogg, Rabi, and Zacharias. Sign of nuclear moments determined by non-adiabatic transition
        Rabi and Schwinger. Theory of non-adiabatic transitions

1937. Bloch. Suggested method of polarizing neutrons
        Estermann, Simpson, and Stern. Scattering of neutrons by ortho- and para-hydrogen
        Feenburg and Wigner. Nuclear spin and theory of beta decay
        Rabi. Molecular-beam magnetic-resonance refocusing experiment proposed
        Schmidt. Theory of nuclear magnetic moments single particle model

1939. Hamilton. Electric quadrupole moment of In^{115} by molecular-beam deflection
        Millman. Millman effect (sign) of nuclear moment from asymmetry in resonance curve
        Rabi, Millman, Kusch, Zacharias. First successful magnetic-resonance experiments

11

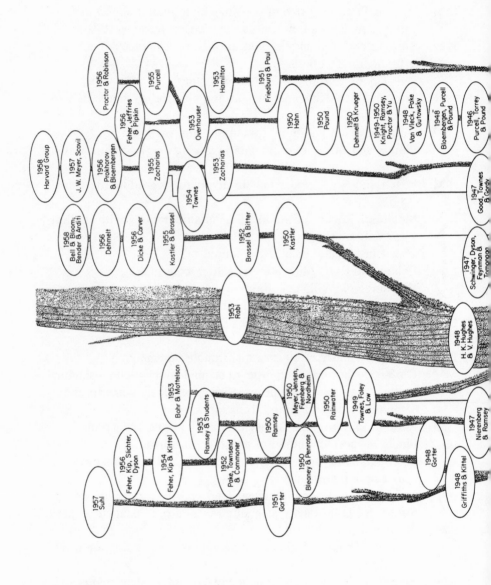

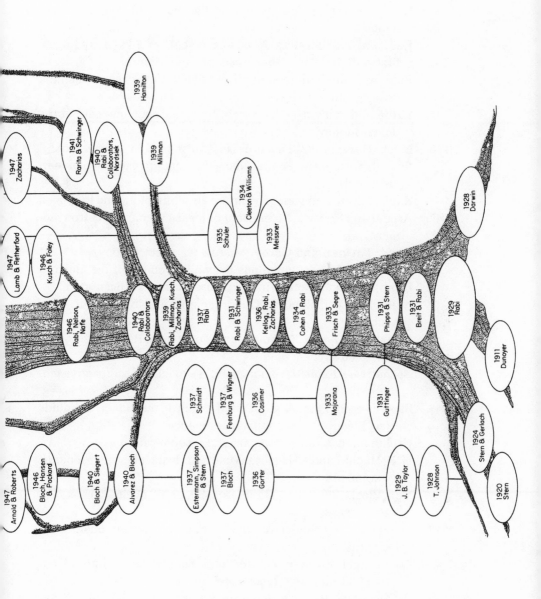

1940. Alvarez and Bloch. Neutron beam magnetic resonance magnetic moment of the neutron

Bloch and Siegert. Refinement of the theory of magnetic resonance

Rabi and collaborators. Nuclear moments of alkalis, hydrogen; first radiofrequency spectroscopy deuterium

Rabi and collaborators, Nordsiek. Electric quadrupole moment of the deuteron

1941. Rarita and Schwinger. Theory of the quadrupole moment of the deuteron; tensor force

1946. Bloch, Hansen, and Packard. Nuclear induction discovered

Purcell, Torrey, and Pound. Nuclear magnetic resonance of matter in bulk

Rabi, Nelson, and Nafe. Hyperfine structure of atomic hydrogen

1947. Arnold and Roberts. Refinement of measurement of neutron moment

Good, Townes, and Gordy. Microwave spectroscopy

Kusch and Foley. Anomalous magnetic moment of the electron

Lamb and Retherford. Fine structure of the hydrogen atom

Nierenberg and Ramsey. Quadrupole effects in magnetic resonance

Schwinger, Dyson, Feynman, and Tomonaga. Revision of quantum electrodynamics

Zacharias. Atomic beam magnetic resonance of radioactive isotopes

1948. Bloembergen, Purcell, and Pound. Nuclear resonance in liquids

Gorter. Electron paramagnetic resonance

Griffiths and Kittel. Ferromagnetic resonance

H. K. Hughes and V. Hughes. Molecular beam electric resonance experiments

Van Vleck, Pake, and Gutowsky. Shape of nuclear resonance line in crystals

1949. Townes, Foley, and Low. Systematics of nuclear quadrupole moments

1949–1950. Knight, Ramsey, Proctor, and Yu. Chemical shifts of nuclear magnetic resonance

1950. Bleaney and Penrose. Electron paramagnetic resonance; hyperfine structure

Dehmelt and Krueger. Electrical quadrupole resonance in crystals

Hahn. Spin echoes

Kastler. First suggestion of optical pumping

Mayer, Jensen, Feenberg, and Nordheim. Nuclear shell structure

Pound. Quadrupole effects on nuclear magnetic resonance

Rainwater. Spheroidal nucleus and quadrupole moments

Ramsey. Separated oscillating field molecular beam experiments

1951. Friedburg and Paul. Multiple focusing for molecular beams

Gorter. Anti-ferromagnetic resonance

1952. Brossel and Bitter. Double resonance experiments

Pake, Townsend, and Commoner. Electron paramagnetic resonance in organic molecules

1953. Bohr and Mottelson. Collective model of nuclear structure; quadrupole moments

Hamilton. Atomic beam magnetic resonance of radioactive isotopes

Overhauser. Overhauser effect; dynamic nuclear orientation

Rabi. Atomic beam magnetic resonance with optical excited states

Ramsey and students. Precise measurement of the magnetic moment of the neutron

Zacharias. Atomic frequency standard based on atomic beam magnetic resonance

1954. Feher, Kip, and Kittel. Electron spin resonance of donors in silicon, color centers, and F-centers in alkali-halides

Townes. Ammonia maser and high resolution microwave spectrometer

1955. Kastler and Brossel. Magnetic resonance of optically pumped sodium

Purcell. Radio astronomy of hydrogen 21-centimeter line

Zacharias. Cesium beam atomic frequency standard

1956. Dehmelt. Optical detection of magnetic resonance

Dicke and Carver. Magnetic resonance in buffered, optically pumped rubidium

Feher, Jeffries, and Pipkin. Dynamic nuclear orientation

Feher, Kip, Slichter, and Dyson. Spin resonance of conduction electrons in metals

Proctor and Robinson. Coupling of ultrasonic vibrations to nuclear quadrupole moment

15

       Prokhorov and Bloembergen. Solid state maser

1957. J. W. Meyer and Scovil. Practical solid state maser

       Suhl. Ferrimagnetic amplifier

1958. Bell and Bloom, Bender and Arditi. Optically pumped frequency standard

       Harvard Group. Radio astronomy of hydrogen 21-centimeter line

CHAPTER

1

Copernicus Comes to Brooklyn

> ... When you are Orthodox, you say prayers for the new moon. When you have an astronomical explanation, the rising of the moon becomes a sort of non-event.
>
> —I. I. RABI

WHEN such powerful early influences as the authoritative teachings of religion, the confining effects of ethnic isolation, and the onerous weight of poverty come together in one person, they can play one upon the other, draw sustenance one from the other and become intensified and reinforced. The total impact of this dynamic intercourse, for ends either good or bad, can be greater than the sum of the individual parts. Religion, ethnic isolation, and poverty dominated the childhood of the boy whose given name was Israel Isaac Rabi.

Israel Isaac was born on July 29, 1898. Like his father and mother before him, he was born in Rymanow, a small town in Galicia, the northeasternmost province of the old Austro-Hungarian empire. Shortly after the birth of his son, David Rabi left Rymanow and emigrated to the United States, arriving at Ellis Island, New York, uneducated and unskilled. The last of nine sons of a poor family, he had been educated to be a good Jew, but not to make a good living. Yet, within a matter of months after his arrival in New York City, David had accumulated the necessary funds to provide passage for both his wife and their infant son. He sent them word: Come to America. Shortly afterward, to the brave best wishes and the sad shaloms of family and friends, Sheindel Rabi and her son left their small town, completely severing the links not only with their homeland but also with their ancestry.

Seventy years later, Rabi returned to Rymanow, which, in the long interim, with the vicissitudes of war and the fiats of peacemakers, had become a town of Poland. Rabi having become, in the same interim, a man of the world, he returned as a famous son of Poland. The Polish government honored him, and the mayor of Rymanow served as his host. There in the town of his birth, of his ancestors, he found no evidence of his own heritage. "It was a small town," Rabi has recalled, "with a nice town square and a great big Catholic church with a large, well-populated, Catholic cemetery next to it." Gone was the wooden sixteenth-century synagogue, burned down by the Germans, and a parking lot occupied the site. Alongside remained the shell of a large, domed cement synagogue. "There may have been a Jew left, I don't know. I asked to see the Jewish cemetery. We got into a car and drove along this very bad road until we came upon a beautiful field." Rabi walked through the field, which sloped down toward a valley and rose again to shape the rolling hills off to the east. Only an occasional stone projecting slightly above the soil, barely visible in the grass, provided silent evidence of a time forever past. Rabi questioned his guide: "Before the war [the Second World War] was the Jewish cemetery as big as the Catholic cemetery?" The response came quickly: "Oh, no, much bigger!" During the war, the gravestones had been leveled. "A whole history of ancestors all . . . all wiped out. Nothing left except to walk through the field. . . . That was that."[1]

Rabi left the quiet field and, for the second time, the town of Rymanow. Now, however, he was departing in a chauffeur-driven car provided by the Atomic Energy Commission of Poland. Seventy years earlier he had left Rymanow in the arms of his young, anxious mother on the way to her husband and to a new world.

When the Rabis were reunited, they, like many Jewish immigrants, settled in the Lower East Side of Manhattan which, at that time, was almost totally Jewish. The city blocks were subdivided into cultural enclaves with Jews from the same parts of Europe banding together. The Rabis lived at 91 Willett Street in the midst of other Jews from Galicia, while David Rabi belonged to the society of the Rymanower Young Men.

The young Rabi spoke English in the streets and Yiddish in his home. David and Sheindel Rabi, on the other hand, were never proficient with English and, as a result, were reticent when they found themselves in an English-speaking environment. Thus it was that Israel Isaac got a new name. When Sheindel enrolled her son in public school, she was asked his name, and responded, "Izzy," the name she and her husband called him. Assuming Izzy to be short for Isidor, the school official put down that name: Israel Isaac Rabi was now, officially, Isidor Rabi. The mistake was never corrected. Later, as a young man, Rabi's response to anti-Semitism was to bring back the second I for Isaac, and, in so doing, to defiantly assert his Jewishness. Throughout his professional career he has been known as I. I. Rabi, the two I's standing for Isidor Isaac. To his friends, to his sister Gertrude, to his wife Helen, he is "Rabi" (pronounced to rhyme with "Bobby") or simply "Rab."

The Rabis were Orthodox Hebrew—a demanding religion. In the regimen of Judaism, however, the life of the Rabis was buoyed up by their faith that God was directly involved with them, an active and interested participant in their daily and hourly affairs. "Even in casual conversation, God entered, not every paragraph, more like every sentence," Rabi has said of his childhood. "There was a certain intimacy with the idea of God, a comfortable feeling. He was a relative in a way. You could deal with Him as Abraham did."

Orthodox Judaism is both culture as well as religion. "Belief has it," writes Israel Rubin, "that the main virtue of the Hebrew slaves in Egypt, on account of which they merited redemption, was their retention of distinctiveness in dress, names and language."[2] Thus, the Rabis named their first-born Israel Isaac—after his rabbi godfather—a name that left no doubt as to the boy's Jewish identity. They spoke Yiddish: "My mother and father could only read and write Yiddish in Hebrew characters." David and Sheindel, however, were determined to provide a secular education for their children (a daughter, Gertrude, was born in January 1903); and from his earliest youth, Rabi knew that he would go to college: "When I look back on it now, it seems absurd, because we had hardly enough money for food."[3]

Rabi's education began, as did that of all proper Jewish boys, in Hebrew school at the age of three. A poor boy, he was brought together with other poor boys into "some evil smelling basement," where an ill-paid teacher with "no idea of pedagogy" held forth. The teacher "opened the Bible, would look at a letter, and say, 'This is Aleph, the first letter of the alphabet.' " But Rabi learned to read, and quickly. He honed his reading skill on the only books available to him—Yiddish books and, of course, the Bible. "I could read long before I went to [public] school, I could read a Yiddish newspaper."

The religious influence in Rabi's boyhood was enhanced by Old World superstition. Rymanow, located in extreme eastern Europe some fifty kilometers from the Russian border, is in the foothills of the Carpathian Mountains—Dracula country, a region famous for its vampires and ghosts, its evil spirits and devils. Rabi heard many hair-raising stories as a child: stories about unaccountably strange things happening to people, stories about face-to-face encounters with ghosts, stories about horrors in the dark times of night. One of his most vivid childhood memories is of looking down a New York street and seeing the full moon poised at the end of it: "One time, I was walking along and looked down the street which faced east. The moon was just rising. And it scared the hell out of me! Absolutely scared the hell out of me."[4]

Another reality served to strenghthen and intensify the Rabis' hold on their religious faith: the reality of poverty. David Rabi, unskilled as he was, worked at a variety of menial tasks: as a night watchman, in a coal cellar, as an iceman, and in a sweatshop where women's blouses were manufactured. Eventually, by saving and borrowing money, he was able to open a little grocery store, which he ran before and after his long day in the sweatshop; during the day, Sheindel Rabi was shopkeeper. In spite of all their hard work, the little store was never successful.

Home to the Rabis was a tiny, two-room flat, one room serving as kitchen, dining room, and living room; and the other a windowless bedroom, barely large enough for a bed. The toilet in the back yard was shared by the other occupants of the building. In these two rooms lived six people: David and Sheindel Rabi; Isidor and his little sister Gertrude; and two boarders. Rabi cannot remember where or how, in those cramped quarters, they all slept.

Home was in a slum—a Jewish ghetto. The streets teemed with activity. There were kids, kids, and still more kids. "The streets were ours," wrote Irving Howe. "Everyplace else—home, school, shop—belonged to the grownups. But the streets belonged to us."[5] There were gangs of Jewish boys, tough boys who roamed the streets and terrorized those who could, and would, be frightened. It took ingenuity to survive; and Rabi, though small for his age, made use of a special gift: he could tell stories. He so fascinated the bullying big boys with Bible stories that he became their mascot.

The neighborhood was a typical slum: "There were lots of prostitutes and saloons. Every intersection had three or four saloons. . . . And there were lots of synagogues."⁶ Synagogues and saloons: contradictory symbols of life in the ghetto of the Lower East Side. Young Rabi could, on the one hand, witness pious and devoted allegiance to religious life and, on the other, observe flagrant disregard of civil law. In their two-room flat, Rabi and Gertrude were thrust into the mature world of adult conversation. "We had relatives coming to our house who expressed different political ideas," Gertrude has said.⁷ Rabi listened and learned. And he read.

Of all the Bible stories, one held a special and unique appeal—the Creation story: "In the beginning, God created the heavens and the earth." Rabi felt that here was something to explore, to understand, and, yes, to question: "[The first verses of Genesis] were very moving to me as a kid. The whole idea of the Creation—the mystery and the philosophy of it. It sank in on me, and it's something I still feel."⁸

Although later he would forgo the practices and the rituals of Orthodox Judaism, basic elements of that religious tradition remain the essence of the man: "There's no question that basically, somewhere way down, I'm an Orthodox Jew. In fact, to this very day, if you ask for my religion, I say 'Orthodox Hebrew'—in the sense that the church I'm not attending is that one. If I were to go to church, that's the one I would go to. That's the one I failed. It doesn't mean I'm something else."⁹ And with a conviction that has been tested by his training as a scientist, and that has endured his active participation in some of the most noteworthy events of this century, Rabi can say today, "My early upbringing, so struck by God, the maker of the world, this has stayed with me."

In 1907, David Rabi moved his family to Brownsville, a community in New York City's borough of Brooklyn. Brownsville was like the Lower East Side, but with a difference. Each was the site of large Jewish populations, whose character was essentially the same.¹⁰ Both communities brought together recent immigrants who had in common their religious faith and their poverty. Brownsville differed from the Lower East Side in being rural: there were chickens and goats in the streets, and the streets themselves were mud when it rained and dust when the sun beat down. Milk could be bought directly from a farmer. Brownsville was, in essence, the Lower East Side with dirt roads and nanny goats. The Rabis, however, were fortunate: they had a nice yard behind their house and, for two years, Rabi was an avid gardener.

The move from Manhattan to Brooklyn was motivated by economics. Since the first little grocery store on the Lower East Side was not bringing in enough money, David Rabi opened a new store in Brownsville.

The family lived in three rooms behind their store. When, at the age of nine, Rabi began to take a more active part in the operation of the store, it became, even more than before, a family operation. After school and on school holidays, he would deliver groceries around the neighborhood. And he would listen. "My father had very little to say and my mother was not very talkative, but for some reason the store became a neighborhood meeting place. Families would congregate there, and the conversation—on a wide range of subjects—was very lively. This is how things were."

In Brownsville, the Rabis lived, as before, frugally amid a mass of humanity living with equal frugality. "I didn't know we were poor," Rabi said later—as did Gertrude, but more revealingly: "There was poverty all around us, but I was very rich. My life was a joy."[11] Rabi remembers being "a close family. We were completely open and we trusted one another. In the grocery store, the money drawer was open, and I could take what I wanted. That's something which I didn't abuse. When there were discussions of the family business, I was part of the discussion, maybe too much a part."

As for education, Rabi was not inspired by school: "I did well in school, but I was no prodigy. Neither did I do any work. I went to class and listened."[12] Inspiration came elsewhere. One day he noticed one of his classmates carrying a strange book, a book that did not come from the school. Rabi had read all of the Yiddish books at home; he knew the Bible stories by heart. A strange book whetted his desire to know its contents. When he asked where the book had come from, his classmate replied, "The library," and thus Rabi was introduced to the local branch of the Brooklyn Public Library, the Carnegie Library.[13]

Here there were more books in one place than Rabi had ever seen. Starting with the A's, with Alcott, he took two books from the shelf and checked them out. But the librarian, suspicious of this small boy, stopped him before he got out of the building, and made him read aloud from one of the books before she would permit him to leave with them. Rabi read for her and then went home with his books. The year was 1908.

The children's books in the Carnegie Library were fun to read, and Rabi read them all. The next bank of shelves held books of science, which were organized by subject rather than by author. Again, he started at the beginning, with A for astronomy. Decades later, he could say, "That was what determined my later life more than anything else—reading a little book on astronomy."[14]

The young Rabi was captivated by astronomy—but not by the usual things that might attract a ten-year-old, such as stars, interstellar distances, galactic sizes, intergalactic distances, or the constellations, or Jupiter's spot and Saturn's rings, or even the craters on the moon. The pages in the little astronomy book that so fixed Rabi's attention described the Copernican solar system.

Nicolaus Copernicus, a Polish astronomer, stirred the world when, in 1543, he published his treatise *De Revolutionibus Orbium Caelestium*. Up to that time, an earth-centered universe had been consistent with the wisdom of the past, with the teachings of biblical scholars, and, most of all, with everyone's common sense. It seemed obvious that the sun rose in the east, circled the earth, and set in the west; nothing indicated that the earth was spinning about a terrestrial axis. A few astronomers, however, like Kepler, like Galileo, saw beyond authorities of the past and were able to ignore the "certainties" of common sense.

Rabi was neither Kepler nor Galileo, but he saw what the Copernican system offered and his mind was receptive to it. His fascination with the biblical creation story, his reading and rereading of it, had raised questions in his mind. The answers he had been given invoked God at every turn: God raised the sun each morning; God darkened the sky each night; God brought the moon to the sky at different times in different shapes.

In the seventeenth century, the astronomer Johannes Kepler had seen the Copernican system as "an inexhaustible treasure of truly divine insight into the wonderful order of the world and all the bodies therein"[15]—a "wonderful order" also apparent to the child Rabi. "It was so beautiful, so marvelous," said Rabi years later, "so simple. Instead of the idea that there is some special intervention every day for the sun to come up, I came home with this great revelation."[16]

That night after reading the astronomy book in the library, Rabi went home "full of delight," walked in, and announced to his parents, "It's all very simple, who needs God?"[17]

Who needs God? Such a question for immigrant parents whose life was simple devotion to God and to their children: "I didn't appreciate what a *blow* this was. Gave them a lot of pain. I was sorry about it, perhaps baffled that they didn't share my enthusiasm. I have guilt feelings about *their* feelings. For my family it was rather tragic: I was the first born, the only son. And I could outtalk them."

Who needs God? The immediate stimulus for the question was Rabi's delight and satisfaction at the Copernican view of the heavens; this question, however, had been in the making during months of open-eyed observations—and testing. Jewish law held that one was not to ride a streetcar on the Sabbath. What if he did? One Sabbath he tried it. He rode the streetcar, half expecting God to wreak havoc on both himself and the streetcar. He waited. No catastrophe occurred. Later he conducted another test: "I remember being in the synagogue and the priests, the *Kohens* [Kohanim], would stand up and with their hands outstretched and covered with a tallis, they would bless the congregation. You were not supposed to look at their hands, you might go blind if you did. Well, I tried . . . with one eye." Since he was not struck blind by his defiant act, his doubts grew about the validity of things he had been taught.

Life conducted according to Jewish law brings dilemmas, moral dilemmas. One such arose in Brownsville:

Of course, you couldn't carry money on the Sabbath. I did once. I bought some candy. It was spectacular. I found I *had* some money in my pocket. I didn't put it there, I don't know how it got there, but there it was. And what to do? I consulted with the other kids, what to do? Well, apparently, you get rid of it. So I spent it and bought some candy. Later the storekeeper told my father and there was hell to pay. Here was a real moral question which I felt was never resolved. They didn't understand the problem I was confronted with. I had the money in my pocket, what am I to do? Go around with it? Whether the sin was having the money in your pocket and walking around with it, or utilizing it—it was all kind of subtle.

There was nothing subtle about the Copernican sun. When Rabi discovered Copernicus in Brooklyn, his life outside the home became increasingly secular as he slowly abandoned the religious practices and rituals of his parents. And they were no match for him:

You have no idea how tough I was. [My father] was a nice gentle man from another culture, another language. . . . I was very hard on him. They [my parents] never spoke English well, not well enough to communicate any subtleties, so there was an enormous gap—a generation gap and, in addition, a cultural gap. They were simple people. My mother was a woman of great intelligence, but very little education. That's true of my father as well. So I was left to myself because of the difficulty of bridging that gap. I would say now that

I was rather insensitive to them. . . . I was the first born, the only son.

Rabi's experiences and reading expanded his horizons beyond the religious system by which his life had been ordered. Whether he sensed a void that needed filling is open to question. The fact remains, however, that at this time Rabi became interested in another system of thought. As one writer has proclaimed, "three groups of influences are at work on [the boy in the ghetto]—the orthodox Jewish, the American, and the Socialist."[18] Furthermore, as another writer has described, "the East Side and Brownsville . . . were seething with social protest. Radicals, social reformers, and all kinds of champions were trying to make the masses cognizant of the deplorable conditions under which they lived."[19]

In this "seething" environment, Rabi happened upon Jack London's *The Iron Heel*. This novel, written in 1907, is a futuristic story set in the 1930s. It dramatically depicts the injustices heaped upon the people of the working class. Moreover, the tenets of socialism are clearly set forth by the story's main character Ernest Everhard, a heroic figure of persuasive knowledge and self-confidence: he explicitly elaborates Karl Marx's theory of surplus value and the materialistic view of history. This book made a powerful impression on young Rabi, and socialism seemed to offer the all-embracing ideas he found appealing. "I became very interested in it, for about two years. I used to go to the local Socialist Club most every night. . . . Among these Socialists, so very symptomatically, never once did anybody address a word to me in the two years I went there."[20] Rabi tried to convert to socialism other students as well as his teachers. His last elementary schoolteacher, a Mr. Howell, was particularly patient with the new disciple of Marxism:

"He brought his lunch to the school, and I brought mine. We would sit there, and he would ask me questions, a whole series of questions: What would I *do* under socialism in this circumstance? In that circumstance? I would very glibly answer all his questions and very confidently." By the end of the school year Mr. Howell's questions had dampened Rabi's enthusiasm for socialism: "I can see how big-hearted he [Mr. Howell] was, because I must have been a pretty nasty and self-confident kid, a snotty kid."

When Rabi entered high school, he took note of his classmates and said to himself, "These people could never run a country."[21] The socialist ideas became discredited in his thinking and he dropped them from his thoughts.

Although his advocacy of socialism as a system to live by came to an end, the influence of some of its ideas continued. For example, he found that the materialistic interpretation of history brought organization and simplicity to his study of history: "It doesn't matter if it's wrong, it's a system, it's a more or less logical thing. . . . It was great."[22]

Many years later, Rabi reflected on this period of his life and on the influences of both religion and socialism.

There's the religious point of view that is universal in its way. If you revolt against religion, where you have nothing, you become an atheist—whatever that means. For me there was this other system which was universal in its way: Marxism. Although erroneous in many respects, it was something and it was positive. There was this faith that human intellect and human effort formed the basis of what humans could do. What Marxism gives you is a view of society and a view of history—an integrated view. It's mostly wrong, but it's a view. You get the habit from this of thinking of things in a holistic way. You see connections.

That was a hell of a big note for a kid of thirteen, fourteen, but I had the advantage of a religious background. Religion is also a system that encompasses everything, but it has something that Marxism doesn't have: religion has color and class. The whole idea of God, that's real class.

While he was reading London and other socialist writers, Rabi was also reading books from the science shelves of the Carnegie Library. For a while he thought of becoming an astronomer, although neither he nor his father had any idea how an astronomer made a living. He discovered electricity and also that he could build electrical devices and do experiments. From magazines published by the late Hugo Gernsback—including the *Electrical Importing Company* and *Modern Electrics*—Rabi learned about radio transmitters and receivers. Soon he was immersed in telegraphy; and, as Gertrude remembers, "Mother's wall in the living room was a radio station and his friends came in and out."[23] Of these activities, Rabi has said: "Whatever I was interested in I could generally get a group to be interested in as well . . . I got some kids together . . . and we strung a telegraph line over two streets . . . I met this kid whose father had a junk shop and he had wire, you know, spools of wire that he thought was junk."[24] By means of stones thrown from roof to roof, wire was stretched through the neighborhood and a telegraph station was set up. Rabi learned Morse code and he got a license.

With the exception of the earphones, Rabi built all the other components of his station: tuner, transmitter, spark coil, and coupler. He also designed a condenser to store electrical energy. His design was sufficiently novel that Hugo Gernsback paid him two dollars for a manuscript describing his design. While he was still in elementary school, Rabi's first scientific paper was published in *Modern Electrics*.

Did Sheindel Rabi like having her living room filled with electrical equipment?

> She couldn't help it. I was a formidable kid. There was nothing much they could do about it when I was set on doing this . . . Did she mind? I don't think she did actually. I amassed quite a bit of apparatus and workshop equipment. My father ultimately bought the house in which the store was, and I put up a big antenna. It was a point of pride to get the news, not from the newspaper, but by picking it up from ships, and so forth.[25]

A thirteen-year-old Jewish boy is expected to celebrate his arrival at the age of responsibility with a bar mitzvah ceremony in the synagogue. On the Sabbath nearest his birthday, he is called to witness the reading of a biblical passage and delivers a talk based on the Torah. Afterward, his parents provide a festive meal for relatives and friends.

But Rabi, this "formidable kid," would have none of it.

> At that time, age thirteen, I was far advanced. I had read extensively and certainly knew about Copernicus . . . and I knew about electricity. The whole Jewish thing, as it appeared to me, began to look like superstition. . . . So to get up there and take all that trouble to read something in the synagogue, I just wasn't going to do it.
>
> What could they [his parents] do? They must have felt badly, but I wasn't so concerned. I was more concerned with the truth, revealed truth. I was a bastard of a kid not to worry about them. I look back now and I consider the sorrows I brought on them, it horrifies me. I wasn't self-righteous about it, I just couldn't figure out how they could miss [these things I knew], they were so beautiful.[26]

In the end, a compromise was reached, and David Rabi's son had a bar mitzvah—but on his own terms. In the annals of this ceremony, Rabi's bar mitzvah was, in all probability, unique.

They had a party at my bar mitzvah, and they brought in some people. They prevailed on me to make a speech, so I made a speech [in Yiddish]. My speech was "How the Electric Light Works," which I described in great detail. I talked about the carbon filament, and then there was something I thought was very clever: getting the [electrical] lead out from the filament.[27]

Rabi's bar mitzvah was not held in the synagogue, but at his home before what he regarded as ancient bearded men.

Rabi was one year older than the average child when he finished elementary school: he had caught numerous childhood diseases and thus he began school one year late. As high school approached, his parents suggested that he go into Hebrew studies at a yeshiva. Predictably, Rabi refused. And, predictably, it was he who decided where he would go to high school.

Boys High was, at the time, the school where all of the smart Jewish boys went. At Boys High he could match wits with some of the best. Boys High was the obvious choice, but Rabi elected Manual Training High School in Brooklyn, which, as its name implies, emphasized manual training. He had four years of crafts such as carpentry, machine shop, foundry work, and printing. Since the school was three miles from home, and he was to spend four years avoiding street gangs as he walked through one hostile territory after another on his way to and from school, his choice was clearly not based on convenience: "I went there purposely. I had been raised in an environment where we didn't see anything but Jews. . . . I wanted to get away from that. I had very definite notions of being an American in a broader sense. I had read a good deal of history and I wanted to be a part of the greater thing; so I went to Manual Training where there were almost no Jews."[28]

According to Rabi, "it wasn't a good school. I doubt whether I did more than ten minutes homework a day."[29]

Along with his four years of shop courses, Rabi also had a full schedule of other subjects—mathematics, chemistry, history, physics, English, and so forth:

Our math teacher was marvelous. The chemistry courses were the strongest, and I took lots of chemistry. My physics teacher was the worst. He was the only teacher with a Ph.D., but he was indescribably bad as a teacher. In fact, all my life I never got good instruction in physics. It was my mathematics teacher who told me that I ought to be reading Maxwell's *Electricity and Magnetism*—not my physics teacher.*

As his shop-oriented high-school curriculum served to satiate his practical desires, his radio station and photography came to an end. He concentrated intensely on reading. "[I] used to get four to five books and finish them in a week. . . . I don't see how I could ever have gotten an education without [the public library]."[30] He read newspapers; he followed the First World War from its opening forays in August of 1914; and he read history, which fascinated him. His high-school history teacher was astounded when Rabi got the highest grade in the state on the New York Regents history exam: "Being small for my age, and shy, I never got known in high school. I knew everything [in history], but never got called on. So [the teacher] was surprised. I said to him, 'I knew all along that you couldn't recognize genius!' "[31]

When Rabi graduated from Manual Training High School in 1916, he was streetwise and self-educated.

*The classic *Treatise on Electricity and Magnetism* by James Clerk Maxwell inspired Rabi's novel approach to his dissertation (see page 43).

CHAPTER

2

The Physicist Emerges from the Wilderness

I discovered that the part of chemistry I liked
was called physics. If someone had pointed that
out to me before, it would have saved me many,
many years.

—I. I. RABI

RABI was destined to be a physicist. In specifics, however, he was
unaware of this destiny until three years after graduating from college.
The years from 1916 to 1922 were Rabi's years in the wilderness—a
wilderness both literal and literary. As his choice of high school reflected his desire to break out of one environment, so his choice of
college was prompted by a desire to get away from still another. Rabi
decided to go "way out west" to Cornell University, in Ithaca, New
York, in Finger Lake country. This area, legendary for its beauty and its
Indians—the Senecas, the Cayugas, and the Onondagas—is also James
Fenimore Cooper country. Rabi had read Cooper, sometime during his
voracious reading bouts, and associated romance with the area. He had
also heard about Cornell's academic program: "It had a greater emphasis on science and engineering than other places had. There seemed to
be a liberal attitude about it, a sense of freedom and novelty."[1]

And so, in the fall of 1916, he entered Cornell University. To pay his way, Rabi had a tuition scholarship won in open competition and a New York State Regents scholarship for one hundred dollars a year. The rest of the money he needed he got from home. "Our parents accepted Cornell," his sister Gertrude said later, "because it was Rabi's wish."[2]

Although he could have found a job on the campus or in town, he did not: "I tried working my way through, getting a job, but I didn't like it. I'd much rather starve and have . . . my time as my own to browse in the library, do what I wanted."[3] He settled for hunger. The food he did eat did not provide the necessary nourishment: "I ate the wrong things. It didn't seem to be reasonable to spend your money on vegetables when you were hungry."[4] As a consequence, he lost several teeth because of malnutrition.

Rabi entered Cornell with advanced standing, but he was not at all certain about what he wanted to do: "I knew I wanted to be a scientist, but having no guidance, I didn't know how to get what I wanted. . . . I was interested in the structure of matter."[5] Yet, he entered Cornell as a student of electrical engineering.

The contradictions are many. On the one hand, Manual Training High School lacked high academic repute. ("It wasn't a good school," said Rabi.) Yet Rabi left that school with a background that gave him advanced standing at Cornell. On the one hand, Rabi was an inveterate reader; yet he did not know that physics would serve his intellectual interests. Real contradictions? Not necessarily. Atomic physics, or the physics concerned with the structure of matter, was just becoming an important part of the discipline during Rabi's public-school days; and the physics textbooks of 1915 would have had little or nothing on atomic structure.

In college, Rabi took chemistry—in part, due to the influence of his roommates; and it was an *unpopular* chemistry course that brought an end to engineering. This infamous chemistry course was qualitative analysis, the bane of many would-be chemists. In this laboratory course a student is given a small sample of material whose chemical composition he or she does not know and instructed to determine the chemical elements present in it. For a student like Rabi with a yen for science, such chemical detective work afforded perhaps the first opportunity to feel something like a real scientist: "I thought it was wonderful—like research. I did very well at it, especially unconventional methods of analysis. Chemistry is a very good introduction to science. It's very tangible and you see things happen. But . . . it didn't appeal to me intellectually, although it appealed to me a great deal in the sense that you could do things experimentally." This appeal prompted Rabi to change his major to chemistry.

His routine at Cornell was the same as it had been in high school.

> I don't think I did more than a few minutes a day, outside of attendance, on any of my courses. I attended regularly because otherwise you would have to make it up. So I attended, listened to the man. He put it on the line. I made up my mind that I would never read in a subject in which I was taking a course. So if I was taking a course in qualitative analysis, I might be reading Freud. I did an immense amount of reading. In this strange way, without taking courses, I got myself a liberal education. If one doesn't try to get high grades, as I didn't, one has a lot of time in college . . . even if you take a heavy schedule, as I did . . . I got an A once, on a bet. . . .
>
> As always, I was very much interested in history. I would read about the history of the subject I was taking, the history of science. So I had a more comprehensive view of the subject than my fellow students. Also, I knew better what would be asked on examinations. Many times I would walk up to the exam with some classmate and say, "I will review you for the exam, I'll ask you some questions," and he would give me the answers he had studied. I'd go in, take the exam, and get twenty percent more than he did. He'd be so full of the subject, he couldn't see the woods for the trees. Because of my more relaxed approach, and the historical, more synoptic view, I got more pleasure out of the thing than the others did, and I didn't have to do as much work.[6]
>
> Again, I didn't have a single teacher who really interested me, or who was very good. I ran into students who were good and got high grades, but nobody who was interesting in the real sense . . . My recreation? Well, Cornell had a good amateur theater group. I'd go to that, and there I developed a taste for bad acting which stayed with me to this very day. When I see good acting, I feel it comes between me and the author. [Cornell] is in beautiful country, and we'd take long walks. . . . There was no fun and games and I did not join a fraternity. I couldn't afford it.[7]

The undergraduate years at Cornell were not happy: "This was where I encountered a lot of discrimination and anti-Jewish sentiment. . . . [Because of this,] I never had enough confidence to get to know any faculty member. I went through all the years not knowing a single faculty member. . . ."[8] Furthermore, the world was at war; a revolution had occurred in Russia: "It seemed strange being up there in Ithaca with the world changing so drastically."

Rabi's unhappiness may have contributed to his decision to join the air force. More likely, however, it was the war and his strong sense of Americanism. His sister Gertrude remembers that "he was very patriotic at Cornell, and he came home in 1917 to join the air force. Mother wouldn't allow it, and she told him to go back to school."[9] Back at Cornell, Rabi did join the Students Army Training Corps and moved into a barracks: "We lived under military discipline and I really loathed it."

Although he had entered Cornell a member of the class of 1920, he graduated, one year early, in 1919, with a bachelor of chemistry. For his senior dissertation he studied the chemistry of the element manganese. Suspected combinatorial forms (then called valence states, now called oxidation states) of manganese had been the earlier subject of a Ph.D. dissertation, but the author had not succeeded in isolating them. Rabi, however, found them and reported them in his senior thesis. Later, these same states of the element were rediscovered by a British chemist and the results were published in the *Journal of the Faraday Society*.

In June 1919, with his baccalaureate in hand, Rabi knew he wanted to go into science, but since chemistry had not captivated his thinking, he was faced with the necessity of getting a job. While his classmates were being snapped up by the chemical industry during his final semester at Cornell, Rabi had received no job offers. Nor did his Jewish classmates receive any. In 1919, Jews did not get jobs in chemical companies, nor did they have access to faculty positions in colleges and universities. They were cut out and passed over. Rabi became obsessed with finding a job: "It became clear to me that somehow or other, if I wanted to pursue my interest [in science], I would have to make money some other way."[10] A job, however, was not going to deter Rabi from his goal. "It's true, I didn't expect a job [in science], but I was going to study this [science] because it interested me. Such things I wanted to know, . . . I couldn't really feel like I was living without knowing them. How I made a living was another matter."

Returning home to Brooklyn in the summer of 1919, Rabi did get a job with the Lederle Laboratories in New York. It was a menial job as a chemist, analyzing various substances such as mother's milk and furniture polish, and he left after a few months: "I really wasn't too good at it. I wasn't interested. I would say I was more fired than left." He next went to work, as a bookkeeper discounting accounts receivable, for a friend of his who had set up a small, private banking business.

Rabi's job as a bookkeeper did not last long either: "Several years went by, and I did practically nothing. . . . I didn't do anything."[11] In this morass he had the support and comfort of three friends: Maurice Finkelstein, Benjamin Ginzberg, and Joseph Lapin. All four young men had finished college with distinction; all four were floundering:

> We didn't have any visible means of support. . . . I used to give little parties and did a lot of talking, . . . very little science talking. After a year or so, I went every day and almost every night to the New York Public Library and read, in science chiefly. In other words, no matter what I was doing, I was quite definite what my interest in life would be, but I wasn't getting anywhere.
>
> This went on for three years, and my parents never said a word to me about it. They must have gone through agonies—their son had gone through college and didn't have a job. Nothing close to his profession.[12]

Rabi looks back with amazement: "It's the most extraordinary thing, they never asked me, 'What are you doing?' I have never seen anything like it. They showed complete faith . . . and love."

"It was Ben Ginzberg who broke the spell. He simply said, 'It's time to quit horsing around.'" And, in the summer of 1922, they all left: Maurice Finkelstein, to Harvard Law School; Ben Ginzberg, to Harvard to work on a Ph.D. in philosophy; Joe Lapin, a Cornell classmate of Rabi's, to medical school, continuing his family's tradition. Rabi turned once more to science and returned to Cornell University as a graduate student: "I went to Cornell simply because I didn't know any other place. It was, so to say, coming back."[13] It was a coming back, not only to Cornell, but also to chemistry. Although Rabi says, "I was really interested in the structure of matter, in atomic structure . . . whatever that meant," in 1922 he did not know that meant physics.

The subject of Rabi's interest, atomic structure, was the most active frontier of physics in 1922; however, it had not yet found its way into student textbooks. Furthermore, the practical character of American physics up to this time contributed to Rabi's misunderstanding of physics. In 1899, physicist Henry Rowland from the Johns Hopkins University had lamented the poor estate of American physics in his address as retiring president of the newly formed American Physical Society:

He who makes two blades of grass grow where one grew before is the benefactor of mankind. But he who obscurely works to find the source of such growth is the intellectual superior and the greater benefactor of the two. How stands our country in this respect? My answer must still be now, as it was fifteen years ago, that much of the intellect of the country is still wasted in the pursuit of the so-called practical sciences which minister to our physical needs, but little thought and money is given to the grander portions of the subject, which appeal to the intellect alone.[14]

Fifteen years earlier, at a meeting of the American Association for the Advancement of Science, Rowland's message had been clearer—and blunter:

Fain would I recount to you the progress made in this subject [physics] by my countrymen, and the noble efforts to understand the order of the universe. I go out to gather the ripe grain and I find only tares. . . . American science is a thing of the future and not of the present or past. . . . What must be done is to create the science of physics in this country rather than call telegraphs, electric lights, and such conveniences by the name. . . . Shall our country be contented to stand by while other countries lead in the race? Shall we always grovel in the dust and pick up crumbs which fall from the rich man's table, considering ourselves richer than he because we have more crumbs while we forget that he has the cake which is the source of all crumbs?[15]

Rowland's addresses, delivered in 1883 and 1899, provided an apt description of American physics at those times. By 1922, however, American physics was stirring, it was coming to life. But, this awakening had not reached Rabi through his experience at Cornell, so he picked up where he had left off—in chemistry.

The chemist, even today, but particularly in 1922, tends to look at matter from without. For many chemists, it is enough to know that alcohol molecules combined with acid molecules produced ester molecules. The physicist, on the other hand, looks at matter from within. The first task is to identify the irreducible entities out of which matter is constructed. The next is to determine the physical properties of these irreducible entities: What are their masses? Do they carry an electrical charge? Are they influenced by a magnet? The irreducible entities themselves come together to form the atoms of the chemical elements. Physicists are fascinated with atoms, particularly the simple atoms. They love hydrogen—the simplest atom of all.

Without knowing it, Rabi wanted to study matter as a physicist. His knowledge was lacking, but his intuition was acute. Knowing that the questions of interest to him were more likely to arise in physical chemistry than in organic or analytical chemistry, he made a decisive change: "I wanted to do advanced work in chemistry; however, I'd taken all their courses . . . so I said to myself, 'I'll study physics. I know all the chemistry this place can teach me [so I'll study physics] and put them together myself.' . . . So I went into physics . . . I soon realized that the part of chemistry I liked was called physics. If someone had pointed that out to me before, it would have saved me many, many years."[16]

As an undergraduate at Cornell some three years in the past, Rabi had had scant physics and very little mathematics. Now that he was to study physics seriously, he was handicapped: "I hadn't had any physics except the kind of physics for chemists. On the other hand, I was older. I had read some. So I registered for advanced courses for which I was not prepared. I knew this."[17] In the face of this challenge, Rabi did something he had never done before, nor has he done since: "I set myself an extraordinary schedule. . . . I had a program which I wrote down. It started from the time I got up every morning to the time I went to bed . . . something for every hour, every minute, lunch and so on."[18] He made this schedule for two reasons: first, he recognized that he needed to devote some time to catch up; second, he was lazy—as he himself readily admits, and his parents recognized. (After it became obvious that Rabi was forsaking the demands of Orthodox Judaism, his father would say to him, "It's not that you're irreligious—you're lazy.")[19]

He followed his minute-to-minute schedule for about six months: "I knew if I broke it once, I'd never go back to it. One Sunday, my friends persuaded me to go out for a walk."[20] That finished Rabi's schedule. "But the back was broken; I was there and I had the feeling I was there."[21]

What is so different about chemistry and physics that Rabi could say of the latter, "I had the feeling I was there"? Physics is parsimonious. A few basic ideas have a validity that extends across nature from the smallness of the atom to the vastness of the galaxy. Furthermore, these same basic ideas capture a variety of factual information in the network of the logical connections between them. The person who sees charm and beauty in the ideas of physics may see no enchantment whatsoever in chemistry. Lacking the simple predictive principles that are the stock in trade of physics, chemists are marvelous in their ability to hold in their heads at all times a vast array of information. Physicists, on the other hand, work from a base formed by a few remembered ideas. Since the advent of quantum mechanics in the mid-1920s, the differences be- tween physics and chemistry have, in principle, lessened. But, in prac- tice, even today—and particularly during Rabi's student days—striking differences remain: "Physics has in it these fundamental insights and general powers that are not there in chemistry."

On March 14, 1923, planning to stay on at Cornell, Rabi completed an application for a fellowship in physics for the academic year 1923–24. He listed as a reference Professor A. W. Browne, of the department of chemistry, who wrote a glowing letter:

> It is with great pleasure that I write this letter in behalf of Mr. I. I. Rabi. . . . During his candidacy for the degree Bachelor of Chemis- try, Mr. Rabi stood very close to the top of his class in scholarship. He is an unusually brilliant student and is very diligent and enthusi- astic in his work. I am sure that he is capable of work of a very high grade, either in physics or chemistry.[22]

Nonetheless, Rabi was not awarded the fellowship: "I can see now why I didn't get the fellowship," he said many years later. "I must have been a pain in the neck, always asking questions. Who wanted that pain in the neck around?"

Without the fellowship, Rabi decided to leave Cornell. He had thought of going to Harvard, but a new interest now joined that of physics. Early in the summer of 1923, Rabi had a visitor. "Go visit your brother at Cornell," said Sheindel Rabi to Gertrude.[23] At about the same time, Helen Newmark was traveling to Ithaca to attend the summer session. Rabi saw Helen when she arrived: "When we got off the train," said Helen, "there was a whole group of young people ready to greet Harry, a well-loved person [also on the train]. Rab turned out to be one of them. He stepped forward, picked up my bag, said to somebody else, 'Take it up the hill; we're going to walk.' So there it was."[24] When Gertrude saw Helen and the look in her brother's eyes, she later told Sheindel, "Mama, you're going to have a beautiful daughter-in-law."[25] In three years, Ger- trude's prediction came true.

Since Helen Newmark was going to Hunter College in New York City that fall, Rabi decided to follow her and go to Columbia—"about," as Helen said later, "the most fortunate thing that ever happened to him."[26]

Rabi was twenty-five years old when, in the fall of 1923, he entered the Graduate School of Columbia University, officially a student of physics.

> At Columbia the atmosphere was immediately different. Cornell had a weakness: they required no examinations in their courses and ... the students became lax. They actually had no advanced courses that were really required so therefore they were not given. ... The Columbia faculty was no better than the Cornell faculty, but [at Columbia] there was a man, Professor A. P. Wills, who believed in solid training. Through his insistence, everybody had to take a course in the partial differential equations of physics and a course in analytical mechanics with LaGrange's equations and Hamilton's canonical equations.[27]

However different the atmosphere at Columbia, Rabi was still a Jew and could not expect to earn his livelihood as a physicist. During his first year at the university, he lived and ate at home with his parents and sister—an arrangement that kept to a minimum his immediate need for money. To help further, he borrowed some money and, with Helen's brother,[28] started a little newspaper, *The Brownsville Bulletin,* which he ran while taking four courses during the fall semester. Both activities suffered. He passed two courses with a grade of P, for "pass"; he withdrew from the third course; and received an INC, or "incomplete," as a grade in the fourth. During the spring semester, he enrolled in only one course. As for the newspaper, it failed after one year.

In the spring of 1924, Rabi had a chance encounter with a professor from the College of the City of New York, who encouraged him to apply for a graduate teaching assistantship at CCNY. After getting an application from Professor William Fox of the department of physics, Rabi asked Ernest Merritt, one of his former professors at Cornell, for a letter of recommendation. It was promptly provided; two weeks later, on June 18, 1924:

> Mr. Rabi made a very favorable impression on us. As you know his training had been chiefly in the field of chemistry before he came back as a graduate student but his interest seems to be more strongly in the field of Physics and he showed so much ability that we were glad to appoint him last year to our scholarship. . . . We have no knowledge of Mr. Rabi's ability as a teacher. His intense

interest and his undoubted ability would make it seem possible, however, that he would be successful at least with advanced and semi-advanced students and I see no reason why he should not be successful also with beginners.[29]

On June 17—one day *before* Merritt's thoughtful letter of recommendation was written—Rabi was appointed part-time tutor in physics by the board of trustees of the College of the City of New York, with a salary of eight hundred dollars a year. "That changed everything. I was on the road. I didn't have to worry and I dropped the other stuff. . . . I had full time, so to speak, to devote to this [physics] without the other necessary distractions."[30] For the first time, his interests and his paycheck were compatible. He moved out of his parents' home and into a dormitory in preparation for the 1924 fall semester.

Between a graduate student and the degree Doctor of Philosophy looms a formidable hurdle—the dissertation. The first step on the path is the initiation of an original research project. The project itself can have dull periods—building equipment, painstaking calibration of an instrument, repetition of routine measurements, tedious analysis—when there is no romance, and discipline and determination are more important than intelligence. When all the research is done, there remains the dissertation. One must sit down and write. The letters ABD —*All But the Dissertation*—are recognized by all academics as the sad, but final degree carried by many once-hopeful students.

To all the vicissitudes that may threaten the success of the research-dissertation process, Rabi brought his own idiosyncrasies and handicaps. Columbia University, between 1924 and 1926, added twists of its own. In the end, however, the result was vintage Rabi.

In 1924 and 1925 and 1926, Rabi wanted to play, so to speak, a violin concerto for his thesis, but Columbia University could supply neither conductor nor orchestra. New music was being written for physics during these years, but all the composers were in Europe—as were almost all of the performers as well. By 1925, the old quantum theory was approaching its final measure: the new physics was a series of clever cadenzas isolated one from the other, and it lacked a theme to tie them together. But new composers were emerging—Dirac, Heisenberg, Pauli, and Schrödinger; and the first notes of the new quantum mechanics would soon be heard. Rabi was learning the new music as best he could —but entirely on his own. No faculty member at Columbia was able to direct a thesis in the new physics.

RABI: Scientist and Citizen

Rabi did the next best thing; he sought out a professor whose research could be regarded as modern physics. X rays had been discovered by the German physicist Wilhelm Roentgen in 1895, an event and a date to mark the beginning of modern physics. Since Professor Bergen Davis was doing research with X rays, Rabi went first to him. The work in Davis's laboratory required access to X-ray machines; and in the fall of 1924, all of the machines were in use. Rabi was not invited to join the Davis group.

It was Professor A. P. Wills who first suggested a thesis topic. A specialist in magnetism, Wills proposed that Rabi design an experiment to measure the response of sodium vapor to a magnetic field. Any substance, when placed between the poles of a magnet, becomes magnetic. But the nature and magnitude of the response varies from substance to substance; this property is its magnetic susceptibility. Wills's proposal to measure the magnetic susceptibility of sodium vapor did not, however, excite Rabi:

> [I recognized that] this was a terrifically difficult thing to do. Sodium at high temperature is, of course, a gas, and it is corrosive and very hard to handle . . . I thought about it for a while and finally I said to myself, "I'm not going to do this." So I went to [Wills] and told him that I didn't think I was good enough to do it. I couldn't tell him I didn't *want* to do it, and besides, I didn't think I *would* be able to do it, and I didn't know anyone else . . . who could do it either. Wills . . . was disappointed, and said he would give the problem to someone else. I said to myself, *"Moichel!* Good riddance." . . . So I was essentially on my own.[31]

The dissertation topic remained unresolved until later that fall when William Lawrence Bragg, a Nobel Prize–winning physicist from England, came to Columbia to give a seminar on some of his latest work. Bragg had just completed a series of experiments in which he measured the electric susceptibility of a group of crystalline substances called the Tutton salts. These salts, such as nickel-ammonium sulphate-hydrate and potassium-sulphate hexahydrate, have an interesting property: while the spatial arrangement of the atoms in this series of crystalline salts is quite similar, their electrical susceptibilities are quite different. Learning of Bragg's results, Rabi decided to measure the magnetic susceptibility of these same crystals.

Since Professor Wills was the logical faculty member to sponsor such

40

a project, Rabi went to him with his proposal. "All right," said Wills, and the project began. "I didn't get any help from him," said Rabi, "nor did I want any. The last thing in the world I wanted . . . was for someone to help me."[32]

The magnetic susceptibility of a substance is determined by its atomic makeup: which particular atoms it contains and how those atoms are arranged. (One can measure magnetic susceptibility without knowing anything about atomic makeup or arrangement.) If a substance—say, a crystal of table salt or a diamond—is suspended between the poles of a magnet, it takes on the properties of a magnet: that is, it becomes magnetized. Draw the substance out from between the poles of the magnet, and the magnetization vanishes. The magnetic susceptibility of a substance is a measure of the degree to which it can take on the properties of a magnet. From a knowledge of this property, information about the structure of materials can be inferred.

Rabi started with the standard way for measuring magnetic susceptibility. First, the material whose susceptibility is to be measured has to be obtained in pure form; thus, the Tutton crystals have to be grown from a seed crystal. Second, the crystals have to be prepared for measurement: in this case, one has to be as skillful as a diamond cutter to cleave one large crystal into three sections, whose facets have different orientations relative to the internal structure of the crystal itself. Third, and finally, the measurement itself: each crystalline section, suspended from a sensitive balance, is lowered into the region between the north and the south poles of an electromagnet. The balance reads differently depending on whether the electric current producing the magnetic field is on or off; this difference is the measure of the magnetic susceptibility.

The first step of the standard approach is trivial, and Rabi began directly. A concentrated solution of the material to be crystallized is made by dissolving a lot of it in water and then suspending, in this saturated solution, a small seed crystal. Slowly material from the solution accretes on the tiny seed crystal, layer upon perfect layer expanding its boundaries. A lovely procedure: one simply waits, luxuriating in the notion that time is doing the job.

And so Rabi luxuriated. As the crystals grew, he did what he *had* to do. He had to teach at CCNY because that institution was providing him with a salary. His teaching load was onerous—sixteen hours in the classroom each week, a full-time job if taken seriously. But since his casual approach to the classroom left him plenty of time to pursue his own interests, as the crystals grew he did what he *wanted* to do. He enjoyed the theater, particularly the opera, and even a poor graduate student could afford standing-room tickets at the Metropolitan Opera. Far and away his greatest enjoyment, however, came from following those events that were taking place in Europe. By 1924, the vexing quantum had brought physics to the point of crisis. At Columbia University, Rabi and his friends could only follow the fascinating development of the quantum by reading the European journals of physics.

Joining Rabi in his enthusiasm were a group of his friends, fellow graduate students: Francis Bitter, who became a world authority on magnetism as a professor at the Massachusetts Institute of Technology; Ralph Kronig, who later left the United States and made significant contributions in theoretical physics as a professor at the Technological University of Delft in Holland; S. C. Wang, whose papers on applied quantum mechanics have been used by generations of spectroscopists; Mark Zemansky, who became a prominent teacher of physics as well as the author of widely used textbooks during his career at CCNY. And there was Rabi: "I organized [this] group to study modern physics, [physics] that the faculty didn't teach. . . . I was getting around to doing things I had done as a little boy, when I organized a group."[33] The group spent their days together, ate together, and talked physics: they talked about the new quantum ideas. Every Sunday these five students got together for a physics seminar, starting at 11:00 A.M. and continuing into the afternoon. At some point, they would adjourn to a Chinese restaurant where Wang would do the ordering. After eating, they would continue their discussions into the late evening. Their enthusiasm was contagious, and soon some professors from New York University began attending their marathon sessions: "We knew very well there was a crisis [in physics]. . . . We were quite familiar . . . with quantum theory and the ideas of [the theory]. We were familiar with the paradoxes of space quantization, . . . with Einstein's problems, and with the difficulties of the light-quantum hypothesis."[34]

Throughout the 1924–25 academic year, Rabi's own graduate courses (he received a "pass" in each of the five courses he took), his teaching at CCNY, and his dissertation research were distractions from his main endeavor: to learn and discuss the new physics. On occasion, he would check to see that his Tutton crystals were still growing. They were.

When the new academic year began in the fall of 1925, Rabi assumed additional teaching responsibilities at City College. To his daytime load of sixteen classroom hours, he added nine hours in the evening. He did not, however, deny his interests. He, Kronig, and the other members of the seminar group read the papers from Europe as fast as they arrived at the Columbia Library: "The *Zeitschrift für Physik* [a leading German physics journal] was so fascinating, something new coming out all the time."[35]

As 1925 slipped into the past and the early weeks of 1926 were gone as well, Rabi had to acknowledge that his research project was not going to do itself: "[I] had to face the very difficult job of cutting and grinding crystals. We had no equipment for that, and the whole business of measuring the magnetic field looked pretty tedious."[36] The method for measuring magnetic susceptibility was not only tedious; it was also difficult, time consuming, and routine. Furthermore, the final result was plagued with uncertainties. For a man of lazy methods, it was too much.

Rabi was still an ardent browser in the library. "One day I happened to be reading, for sheer pleasure, Maxwell's *Treatise*."[37] The Scottish physicist James Clerk Maxwell was the founder of the modern theory of electromagnetism, and his *Treatise on Electricity and Magnetism* (1873) is a classic. As he read, Rabi found himself thinking, "This is it!" "It" was a way to measure the magnetic susceptibility of the Tutton crystals without the cleaving, the grinding, the calibrating, and all the onerous, time-consuming demands of the old standard method. The new method conceived by Rabi not only circumvented all the work that he had been avoiding for months and months, but also promised to give much more accurate results.

Now he began his dissertation in earnest. Dedicated vigor replaced lethargy as he assembled the modest equipment required to carry out the experiment: a magnet, a torsion balance, and some odds and ends of glassware. Between the pole faces of the magnet, he clamped a piece of glass tubing that could hold a liquid solution. That was all the equipment needed and that was all the set-up required.

The experiment centered on two comparisons. First, the crystal whose magnetic susceptibility was to be measured was lowered, via a glass fiber, into a solution (held in a tube between the magnet-pole faces) whose own susceptibility could be increased or decreased. When the susceptibility of the surrounding solution matched that of the crystal, the magnet could be turned on and off without disturbing the delicately suspended crystal. Since minute changes in a crystal's position could be detected, this first comparison was a precise method for making the susceptibility of the solution exactly equal to that of the crystal. Now, it remained to measure the solution's susceptibility in order to determine the crystal's susceptibility.

Thus, the second comparison was between the solution and water. The magnetic susceptibility of water was known precisely. Samples of the solution and water were suspended between the poles of a magnet, and their weights compared. Their weights were in exactly the same ratio as their susceptibilities. From the weight ratio, the susceptibility of the solution was determined—and was, of course, the same as the crystal's. Done!

The old method of determining magnetic susceptibilities was crude: a brute-force approach. Rabi's method had style:

The standard way of doing the problem was so boring to me and so difficult I just couldn't get down to it. I might never have finished my dissertation if I had had to do it that way because I am not an activist in this sense. I like experimental physics, but I'm not an activist and I never was, especially at that time, when the world was so full of new theory, new ideas, and otherwise. . . . I mean, I was a young man and there was opera going on, plays, and other things.[38]

Rabi's method was so easy and so quick that he was able to measure a whole series of crystalline substances, more than had ever been done before, and with results that were unexcelled in accuracy. All of this he did in just six weeks: "It was so simple that I got no experimental experience out of it."[39]

He got neither experience nor recognition:

It taught me a lesson. This paper [my dissertation] was published; it was the first paper in that issue of the *Physical Review;* it was abstracted in *Physikalische Berichte* and *Physical Abstracts* . . . and nobody saw it.[40] *Absolutely* nobody saw it. [J. H.] Van Vleck, who was interested in this field, learned of it some years later through a reference in an Indian journal. It [my dissertation] was seen by K. S. Krishnan[41] who started his whole career in magneto-chemistry using these methods, but *nobody else* ever saw this thing; I saw no reference to it or anything. It shows that when you have something and you just introduce it on the world, they won't look at it. It has to be brought in and gradually; it has to have backing. I hadn't read a paper on it to the Physical Society or anything of that sort; it was just written and there it was.[42]

Rabi was bothered by the lack of response to his published dissertation. He takes his physics personally. It is *his* physics, *his* creative effort, between him and nature.

Even during this early period when, as a graduate student, Rabi was discovering physics, he displayed aspects of what would later be part of his distinctive style in physics. He eschewed the routine, was uninspired by the ordinary. Faced with a long, dull experiment, he was able to find an ingenious alternative that was both quick and witty; and his instinct led him to home in on the crucial question. In the years ahead, all of these attributes would show themselves again and again.

On July 16, 1926, Rabi sent his dissertation, entitled "On the Principal Magnetic Susceptibilities of Crystals," to the editors of *Physical Review,* the major American journal of physics. On the next day, Dr. I. I. Rabi and Helen Newmark were married.

CHAPTER

3

Learning the Melody

People of my generation went abroad, mostly to
Germany, and learned not the subject, but the
taste for it, the style, the quality, the tradition.
We knew the libretto, but we had to learn the
music.

—I. I. RABI

IN 1913, when Rabi was a sophomore at Manual Training High School
in Brooklyn, quantum ideas were first applied to the question of atomic
structure. This step was taken by Niels Bohr, the Danish physicist
whose influence during the bewildering years of the old quantum theory
(1913–24) and through the formal development of the new quantum
mechanics was paramount. Bohr's 1913 atom was a bizarre hybrid in
which the smooth continuity of classical physics was combined with the
disjointedness of quantum behavior.

Bohr started with the simplest of all atoms—hydrogen. He adopted
the nuclear model of the atom proposed two years earlier by his mentor,
the British physicist Ernest Rutherford. In this model, the atom is a
miniature solar system. Electrons, with a negative charge, orbit around
a massive nucleus that carries a positive charge. Electrical forces hold
the atom together just as gravitational forces pull the planets to the sun.
The orbits of the electrons are smooth paths determined by the principles of Newtonian physics.

To this model, Bohr imposed an *ad hoc* quantum idea: he assumed
that the energy of the hydrogen atom is quantized; that is, that the total

46

energy of the hydrogen atom can have only certain values, a select set of discrete values. This discreteness of energy results in a discreteness of electron orbits, allowing only certain orbits with specifically prescribed radii. Immediately, physicists had to deal with the peculiar situation of the electron that moves in a smooth orbit, according to the well-known laws of Newton's physics, while at the same time being constrained to move only in those orbits allowed by Bohr's quantum condition.

Bohr had a reason for postulating discrete energy states: he wanted a way to explain the unique spectral light emitted by hydrogen atoms. He achieved this by postulating quantum transitions—electrons jumping from one orbit to another and, in the process, emitting (or absorbing) light. Emission occurs when an electron jumps from a high-energy orbit to one lower in energy; if the jump is in the other direction, absorption occurs. In Bohr's model, the emitted (or absorbed) energy is radiant in nature and has just those discrete frequencies observed in the hydrogen spectrum.

Bohr's model gave an account of the hydrogen spectrum. Again, however, the situation was bewildering: on the one hand, the electrons move in their orbits in a continuous, predictable fashion. On the other hand, when they make quantum jumps, they do so discontinuously and unpredictably. When an electron jumps *from* orbit number 3, what determines its destination? What determines whether the electron ends up in orbit number 2, or in number 1? The model proposed by Bohr could not answer these questions. Moreover, the extension of his ideas beyond the hydrogen atom grudgingly ground to a halt with the next simplest atom—helium.

For the next dozen years after the appearance of Bohr's famous paper, new successes and failures alternately raised and dashed physicists' hopes for a theory of atomic structure. The principal idea of the old quantum theory, that atoms exist in discrete energy states, gained empirical support in 1914 when the German physicists James Franck and Gustav Hertz sent a stream of high-speed electrons through a gas of mercury.[1] Their data showed that, when an electron collides with a mercury atom, the latter absorbs energy only in discrete amounts. Furthermore, the size of the energy packet transferred *to* the mercury atom in the collision is the same as that of the energy packet radiated *by* the mercury atom in the formation of its spectrum.

The spectra of another group of atoms, the alkali atoms, provided both joy and disappointment: joy, because the gross features of the spectral lines seemed to agree with Bohr's ideas; disappointment, because the bright yellow emission line of the alkali atom sodium turned out to be, in fact, two lines close together. There was no explanation for the presence of the two lines.

Each energy state in Bohr's atom was labeled with a number—a quantum number. Spectral lines were equated with the mental image of an electron undergoing a transition between states with different quantum numbers—that is, between different numbered orbits. As we have seen, this simple model left many questions with no answers.

Suppose a sample of gas—say, hydrogen—is placed between the north and the south poles of a magnet. A magnetic field fills the space between those poles, and the atoms (or molecules) of the gas are in that space. The magnetic field exerts a pronounced influence on the observed spectrum: spectral lines are split into separate, distinct components. When the magnet is turned on, producing a magnetic field, one spectral line becomes two or three or four or more distinct lines, each with its own distinct frequency. This splitting is called the Zeeman effect after its discoverer, the Dutch physicist Pieter Zeeman.

It was Arnold Sommerfeld of Munich, Germany, who, in 1916, provided an explanation of the Zeeman effect.[2] Each transition requires two quantum states; therefore, the magnetic field must subdivide the principal energy states postulated by the Bohr model into two or more energy states. This division would provide additional starting and ending states and would account for the additional spectral lines. But the question remains: Why are there more energy states when atoms are in the presence of a magnetic field? Sommerfeld answered as follows: The magnetic field provides a direction in space with respect to which the electron orbits in the atom can orient themselves. However, and here is the crux of the matter, only certain spatial orientations are allowed. Since each orientation corresponds to a slightly different energy, more energy states are possible in the presence of a magnetic field.

The spatial orientations postulated by Sommerfeld (and independently by the Dutch physicist Peter Debye[3]) were a new form of quantization, appropriately called space quantization. Once again, there was joy and there was disappointment: the idea of space quantization accounted for some Zeeman splittings of spectral lines, but not for others.

Of all the ideas of the quantum theory, space quantization was perhaps the most bizarre. Even Sommerfeld found it surprising. It was *ad hoc* in nature, and the question remained: Was space quantization purely fiction, a curious idea whose only significance would be the "explanation" of a single phenomenon? Otto Stern, then in Frankfurt, Germany, conceived of a way to put Sommerfeld's idea to the test. From 1921 to 1922, just before Rabi entered graduate school at Cornell University, Stern was in the early stages of his molecular-beam studies, the work that would bring him the Nobel Prize in 1943. It was at this time that he and his Frankfurt colleague, Walther Gerlach, performed their famous experiment. It was also the time when the perplexities and the attendant frustrations of the old quantum theory were reaching their peak.

Because of the orbital motion of a single electron, an atom can possess a magnetic moment: that is, an atom, when "looked at" from the vantage point of a neighboring atom, appears to have a tiny bar magnet tucked away inside itself. Sommerfeld's spatial quantization allowed only selective, discrete orientations of this atomic magnet relative to the direction of an externally applied magnetic field. This was the basis of the Stern-Gerlach experiment.

In this experiment, silver atoms flew with great speed through a highly evacuated chamber. They began their flight by escaping from a small aperture in an oven whose temperature was high enough to vaporize silver metal. Additional apertures were set up so that those silver atoms that entered the evacuated working chamber did so as a well-defined, ribbonlike beam. At the opposite end of the evacuated chamber was a beam detector—a flat piece of cold glass. A mirrorlike deposit formed on the glass plate where silver atoms from the beam struck and adhered to it. Between the source of silver atoms (the oven) and the detector was a long magnet so situated that the beam of silver atoms passed between and along the full length of the pole faces.

The pole faces were shaped to produce a non-uniform magnetic field: specifically, the field grew weaker from the north pole to the south pole. When silver atoms with their intrinsic magnetic moments entered the non-uniform magnetic field, a force was exerted on them. The size of this force as well as its direction depended on the orientation of a silver atom's magnetic moment relative to the external magnetic field. Moments tending toward the parallel configuration were pushed toward the south pole; those tending toward the antiparallel orientation were pulled toward the north pole; moments at right angles to the external field were neither pushed nor pulled; they were not deflected by the non-uniform field.

Silver atoms left the hot oven with their magnetic moments oriented in higgledy-piggledy fashion. This was a fact; there was no doubt about it. As the randomly oriented silver atoms entered the region of the non-uniform magnetic field, physicists predicted that some atoms would be pushed, some would be pulled, and some would pass through undeflected. A *continuous* gradation of deflections should occur; therefore, the beam, narrow on entering the field region, should be widened as it leaves. On the cold glass detector plate, one should see a continuous mirrored smear over the widened dimension of the beam, dense at the widened-beam center and tailing off to each side of center. That was the conventional wisdom.

Stern and Gerlach saw something very different. Instead of a continuous mirrored smear, they saw two distinct arching smears with *nothing* in between, *nothing* in the middle. In just the position where most of the silver atoms should have struck the detector, there was nothing. What did this mean? The result implied that only two distinct orientations of the silver atoms are allowed in the magnetic field. Although the result confirmed the idea of space quantization, no one—Einstein, Bohr, Sommerfeld, Stern—seemed to understand or agree upon a detailed interpretation. How do the silver atoms take up their specific orientations? There was no hint of an answer.

The 1922 Stern-Gerlach experiment stunned I. I. Rabi. It intrigued him; the mystery of it bore into him. Almost sixty years later, when leading physicists of the twentieth century were asked to identify important events in their careers, Rabi responded by recalling this experiment: "The results of the experiment were astounding. The whole thing was a mystery. This convinced me, once and for all, that the direction of the ingenious classical mechanism was out. We had to face the fact that the quantum phenomena required a completely new orientation."

Until he encountered the Stern-Gerlach experiment, Rabi was skeptical about the quantum theory. The system of ideas underlying the Bohr atom and the contorted attempts, valiant though they were, to extend these ideas to other atomic phenomena, had, as far as Rabi was concerned, a contrived silliness about them. Then came space quantization and its empirical verification by Stern and Gerlach. Here was an incontrovertible experimental result that was, and remains even yet, the most impressive evidence for the fundamental difference between the macroscopic physics of tennis balls and the microscopic physics of atoms:

> Here was a mystery that was beyond my way of thinking. These atoms had to orient, but how? I was great at inventing mechanisms, but there *was* no mechanism. So I looked at the Bohr atom again and said "O.K., we've given up a lot, but you have to give up a lot."

I felt like a young fellow whose town had been destroyed. Who's going to rebuild? It was up to us, the young generation of physicists.

Rabi was, as a graduate student, so excited about the Stern-Gerlach experiment that he was asked to give a departmental seminar on it.

While the dramatic result of this experiment excited physicists, it also was a distressing reminder that their subject was in a state of crisis: there was no coherent, comprehensive explanation of atomic behavior or atomic structure. Since crises spawn opportunities, it was a heady time for Rabi and the other young physicists at Columbia University. They avidly read and discussed:

- The French physicist Louis Victor de Broglie's 1923 paper on the wave nature of matter.[4]
- The Austrian physicist Wolfgang Pauli's 1925 paper on the exclusion principle which restricted the behavior of electrons in an atom in such a way as to lay the groundwork for understanding why atoms of different elements have distinctly different physical and chemical properties.[5]
- The 1925 paper by the Dutch physicists S. A. Goudsmit and G. E. Uhlenbeck proposing that the electron has its own intrinsic magnetic moment.[6]

These papers, and others, were soon to be incorporated into the formal structure of a new mechanics of the quantum.

The birth of quantum mechanics, in a formal sense, occurred over the period from 1925 to 1927. In fact, there were several births. Werner Heisenberg's formulation of quantum mechanics came first, in mid-1925 —a version, however, that was soon couched in a mathematics unfamiliar to the vast majority of physicists.[7] For this reason, Erwin Schrödinger's version of quantum mechanics, which came in early 1926, was immediately welcomed.[8] The versions put out by these two German physicists seemed to bear no resemblance; but by the middle of 1926, Schrödinger was able to demonstrate the mathematical equivalence of his version with that of Heisenberg.

The group at Columbia were clearly more at ease with Schrödinger's version. They read it immediately and studied its contents, and Rabi was eager to take up Ralph Kronig's suggestion that they "do something with this Schrödinger method just to learn it better."[9] Since Schrödinger's paper had just been published the field was wide open. Rabi and Kronig proceeded carefully, looking through the literature—recent journals and books—to find an appropriate topic.

Schrödinger had used his method of quantum mechanics to determine the allowed energies of an atomic system such as hydrogen. Kronig and Rabi decided to extend Schrödinger's quantum mechanics to molecular systems.* They set up the Schrödinger equation, a three-dimensional, second-order partial differential equation, for their specific system—a symmetric top. After routine preliminary steps, they confronted a mathematical equation that neither one of them had the faintest idea how to solve. They stood at an impasse.

Kronig, the most experienced of the group, had finished his Ph.D. a year earlier, in 1925, and had already been to Europe where, as a traveling fellow of Columbia University, he witnessed firsthand the feverish state of European physics. But he could not solve the equation. Nor could S. C. Wang, who took inspiration from the Kronig-Rabi project and later extended their work to more complex molecular systems. Neither could Bitter, nor Zemansky.

Rabi's penchant for eschewing the onerous demands of daily work by escaping to the peaceful serenity of the library broke the impasse. This was a time when he should have been busy. Not only was he teaching twenty-five hours a week at CCNY, but he was also under pressure to finish his dissertation, to keep on top of developments in the new quantum mechanics, and to work with Kronig on their quantum mechanical problem. Nonetheless he was sitting in the library reading for pleasure the original works of Carl Gustav Jakob Jacobi, eminent mathematician of nineteenth-century Germany. As he browsed through the pages of Jacobi, an equation seemed to leap from a page. "My God!" he thought. "That's our equation!" The equation had the form of a hypergeometric equation, which Jacobi had already solved. The solution was expressed in terms of a hypergeometric series; and, in terms of this series, the intractable equation could now be solved.

As Rabi put the finishing touches on his doctoral dissertation, he and Kronig were applying Schrödinger's quantum mechanics to their problem. Their results established that the symmetric top could have only a discrete set of energy states. They set up a computational assembly line to calculate the quantities that would give the intensities of the quantum transitions. After finishing their project, they sent their manuscript to the editor of *Physical Review*. It was rejected. The editor insisted that the manuscript be shortened. On November 4, 1926, just a

---

*Specifically, they solved the Schrödinger equation for the symmetric top and found the energy states of such a mechanical system. Since many molecules are symmetric tops, their results could be applied to the study of molecular spectra.

few months after the appearance of Schrödinger's original papers on quantum mechanics, Kronig and Rabi sent their shortened version of the symmetric-top paper back to the editor. It was accepted and appeared in the February 1927 issue of *Physical Review,** one month after the publication of Rabi's dissertation.

There was no question about what he wanted to do next: he wanted to go to Europe. Rabi was in his third year as a tutor at City College; it was a miserable job, and he was hired on a year-to-year basis. The very nature of the tutor's position precluded permanency. Furthermore, the work load was heavy—still twenty-five hours each week; and the pay was insultingly low (universities then, as today, exploited teachers who had to accept nonregular faculty appointments). But it was a job and, more significant, it was a job teaching university-level physics. Rabi had neither hope nor thought of a better university position—not in 1927, not for a Jewish physicist.

While Rabi had his problems, the physicists in Europe had their problems as well. By the summer of 1926, there had appeared a third version of quantum mechanics. To the matrix formulation of Heisenberg with its strange mathematics and to the wave equation version of Schrödinger with its strange wave function, the English physicist Paul Dirac added his approach with its Poisson brackets by which the equations of classical physics could be transformed into their quantum-mechanical equivalent. All of these versions were highly abstract; and before quantum mechanics could be considered complete, it would be necessary to interpret these equations and then extract from them their physical meaning. In other words, a mathematical formalism, however consistent and complete, is not a physical theory. To be a working theory, the symbols of a mathematical formalism must be defined and understood so that a dialogue can be carried out with nature: specific verifiable predictions made, experiments designed, and experimental results interpreted.

Schrödinger's wave equation was an immediate success because it could be, and was, applied to a variety of problems, of which the application made by Kronig and Rabi was just one. What, however, did the wave equation really mean? Schrödinger's own interpretation was proving to be inadequate. What was the meaning of the wave function that

---

*Ironically, the same problem was also being solved by two German physicists, Fritz Reiche and Hans Rademacher, at about the same time. Their 59-page paper, published in *Zeitschrift für Physik,*[10] contained much of the information that had been eliminated from the Kronig-Rabi paper.

came by solving the Schrödinger equation? Max Born, physicist from Göttingen in Germany, responded in probabilistic terms, declaring that the solution of Schrödinger's equation is a probability amplitude whose down-to-earth physical meaning was to be found by squaring it. The implications of Born's interpretation were profound.

In order to understand them, let us consider the application of the Schrödinger equation to the hydrogen atom. When the equation is set up and solved, there in all its abstract splendor is the probability amplitude. The probability amplitude is not a number; it is a function dependent on such parameters as the distance from the nucleus of the atom. The square of the probability amplitude at a particular point gives the probability of finding the electron in the immediate vicinity of that point. If, for example, the square of the probability amplitude is ½ for a particular location, then there is a fifty-fifty chance of finding the electron in that specific location. Is the electron there or isn't it? The theory cannot say. The best it can do is to say that on the average the electron will be there half of the time and somewhere else the other half.

The probabilistic character of the information obtained from the theory was, if true, a profound change. The sweetness of physics had always been the definiteness, the unambiguousness of the answers it provided. The time of a solar eclipse could be predicted exactly, with no ambiguity. Schrödinger was so unhappy with this development that he wished he had never written his papers.

Still another profound change was taking form in Europe, because something was still lacking in the new quantum mechanics. Suppose a measurement were made that would give the instantaneous location of the electron as it moves around the proton in a hydrogen atom. Could such a result be accommodated by the new theory? No, the theory gives only a probability, not a number giving the location of the electron. Is the theory lacking? Perhaps.

Suppose, on the other hand, physicists were deceiving themselves as they thought of measuring the exact location of an electron. Werner Heisenberg was thinking deeply about measurements and the quantum during the final weeks of 1926. Whenever a measurement is made, there is of necessity interaction between the object of the measurement and the measuring device—a measurement jolt. In the smooth world of classical physics, the size of this jolt can be reduced continuously to any arbitrary small value so that the behavior of the object being measured is essentially unaffected. This cannot be the case in the discrete world of the quantum where the size of the measuring jolt can be reduced only in discrete quantum steps. These steps are limited; in fact, the measuring jolt can be reduced only to the size the jolt has in its lowest quantum state. Heisenberg was able to demonstrate that the size of the measurement jolt, even at its smallest, is sufficient to alter the behavior of atomic-sized objects. Thus, in the very act of measuring, desired information is lost. This line of reasoning brought Heisenberg, in the spring of 1927, to an enunciation of his momentous uncertainty principle, the capstone in the formal structure of quantum mechanics. In a sense, the uncertainty principle excuses the theory for what it cannot provide anyway; in another sense, it makes the theory complete. When Pauli first heard of it, he said, "Now the light dawns in quantum mechanics."[11]

Even more than Born's probabilistic interpretation, Heisenberg's uncertainty principle sent shock waves through and even beyond the profession. Always implicit in the thinking of physicists had been the axiom of determinism: if we know the present exactly, the future can be predicted exactly. In his 1927 paper, Heisenberg wrote: "We *cannot* know, as a matter of principle, the present in all its details."[12] Hence, the strict causal links to the future are broken. The impossibility of making exact predictions about the future behavior of an electron brought consistency to the probabilistic nature of the quantum-mechanical description of an electron. Everything did not, however, become smooth, simple, and complete; the physical and epistemological implications of both the probabilistic interpretation and the uncertainty principle remain topics of intense scholarly discussion up to the present day.

The years immediately following the formulation of quantum mechanics were exhilarating for theoretical physicists. And, as of May 10, 1927, Rabi was to be a part of that excitement. On that date, he was appointed a Barnard Fellow for the period September 22, 1927, to June 8, 1928, with a stipend of fifteen hundred dollars. He immediately applied for a leave of absence from his teaching position at CCNY.

When his application was denied, it was an all but crushing blow. He had not been able to find a position as a chemist after graduating from Cornell in 1919; he shuddered at the memory of the odd jobs he had held. He now had a Ph.D. in physics, but things were no different: the prospects of getting a job as a physicist were small to the point of hopelessness. Furthermore, he was now almost twenty-nine and married, with responsibilities to his wife. "I determined," Rabi said later, "that I would live only one life and I was going to do this. I was going to Europe." Helen agreed. On June 2, 1927, the College of the City of New York accepted his resignation.

Rabi left New York in July, but his specific destination was unknown. He had made no formal arrangements to visit any particular place or to work with any particular individual. No cables had been sent; no letters had been written. Wherever it was he decided to go, he would arrive unannounced. Such was the informality of the times, and such was the nature of Rabi. "I shall work with Schrödinger," he thought; and when his ship docked, he headed for Zurich and the university. Finding a seminar in session when he arrived at the physics department, he slipped into the back row of the lecture room and, much to his chagrin, discovered that he could not understand a word that was being said, even though he knew German. He saw two men in the room whom he immediately recognized as American by the cut of their shirts. One of the Americans was J. A. Stratton, who eventually became the president of the Massachusetts Institute of Technology; and the other was Linus Pauling who was to become a famous chemist. They reassured Rabi that the seminar speaker was speaking not German but *Schwyzertutsch,* a Swiss dialect. They celebrated both Rabi's relief and his arrival by going to Pauling's apartment for drinks.

When Rabi went to see Schrödinger, he met with disappointment: the German physicist had resigned his position and was about to leave Zurich for Berlin where he was to succeed Max Planck as director of the Theoretical Institute of Berlin. Without Schrödinger at Zurich, Rabi had to go elsewhere, and he decided on Sommerfeld and the University of Munich. Linus Pauling gave him a good tip about a pension near the university. He arrived in Munich late in the day and managed to find the pension just in time to register for the evening. The next morning at breakfast, Rabi saw the most German-looking man he had ever seen, reading the *American Mercury.* It was Edward Uhler Condon from the University of California, Berkeley. The American physicist had been with Born in Göttingen for almost a year and was stopping briefly in Munich on his way back to the United States. A second American in Munich was H. P. Robertson from the California Institute of Technology. The friendship established in Munich between these three American physicists was to grow and flourish throughout their lives.

Upon meeting Sommerfeld, Rabi simply said, "My name is Rabi. I've come here to work."[13] And with that, Rabi was accepted. Sommerfeld showed Rabi around the Institute and introduced him to other visitors and to his students. One graduate student was Rudolf Peierls and another, who was sitting under a naked light bulb at a desk in the basement, was Hans Bethe.[14] "I remember Rabi as a very joyful young man,"

56

Bethe has said. "There were these two jolly Americans [Condon and Rabi] who stuck really quite close together. They seemed to know physics."[15]

Rabi began a computation in which he attempted to calculate, from Schrödinger's theory, the magnetic susceptibility of the hydrogen molecule. Since the research journals were kept in Sommerfeld's office, anyone who wanted to consult one had to gain access to the office through an assistant. *"Ist der Herr Professor verhastet?"* Rabi asked the assistant, who informed the young American that his German was in error. Rabi had actually asked, "Is the professor arrested?"

In his weeks in Munich, Rabi was thoroughly introduced to European life. Sommerfeld invited the members of his research group to tea in the garden; and while sipping tea, they discussed quantum mechanics. In these discussions, Rabi recognized that "although I'd never studied under great teachers, I was better prepared than more than ninety-five percent of the German students."[16] But between parties and looking around Munich with Ed Condon and Bob Robertson, Rabi accomplished little at Sommerfeld's Institute.

The ninety-seventh annual meeting of the British Association for the Advancement of Science was held in Leeds, England, from August 31 to September 7, 1927. This was a spectacular affair, and, in a letter, Professor Wills, Rabi's dissertation advisor at Columbia University, had told Rabi that if he could get to the British Association meeting, he would always remember it as one of the most stimulating of his career, both because of the papers presented and, even more, because of the number and character of the scientific men whom he would meet. At this annual meeting, the English mathematician E. T. Whittaker was to give a paper on the outstanding problems of relativity theory; and R. A. Millikan, an American physicist, was to give an evening lecture on new research in cosmic-ray physics. Two other papers, however, caught Rabi's attention: first, Peter Debye was giving a paper on the polar properties of molecules (Rabi was still thinking about magnetic susceptibilities, and Debye's paper might prove edifying); but of most interest was a paper on recent progress in quantum mechanics to be given by none other than Werner Heisenberg.

While the meeting of the British Association was reason enough to make the trip from Munich to England, Rabi had a better reason: Helen was on her way from New York to join him and would arrive in London just as the meeting ended. Besides, Rabi was looking elsewhere. Sommerfeld was a wonderful old man and Rabi had enjoyed his summer weeks at the Institute, but for Rabi, the magic sparks were not flying in Munich. He would go to England, attend the meeting in Leeds, meet Helen, and then go on to Copenhagen, to the Institute for Theoretical Physics headed by Niels Bohr.

The Rabis arrived in Copenhagen in mid-September. As soon as they got off the ship, Helen and Rabi found a place to check their luggage, bought a map of the city, and walked to the Institute. And, as Rabi had earlier in Munich, he knocked on the door of the Institute and, to the blonde secretary who appeared, said, "My name is Rabi. I've come to work here." Once again, he had not written ahead to make formal arrangements.

Moreover, at this time, Bohr's Institute was practically deserted. The summer of 1927 had been a demanding one for Bohr and his flock of young physicists, as they carefully and methodically thought through the implications of Heisenberg's new uncertainty principle and integrated it into a comprehensive view of quantum mechanics—a view that became known as the Copenhagen interpretation. By September everyone was exhausted; and when Rabi arrived, they had all gone on a holiday. Nevertheless, Rabi was given a key to the Institute and the name of a pension. After taking Helen to the pension, he returned alone to the Institute and immediately started work on his calculation of the magnetic susceptibility of molecular hydrogen.

The quiet time during those first days at Bohr's Institute gave Rabi the chance to explore it. Like all legendary places, there was a mystique about it, a mystique that seemed to emanate from the very stones in the walls: "It was an inspiring place, a place where you'd be ashamed to have a trivial idea."

Gradually people began to return from vacation; and finally, in October, Bohr himself showed up. The Danish physicist was surprised by the presence of the young American, but invited Rabi into his office and discussed the work that was in progress. Bohr talked in a quiet, halting fashion and, as he outlined his work, paced back and forth. He had just bought a new pair of shoes, which squeaked at each step. Between Bohr's soft voice and his noisy shoes, Rabi understood little of what he had to say. Bohr's aura, however, was almost blinding: "When Bohr is about," wrote Rabi to the physicist George B. Pegram back at Columbia, "everything is somehow different. Even the dullest gets a fit of brilliancy."[17]

But, alas, beautiful Copenhagen and the Bohr Institute were not to last. Bohr asked Rabi to leave—a dismissal that carried with it a surprise and, as it turned out, a lovely one. Unbeknownst to Rabi, Bohr had arranged for both Rabi and Yoshio Nishina, a Japanese physicist also visiting the Institute, to go to Hamburg and work with Pauli. At the end of October, after spending a short six weeks in Denmark, Rabi and Helen were on their way to Germany.

The weeks in Copenhagen had not been good for Rabi. Having shown up at the Institute with no entrée whatsoever, he was barely tolerated. Even Ralph Kronig, his friend from Columbia and co-author of the symmetric-top paper, who was also there at the Institute, snubbed him completely. Kronig was angry with the United States and was cutting all ties with his native country. Rabi, an enthusiastic American, was caught in the backwash of his old friend's bitterness. "We weren't enemies," Rabi said later, "but it clearly was of no advantage to him to know me. I don't know what Kronig told Bohr, or what picture he gave of me. I'm sure it was not terribly flattering or they wouldn't have sent me off."

Hamburg was different. After four months of ad-libbing his way from Schrödinger's Zurich to Sommerfeld's Munich to Bohr's Copenhagen, Rabi now had, so to speak, a script—and one provided by the eminent Niels Bohr: "I was a little concerned that I hadn't been consulted about it [the appointment in Hamburg], but it wouldn't have been good if I had been. I wouldn't have written. What they did was just perfect. I was going to a better institute." While as a center for theoretical physics, Hamburg did not have the reputation of a Munich or a Copenhagen, Pauli could stand toe to toe with the best of the theoretical physicists; and his reputation went far beyond his own theoretical work. An acerbic critic of other physicists' work, he was anything but subtle in his personal relationships. Upon meeting the youthful Pauli, the distinguished Paul Ehrenfest, an Austrian physicist, was prompted to say, "I like your papers better than you." Pauli retorted, "That's strange because I like you better than your papers."[18]

Rabi was lucky. In an early conversation with Pauli, Rabi brought the great man up short:

Interestingly, I managed to get the first blow in. We were talking about something and I wanted to disagree, but my German wasn't very good, so I said, *"Das ist Unsinn!"*—'That is nonsense.' . . . Later it turned out that the disagreement was purely linguistic. . . . It was a misunderstanding. . . . He never attacked me the way he did some of the others. We got along very well.[19]

Rabi had come to work with Pauli, but there was in Hamburg another professor—Otto Stern—who would have a determining influence on Rabi's professional career. This was the Stern who, along with Gerlach, had performed the experiment confirming space quantization—the experiment that had totally altered Rabi's view of the old quantum theory. In 1923, Stern had left Frankfurt, where the classic experiment was done, to assume the directorship of a molecular-beam laboratory at the University of Hamburg.

There was another happy circumstance for Rabi: working in Stern's laboratory were two postdoctoral fellows whose native language was English: Ronald Fraser, from Scotland, and John Taylor, from the University of Illinois. Rabi became a regular visitor to Stern's laboratory in order to talk with them, and the three men and their wives became close friends.

While he and Nishina were doing theoretical work with Pauli on the dispersion of X rays, Rabi began following the molecular-beam experiments of Fraser and Taylor. Neither of these physicists were theoretically inclined, and Rabi was able to provide helpful background and to answer some of the questions that grew out of their experiments. Thus, Rabi, though working for Pauli, moonlighted in the molecular-beam laboratory.

The molecular beamist wrestles with nature, and the outcome of the bout hinges on tiny effects. When a beam of atoms is sent through a *non-uniform* magnetic field, an atom with a magnetic moment is deflected. By measuring the size of the deflection, one can determine basic magnetic properties of the atom. In practice, however, the deflections are small, often too small to be measured accurately. Even worse, the strength of the magnetic field must be accurately known for all points along the path traversed by the atom. In other words, the non-uniform magnetic field must be calibrated—a calibration that is almost impossible to accomplish with accuracy.

By contrast, the strength of a *uniform* magnetic field can be determined with much greater precision. If only a uniform field could be used to deflect atoms. Rabi wondered. As he visualized a beam of atoms entering a non-uniform magnetic field, he saw with his mind's eye something else: a beam of light striking a glass prism. A light beam bends as it leaves the air and enters the glass. Rabi saw an analogy. If a beam of atoms were sent into a *uniform* magnetic field *at a glancing angle,* their direction of flight would be bent as they entered the field. Once again, the size of the deflection would depend upon the magnetic moment of the atom. With Rabi's scheme, however, a uniform, rather than a non-uniform, field does the deflecting; and it can be calibrated precisely.

The insight came to Rabi during December 1927, and he casually mentioned it to Stern. The response was quick and direct: "Why don't you *do* the experiment and see if your idea works?" Rabi was chagrined. He had purposely come to Europe to do theoretical physics and was reluctant to undertake an experimental project. Both Fraser and Taylor urged him to do it. They, along with others, pointed out what an honor it was to be invited by Stern to do an experiment. Rabi agreed: "I had no job, and I had a wife to support. . . . I was in no position to refuse an honor."[20] So Rabi began the experiment—his first in molecular beams.

When Rabi began his molecular-beam experiment early in 1928, he had to start from the very beginning. His ingenious dissertation research, completed in a mere six weeks, had not given him the broad experience in experimental techniques he needed. Now he was faced with a complicated experiment. It required high vacuum methods: How does one find a leak in a vacuum system? It required a beam of atoms: How does one stabilize the beam intensity? It required beam detectors: How does one build a detector? It required magnets and power supplies: How does one stabilize power supplies and calibrate magnetic fields? All of these questions had to be answered, and all of the answers had to be carefully orchestrated so as to sing together harmoniously. Such orchestration required knowing experimental techniques, knowing little tricks, and knowing where to kick the apparatus and when to do so. All this Rabi learned from John Taylor, an extraordinarily gifted experimentalist.

Toward the end of 1928, the molecular-beam experiment was reaching its conclusion. Taylor watched as Rabi sent a beam of potassium atoms down the apparatus. For the normal Stern-Gerlach experiment, a magnetic field is set up in between the atom source and the detector. For Rabi's experiment, the detector—a photographic plate—was itself between the poles of a magnet. The atoms entered the field at an oblique angle. If Rabi's idea was valid, the entering beam should be split into two components. Everything was working well, and Rabi and Taylor waited; they were taking a time exposure with potassium atoms instead of with light. When they were confident that enough time had passed to give a good exposure, they stopped the beam and carefully took out the photographic negative. As the developing liquid acted, a smear began to appear—then another; they grew more distinct: each smear had sharp edges, and the inner edges were well separated. There were definitely two well-defined beams. The photograph bore dramatic witness to the soundness of the idea Rabi had casually proposed a year earlier.

Rabi was ecstatic about his experimental triumph. He had many copies of the photograph made and, like a proud new papa, sent them to Bitter, Condon, Zemansky, and other friends back home. No one in Hamburg escaped Rabi's delight. Stern's response was both gracious and wise. "First, publish a letter to *Nature*," he said. "If you publish it first in German, they'll think it's my thing, and it is yours."[21] In December 1928, Rabi sent a letter, "Refraction of Beams of Molecules," to the English journal *Nature* and a longer, complete description of his experiment to *Zeitschrift für Physik.* The impish Rabi, a twinkle in his eye, wanted to exploit the way German words can be linked together and to make the title of his German paper one long German word—

"Molekularstrahlenablenkungsmethode"—

but Stern said no. Instead, the title was *"Zur Methode der Ablenkung von Molekularstrahlen"* (On a Method of Deflecting Molecular Beams). The letter appeared in *Nature* in February, 1929, and the full-length German article came out two months later.[22] Following Stern's advice, Rabi got full credit for his novel method, and to this day, the field configuration he originated in Hamburg is known as the Rabi field.

The year 1928 was a happy one for Rabi, with invigorating work, stimulating people. There were at Hamburg, besides Pauli and Stern, Professor W. Lenz; Walter Gordon, of the Klein-Gordon equation; and, for a time, Pascual Jordan, an important participant in the development of quantum mechanics. There, too, were Fraser, Taylor, and Nishina. Most of these men were bachelors, and they ate lunch together almost every day. The lunchtime conversations—ranging over physics, German life, politics, movies (Stern was a movie aficionado), and anything else that came to mind—were so interesting that the professors were willing to compromise with the poor postdoctoral fellows and eat at cheap restaurants.

Pauli's presence at Hamburg attracted Bohr, Born, and other well-known scientists: "It was a place where people were in and out all the time . . . The seminars were marvelous and the colloquia were very interesting, very high level."[23] Rabi was able to observe different kinds of minds at work: "Lenz, for instance, had a mind like a steel trap. He could make up things on the spot, although he never accomplished very much. There was Stern with his marvelous physical intuition and point of view, and Pauli with his tremendous solidity."[24]

Observing the physicists and the life in Hamburg, Rabi gained important insights about himself and about his country. For the first time he witnessed first-rate minds at work. Neither at Cornell nor at Columbia had he seen scientists who could be compared with Bohr, Pauli, Stern, or Heisenberg; and for Rabi these men were at the top of their profession. In the rank of physicists below them, Rabi found that he was equal to or better than the best. He came to realize that his own education had not been as defective as he had imagined.

> I was better prepared to read the literature and to do something with it than most of the Germans at my level. . . . When you looked around the second tier [those on the level just below the great men that were there], you found that it didn't exist.[25]

Furthermore, said Rabi,

> Of the students I saw around Stern, any one of our better students could have run away from them when it came to experiments . . . and in basic education. It was clear to me then that [the American] system was a lot better for us as a system; What we needed were the leaders.[26]

"What we needed were the leaders." This conviction, which grew in intensity throughout Rabi's two years in Europe, had taken form back in Munich. He chafed under the general contempt toward American physics. In response to the anxiety of a German student who had been granted a fellowship to go to the University of California, Berkeley, Sommerfeld said, with a touch of scorn, *"Nehmen Sie das nicht so ernst. Das Leben in Amerika ist gar nicht so schwer. Dort kann jeder junge Mann* assistant professor *werden* [Don't take all this so seriously. Life in America is not so difficult. There any young man can become an assistant professor]."[27] The implication of such remarks, that the standards for professorial posts in America were much lower than those in Europe, irked the Americans. Rabi, Ed Condon, and Bob Robertson promised each other that they would put an end to the second-class status of American physics.

The judgments and comments of the German physicists went beyond

American physics, extending to America itself, as not only Rabi but also Helen noticed. At a drawing class she was taking in Hamburg, her instructor showed his surprise that she, an American, could produce a drawing of quality.

In early 1928, Rabi received a letter from his old friend Ben Ginzberg in which he comments on Rabi's rediscovery of America. Ginzberg goes on to suggest that he and Rabi had been unduly pessimistic about intellectual and cultural conditions in America. Ginzberg's remarks were obviously in response to a letter from Rabi expressing patriotic views. "The Germans' misunderstanding of the United States was so great," said Rabi later, "that I was known as a chauvinist because I would argue with them all the time. There were plenty of things in the United States I didn't like—plenty of things. But not what they [the Germans] talked about. They didn't like the things about us that were good. After all, we had an honest-to-goodness democratic system—you could live with it."[28]

Rabi introduced a liveliness to the sober atmosphere of Stern's institute. The unusual aroma of coffee began to waft through the corridors, and, with it, the sound of Rabi's high-pitched laughter. The operatic arias, Jewish folksongs, and ribald German ditties that emanated from the Taylor-Rabi laboratory were sometimes so loud that workers on other floors had to ask them to be quiet. Then there was the matter of work schedule. The doors of Stern's institute opened at exactly seven o'clock in the morning and closed exactly at seven in the evening—a schedule kept by the Europeans with Teutonic precision. Not so the Americans, who came in late in the morning and were going strong by early evening. They persuaded Stern to allow them to work their own hours. In the evening, Helen Rabi and Gladys Taylor would arrive: "We would come over about ten," Helen has said. "They had a bunsen burner, and we'd boil eggs or something of that sort."[29] In the late hours, the lab was a rollicking place; no one else was there so they could sing with abandon.

And the impetuous Americans were successful: the results of Rabi's method were coming in. In fact, the experiments went so well that Stern said he would have to adopt the "American work method" *(Amerikanishe arbeiten methoden).*

With the fire of physics so hot and with so many irons to be shaped, Rabi could not be content doing any one thing. Early in 1928, Dirac's famous paper was published in which he generalized Schrödinger's equation by incorporating into it the considerations of the theory of relativity.[30] In this 1928 paper, Dirac applied his relativistic quantum mechanics to the hydrogen atom. Wonderful things happened. Properties of the electron which had heretofore been unaccounted for by any of the versions of quantum mechanics suddenly became direct consequences of Dirac's new theory. Dirac's electron had an intrinsic spin (angular momentum) and exhibited behavior as if it were a tiny bar magnet. In a theoretical paper, Rabi put Dirac's electron into a magnetic field, set up the appropriate Dirac equation, and solved it exactly. Rabi was hopeful that his theoretical calculation would reveal still further properties of the electron, but it did not. Early in May 1928, he sent his paper *Das freie Elektron im homogenen Magnetfeld nach der Dirac-schen Theorie* (The Free Electron in a Homogeneous Magnetic Field Based on Dirac's Theory) to *Zeitschrift für Physik,* where it was published later that year.

Early in 1929, with the molecular-beam experiment behind him, Rabi left Hamburg. The Barnard Fellowship having expired the previous June, his work and travels were now financed by an International Education Board Fellowship, granted by the Rockefeller Foundation and carrying a stipend of $182 a month for living expenses. During the first week of the new year, he was on his way to Leipzig where he hoped to get back to theory under the tutelage of the great Heisenberg. As usual, Rabi ignored the formalities of writing a letter to make arrangements; and his arrival in Leipzig was a surprise both to Heisenberg and to the Rockefeller Foundation. With a touch of coolness—"I judge from your letter that you anticipated this authorization"—the Rockefeller Foundation acknowledged and "authorized" his shift from Hamburg to Leipzig.[31]

In Leipzig, Rabi met for the first time the American physicist J. Robert Oppenheimer and the Hungarian physicist Edward Teller. In many ways, the three men could not have been more different, and these differences would become, in the years ahead, the ingredients of high drama. Between Rabi and Oppenheimer a bond of mutual respect took shape in Leipzig, a bond that would develop and grow strong in the decades ahead. For Rabi and Teller, it was another story: a chasm of bitterness would come to separate these men, a chasm across which Rabi was unwilling to extend a hand.

At the time Rabi arrived in Leipzig, Heisenberg was interested in consolidating the new theory of quantum mechanics by applying it to specific physical problems. In this context, Rabi began working on a problem that he had been thinking about: the application of the new quantum mechanics to solids. Specifically, he wanted to calculate the elastic properties of solids, such as their compressibilities, and selected the alkali metals as the solids he would study.

Rabi's work on the theory of solids produced no results, in part because his sojourn in Leipzig did not last. Heisenberg was preparing for an extended lecture tour in the United States and was to depart from Leipzig on March 1. In the meantime, Pauli had become a professor of physics at the University of Zurich; and on March 1, 1929, Rabi and Oppenheimer left Leipzig for that city. Again, Rabi made no formal arrangements. The Rockefeller Foundation, which earlier had suggested to Rabi that "it would be preferable to determine now what you wish to do, rather than to develop your ideas step by step," wrote with resolve on March 4, 1929, "What is,—is, and I am recording the fact that you are to be with Professor Pauli as of March 1st."[32]

The following months in Zurich were wonderful. In addition to Pauli's stimulating presence, there were Paul Dirac, Walter Heitler, Fritz London, Wheeler Loomis, John Slater, Leo Szilard, Eugene Wigner, and John von Neumann—some of the finest minds in physics.[33] Rabi talked and listened, argued and learned. The wonder of Zurich, however, paled when, on March 26, Rabi received the following cable from Columbia University:

OFFER LECTURESHIP HERE NEXT YEAR THREE THOUSAND SALARY WRITE

Rabi's offer came, in part, due to the good offices of Werner Heisenberg, who had been at Columbia University earlier that month when George B. Pegram, chairman of the physics department, was searching for a theoretical physicist to teach the new quantum mechanics. An offer had already been extended to Ralph Kronig, but he had turned it down. Pegram asked Heisenberg for his recommendation of a physicist to fill the position. Shirley Quimby, then a young professor at Columbia University, recalls that moment:

I remember very well sitting in Pegram's office with Heisenberg. Pegram was anxious to have somebody who was a hotshot and knew developments in quantum mechanics. I remember hearing Heisenberg giving Rabi a big buildup, a big buildup. He talked about his ability as a physicist. That was how he [Rabi] happened to be selected for the faculty. I think it was largely on Heisenberg's story.[34]

Rabi accepted Columbia's offer immediately. He was elated. Helen was pregnant. He had a job, in physics, at Columbia, in New York City. No more was needed; no more was wanted. Rabi's final weeks in Zurich were ebullient. The Swiss Alps were a joyous climax to a voyage of inspiration. He had seen them all—Schrödinger, Sommerfeld, Bohr, Pauli, Stern, Heisenberg, Dirac, Born. His knowledge of physics had been shaped by the masters of the subject.

On August 1, 1929, he boarded the SS *President Roosevelt* in Cherbourg. As the ship slipped out from its berth, Rabi was content: he had come to Europe knowing the words of physics, he was returning to America knowing its melody.

CHAPTER

4

Classroom Lecturer

I was fortunate at Columbia, there was no publish or perish thing.

—I. I. RABI

WHEN the SS *President Roosevelt* slipped into its New York berth in early August of 1929, Rabi's apprenticeship in physics was over. As he disembarked, he was at the same time embarking on thirty-nine years as a professor. Beginning as a lecturer, the lowest academic rank that Columbia University offered, he finished as Columbia's first University Professor, an honor bestowed on only a few since the rank was created. As University Professor, he was given carte blanche to do as he pleased: he could teach or not teach; he could teach a course in the physics department or in any academic department he chose.

Lecturers are not usually expected to do research, as they are re-quired to carry a heavier-than-average teaching load. Rabi's lectureship, however, did not follow the typical pattern. He was appointed to the faculty of the department of physics for the explicit purpose of bringing the new quantum mechanics to Columbia University.

At that time, anyone who wanted to learn quantum mechanics had to dig it out of the pages of such technical journals as *Zeitschrift für Physik, Annalen der Physik, Philosophical Magazine,* and *Physical Review.* While Harvard physicist Edwin Kemble's famous review arti-cle on the subject was published in two parts during 1929 and 1930 in *Reviews of Modern Physics,* the early textbooks were still to come.[1]

Rabi's assignment, to teach quantum mechanics from the original sources, was a formidable task.

His appointment as lecturer, however, connoted more than the teaching of quantum mechanics. George Pegram, chairman of the physics department, had tried for years to bring a theoretical physicist to the department. In those days, more so than today, the distinction between theoreticians and experimentalists was obscure, and often was made more in terms of the courses one taught than in terms of research activities. Regarding Rabi as a theoretical physicist, Pegram asked him to teach a course in statistical mechanics and an advanced seminar on quantum mechanics. To the credit and foresight of Pegram, he must have recognized what a formidable task it would be to teach these two courses, particularly quantum mechanics; and although the full professors in his department were teaching fourteen hours each academic year, he gave his new lecturer a teaching load of only four hours—two hours each semester.

As a teacher, Rabi was a novice. His heavy teaching load at City College during his graduate student days had been demanding of his time, but not of his creative energies. He had never had the full responsibility of organizing and teaching a course: assigning homework, writing exams, and evaluating student performance. Furthermore, since he himself had never had a course in either statistical mechanics or quantum mechanics, he could not draw from the organizational example of another professor. While he knew these subjects, he had learned them on his own—from the pages of journals, from informal discussions with other physicists, and from his years in Europe. Now he was faced with students who knew little or nothing about either subject:

> I read very hard on the preparation of this course [statistical mechanics]. I remember working from early morning till late at night, and indeed I was so well prepared by the time each lecture came about that the students understood practically nothing, because I spoke to them as one expert to another.[2]
>
> [The second semester] I gave that course in quantum mechanics and when I look back on it, I am amazed. I was a new teacher. I gave everything I knew in the first hour and then the question was "What'll I do next?" In a two-hour course I gave the whole of quantum mechanics, through matrix mechanics [the Heisenberg form of quantum mechanics] and Dirac theory. Preparing those lectures, which were not trivial, took me full time, every day.

"Full time, every day" meant that there was little time left for doing physics. Rabi's plan had been to continue the theoretical solid-state research he had started in Leipzig; that is, applying quantum mechanical theory to solids and attempting to calculate such properties as elasticity. "I had some ideas—good ideas actually—about solid-state properties, but they bored the hell out of me."[3] Besides, there was Professor Quimby in solid state at Columbia.

Under the best of circumstances, teaching and research compete for a professor's attention. In Rabi's case, teaching and research played against each other during his first year at Columbia: on the one hand, boredom with his solid-state research encouraged him to spend time teaching; on the other hand, the pressures of organizing a new subject from scattered resources kept his research from becoming a vital, interesting part of his daily routine.

Early in the academic year, on September 24, 1929, Rabi and Helen's first daughter, Nancy Elizabeth, was born. They were living then with Helen's parents. Throughout the year, Helen watched Rabi become more and more consumed by his work. She had married a man who, even in the busiest of times, would, for sheer enjoyment, go to the library and read or to the opera. Now, she watched, as he sat silent at dinner during a conversation on socialism. (Helen's father, Alexander Newmark, worked with the leader of the Socialist party, Norman Thomas, and was well known in the early New York socialist movement.) The same Rabi who as a young boy had been infatuated with socialist ideology, who still finds interesting the Marxist view of history, sat silent. Increasingly, his mind was on physics.

Even as a new lecturer, Rabi was like an open window in a stuffy room. He was teaching the most advanced courses in the department; he was infused with the confidence that comes from being in the mainstream of a fast-moving subject; he knew firsthand the leading physicists in the world, and he knew their physics as well: "My position in the department essentially was that of theoretical physicist and I was consulted on many occasions by my colleagues in the department, since I'd brought back this knowledge of quantum mechanics from Europe, and it impinged naturally on every problem which confronted the department."[4] Professor Quimby, only six years older than Rabi, said, "He was the only one, the only live wire in the outfit."[5]

At the conclusion of his first year, Rabi was promoted to assistant professor even though he had published no papers.

His year as lecturer was probably his finest as a *classroom* teacher.

Within months after the end of the academic year, he began to build his molecular-beam apparatus, and his research soon became a passion. Throughout the 1930s, Rabi allotted no time to prepare for his classroom teaching. Sidney Millman, an early Rabi student (Ph.D. 1935) and later executive director, Research, Physics and Academic Affairs at Bell Labs, recalls, "He projected to his students an interest and understanding in depth of the quantum theoretical concepts. He also left the impression among students that his interest was even greater in research than in the meticulous preparation of the lectures for the course."[6]

Rabi's attention was elsewhere and the classroom fare he presented to his students was confused and disorganized. As his colleague Shirley Quimby recalled, "You never got a good set of notes from his students. . . . He never got good sets of notes for himself."[7]

Nonetheless, something happened in Rabi's classroom. Frank Press, president of the National Academy of Sciences, took courses from Rabi:

> He was unusual; if he made a mistake, a very simple mistake, . . . the next thirty minutes or so would be spent trying to find that mistake. However, in terms of giving perspective to the significance of a particular discovery, the state of the art, the humanistic aspects of science, a sense of excitement—he was without peer. His influence on me as a young student . . . was really special.[8]

Leon Lederman, director of Fermilab, has affirmed "how bad Rabi's lectures were but how successful his teaching was. There was a sort of electricity in the air. After a confused lecture, we'd rush to the library, open the journals and books, and try to dope out what in the world he had said."[9] Irving Kaplan, longtime professor at the Massachusetts Institute of Technology, said, "Harold Urey [Columbia professor] and I. I. Rabi were the worst teachers I ever had, but it is because of them that I am a physicist."[10] Norman Ramsey, a Rabi Ph.D. student (1940) and today Higgins Professor of Physics at Harvard University, remembers Rabi's courses as extremely enlightening but their organization as "really pretty dreadful. He'd get stuck in the middle. He was working it out from scratch. . . . You really got to appreciate him if you concentrated on individual points of view and detail, which was absolutely superb and extremely important—much more important than the material actually covered."[11] William Nierenberg, a Rabi-Ramsey Ph.D. (1947) and recently retired director of the Scripps Oceanographic Institute, both echoes an old theme and adds a new one:

He was simply an awful lecturer; that's all there is to it. He could have taken the time to prepare. . . . He just assumed that he would remember. I'll tell you something great about him: he was always available, incredibly available, after class for discussion. He would take the time. He had full patience to work with his students. A couple of us would come to see him after class; if it's an hour, or two hours, he would stay.[12]

As Quimby has confirmed: "His door was always open, . . . blackboard too."[13]

In the strict sense of the term, Rabi never was a great classroom teacher. As his wife said:

He's not very good at explaining things. He tells the story of his oral examination for his doctor's degree. They told him to explain it. So he explained it. He got no reaction, nobody asked him questions. So he started over and explained it again. He explained it three times. Finally they said all right, but he doesn't think they understood what he told them. . . . He takes so many things for granted in his own mind that he doesn't stop to explain anything in detail. He jumps.[14]

Yet, good teacher or bad, the impact he had on his students was profound: he altered their lives. And for this, he was honored. The citation presented to Rabi, the Oersted Medalist of 1981, reads in part: "For his pervasive influence on American physics through his own work and through the contributions of his many illustrious students."[15] The Oersted Medal, the highest honor given by the American Association of Physics Teachers, is awarded in recognition of an "outstanding contribution to the teaching of physics." Over the years such renowned physicists as Robert Millikan, Arnold Sommerfeld, Edward Purcell, Richard Feynman, and Victor Weisskopf have received this award. For weeks after Rabi received it, he carried the bronze medal in his pocket. He showed it to friends and associates. He had received many, many honors, but the Oersted Medal was something special: it recognized Rabi the teacher.

5

Nearer to God

When I discovered physics, I realized it tran-
scended religion. It was the higher truth. It
filled me with awe, put me in touch with a sense
of original causes. Physics brought me closer to
God. That feeling stayed with me throughout
my years in science. Whenever one of my students came to me with a scientific project, I
asked only one question, "Will it bring you
nearer to God?" They always understood what I
meant.

—I. I. RABI

IN 1928, while Rabi was still in Hamburg, Otto Stern took Rabi to
Göttingen to visit Max Born—shortly after the publication of Paul
Dirac's epoch paper "The Quantum Theory of the Electron." Physicists
were euphoric. In this paper, Dirac had combined the new quantum
mechanics with the older theory of relativity and was able to account
for two fundamental properties of the electron: its spin and its magnetic
moment. With Rabi looking on, Born told Stern that physics would be
over in six months. Such megalomania is a disease that afflicts some
physicists, particularly theoreticians, after a success such as Dirac's.

Of course, Born was wrong. Still, the fact remained that after the work
of Dirac, the electronic structure of atoms could, in principle, be accounted for. After, let us say, 1930, questions about the atom's electrons
were concerned more with consequences of the fundamentals than with
the fundamentals themselves. (As we shall see, Rabi's postwar work

once again brought up fundamental questions about the electron.) An atom's electrons determine its chemical behavior; and now, to a large extent, interest in studying the electronic structure of atoms passed from physicist to chemist—a transition that, for several reasons, had a direct influence on Rabi.

Rabi wanted to be a theorist. (He had carried out his molecular-beam experiment in Hamburg only because Stern's invitation to do so had been too great an honor to spurn.) He came to Columbia as a theorist, taught theoretical courses, and, for about two years, went through the minimal motions of doing solid-state theoretical research. By his own standards, however, he was failing.

From the beginning Rabi's resolve to do theoretical physics was compromised. When he accepted the position of theoretical physicist at Columbia, he kept the door open for doing experiments. In the May 1929 letter where Pegram identified the courses that Rabi would be teaching during the 1929–30 academic year, the chairman of the physics department also picked up on a comment Rabi had made in an earlier letter: "We are glad that you have in mind that you would like to do, or at least direct, some experimental work. Perhaps one or more of our well prepared students will want to work with you on your molecular stream experiments."[1] (In the early days of molecular-beam research, the beams were sometimes referred to as "streams" or "rays.")

Other indications affirm that the subject of molecular beams was asserting itself in Rabi's thoughts. Early in 1930, Rabi and Ronald Fraser, who was still working in Stern's Hamburg laboratory, exchanged letters in which they discussed a molecular-beam experiment involving a meta-stable form of the atom neon. Fraser thought such an experiment would be very difficult. A little later in 1930, Rabi was writing letters to other experimentalists, raising questions about one of the most irksome problems in molecular-beam experiments: beam-particle detection. Clearly, throughout his first year and a half at Columbia, Rabi had to suppress thoughts about molecular beams in order to concentrate on his solid-state theory.

What is the captivating charm of molecular beams? It is the elegance of simplicity coupled with the allure of power. First, consider the simplicity. The object of study in a molecular-beam experiment is a particle —either an atom or a molecule. The source for such beam particles can be an oven that contains a sample of the material—for example, a piece of sodium metal—and is heated to a temperature sufficient to create a vapor of the sample. The oven itself is housed in a stainless steel cylinder about 25 centimeters in diameter and 100 centimeters in length. Portholes are built into the side of the cylinder, and high-speed vacuum pumps are used to maintain the best vacuum possible within the cylindrical chamber. When the gaseous particles diffuse out of the hot oven, some of them make it through a succession of narrow slits. (Those that do not are quickly removed by the throbbing vacuum pumps.) After the last slit, the particles emerge into the working volume of the chamber as a well-collimated beam of particles all moving parallel to the long axis of the cylinder. The particles in this ribbonlike beam are isolated not only one from the other, but also from their environment. The residual pressure in the working chamber is so low that particles can pass through the entire apparatus without colliding with any other particle. Each beam particle is splendidly isolated, outside the range of influence of any other atom or molecule. It is this quiet isolation that creates the simplicity: individual particles can be studied in seclusion without the disturbing influence of noisy neighbors.

The power of the molecular-beam method lies in the opportunity it affords to exert predetermined influences upon individual atoms or molecules. As beam particles move along their solitary path, they can be pushed or pulled by magnetic or electric forces in precisely known ways, and their response to these external forces can be measured. Some intrinsic property of the beam particle itself makes it sensitive to the external influences; and by measuring the response of the particles to these outside forces, one is at the same time measuring the specific intrinsic property. When one designs an experiment that delicately nudges an unseen atom in such a way as to reveal a basic inner property of that atom, and when one then determines that property with a precision and accuracy that renders crude the well-known facts of everyday life, it is an experience never forgotten.

In a molecular-beam apparatus, atoms or molecules leave the source, fly through the working region of the chamber, and impinge upon a detector. The larger the number of particles incident upon the detector, the larger is its response.

A molecular-beam experiment involves two basic steps: first, the adjustment of the beam so that the particle current (the number of particles per second) registered by the detector, in the absence of any externally applied force, is steady; second, the exertion of a specifically designed force directly on the beam particles as they move through the working region of the chamber, and the observation of how the particle current changes. Changes in the detector readings are correlated with the external influences that are applied to the beam particles. These basic steps occurred in the Stern-Gerlach experiment (pages 48–51); but, as dramatic as it was, this experiment was only qualitative: it established that the magnetic moment of the silver atom could take only one of two orientations with respect to the direction of the magnetic field—approximately parallel and approximately antiparallel. Suppose, however, that one wanted to measure the magnitude, the size, of the silver atom's magnetic moment? Suppose, further, that one wanted to measure it precisely? To accomplish these goals a more refined experiment is required.

The particles out of which the silver atom is made—and all other atoms as well—possess their own intrinsic properties. They have mass: the proton is 1,836 times more massive than the electron. They can have a charge: the proton is positively charged; the electron, negatively; and the neutron carries no charge. They have spin: an intrinsic angular momentum with an accompanying magnetic moment. Angular momentum is quantized: that is, it can have only certain discrete values. Furthermore, angular momentum can have only certain orientations with respect to a defined spatial direction—this is the strange business of space quantization. Since the magnetic moment of a particle is either parallel or antiparallel to its angular momentum, the magnetic moment is likewise restricted to certain spatial orientations.

The silver atom is a composite of these particles—forty-seven electrons, forty-seven protons, and sixty (or sixty-two) neutrons. The intrinsic properties of all these particles combine to give the silver atom its basic properties. For example, the forty-seven negatively charged electrons together with the forty-seven positive protons leave the silver atom with no net charge. The spins of the particles can also add together and, in the process, cancel each other out; in fact, the spins of forty-six of the electrons in the silver atom add together pair by pair to give zero spin. The forty-seventh electron is left over, and it is this last electron that gives the silver atom its atomic magnetic moment.

Now suppose one wants to measure the magnetic moment of the silver atom. As in the Stern-Gerlach experiment, a beam of silver atoms can be sent through a non-uniform magnetic field, a field whose non-uniformity is directed across the beam. As silver atoms move through the non-uniform magnetic field, they are deflected: the larger the non-uniformity of the field, the larger is the deflection; the larger the magnetic moment of the silver atom, the larger is the deflection. In order to determine the size of the magnetic moment of the silver atom, one must first *know* the non-uniformity of the magnetic field. In other words, the field must be calibrated—a task that, while possible, is both difficult and subject to error. Second, one must measure the exact amount by which silver atoms are deflected—another difficult task.

The problem is with velocities. If it were possible to isolate one silver atom whose velocity was known exactly, and measure its deflection, the problem would be solved. But we cannot do this. We must work with trillions of silver atoms, each one moving with an *unknown* velocity. Slowly moving atoms are deflected by a large amount because they are in the deflecting field for a longer time. By contrast, fast-moving atoms zip right through the non-uniform magnetic field, and the deflecting force acts only briefly. This range of velocities—from slow to fast—is translated into a range of deflections—from small to large. The nineteenth-century physicist James Clerk Maxwell showed how these velocities are distributed around an average velocity which itself depends on temperature. (The higher the temperature of the source oven, the larger the average velocity.) The deflections, therefore, are distributed around an average deflection. It was Otto Stern who showed how Maxwell's velocity distribution can be transformed into a deflection distribution.

Stern did much more; in fact, the whole development of the molecular-beam technique as a precise, quantitative method of research was the work of Stern and his many collaborators in Hamburg from 1923 until his laboratory was dismantled by the Nazis in the summer of 1933. There emanated from Hamburg, over those years, a series of papers that established the field of molecular beams; these papers all carried the subtitle *Untersuchungen zur Molekularstrahlmethode* (Studies on the Molecular Beam Method) and were numbered consecutively from 1 (in 1926) to 30 (in 1933). Rabi's Hamburg experiment, for example, was the subject of paper 12 in the *U.z.M.* series and Stern's theoretical method for transforming a velocity distribution into a deflection distribution was the subject of paper 5 (1927).

The magnetic moments of several atoms had been determined with the molecular-beam method. Quantum-mechanical theory predicted that the magnetic moments of atoms should have a magnitude approximately equal to 1 Bohr magneton (a special unit for expressing magnetic moments). The experimental results, published in the *U.z.M.* series, were in agreement with these theoretical predictions.

In 1930, Rabi knew all this. The question was, What to do? Stern was working with atoms, and the agreement that he and his assistants were finding between theoretical predictions and experimental results was a testimony to the fact that the basic questions about the atom were pretty well understood. Besides, that was Stern's bailiwick. Rabi wanted fundamental questions, *new* fundamental questions.

He wanted to command his own research field. Shirley Quimby was doing solid-state research at Columbia, so he could not do solid state. The great Stern was doing atomic physics, but Rabi did not want to work in his shadow. There was still much to be done in atomic physics, but Stern was doing basic research, and much of what remained had too strong a flavor of chemistry about it to suit Rabi's taste. Chemistry at Cornell had been a good introduction to science, as he has admitted; but when he discovered physics and left chemistry, he had no intention of ever returning. The research problems that attracted him—and, even more, those that repelled him—can be understood as a flight from chemistry. He was uneasy with any problem that brought atoms into contact with each other. He avoided liquids and solids: rubbing atoms together was too close to chemistry.

Rabi's instinct for basic questions is acute. J. M. B. Kellogg, a long-time postdoctoral fellow in Rabi's laboratory, wrote to him in 1947: "Your own ability to hit the jackpot is old stuff."[2] In 1931, the "jackpot" was far beneath the atom's electrons where the mysterious nucleus resides. The nucleus, massive core of the atom, is quarantined from the outside world by electrons. The nucleus is farther, in nuclear dimensions, from its swarming electron family than is our sun, in solar dimensions, from its planetary leftovers. What is the nucleus? The nucleus of the silver atom is a composite of forty-seven protons and either sixty or sixty-two neutrons, but this was not known in 1931. The neutron itself was not discovered until 1932.

The magnetic properties of the atom—due both to the motion of electrons about the nucleus and to the intrinsic spin of the electron—were first recognized through spectroscopic studies. Bright spectral lines, looked at carefully, were actually several bright lines spaced close together. In some cases, spectral lines were split into many components spaced so close together that experimental techniques were strained to the limit to resolve them. In order to account for these hyperfine splittings, Pauli, in 1924, postulated nuclear magnetic properties: specifically, he postulated that the nucleus has a spin and an accompanying magnetic moment.

In principle, nuclear magnetic properties could be determined through the analysis of atomic spectra. Practice was another matter. The spectrum of the element sodium, for example, was the subject of a long paper

78

published in 1928.[3] The conclusion of this study was that the spin of the sodium nucleus had to be extraordinarily large. In 1931, Harold Urey, Rabi's colleague at Columbia, re-examined the spectrum of sodium and concluded that "the spin of the nucleus is probably $5/2$ or less."[4] The disagreement between investigations and the uncertainty conveyed by the words "probably" and "or less" are both testimonies to the difficulties—in the early 1930s—of determining nuclear magnetic properties via spectroscopy.

There it was. The nuclear spin of sodium was uncertain, and Rabi was restless with solid state.

> I didn't come to do solid state. I was more interested in the fundamental properties of things ahead. Of course, I didn't realize then the tremendous strides that were to be made in solid state; but still, I didn't think solid state brought me very much nearer to God. Finally, I said to myself, "I'm not doing very well in theory. I don't have very interesting ideas, ideas I can really get down to. Well, I'll go back to molecular beams."

Molecular beams—"nearer to God." For Rabi, the metaphor that equates doing good physics with nearness to God is a guiding principle. It is not molecular beams *per se* that are the basis for the metaphor; rather, it is that molecular beams, as an experimental technique, give access to fundamental insights and fundamental knowledge about the world: fundamental knowledge is the product of good physics. And for Rabi, good physics draws one "nearer to God."

> Coming from an orthodox Jewish background, there was one God. The world was a creation of His, and therefore it must have a meaning and a coherency. When I chose physics, I was no longer practicing the Jewish religion, but the basic attitudes and feelings have remained with me. Somewhere way down, I'm an Orthodox Jew.
>
> To choose physics in the first place requires a certain direction of interest. In my case it was something that goes to my background, and that is religious in origin. Not religion in a secular way, but religion as the inspirer of a way of looking at things. Choosing physics means, in some way, you're not going to choose trivialities. The whole idea of God, that's real class . . . real drama. When you're

doing good physics, you're wrestling with the Champ. You have one life to do it in, you don't want to waste it.

The year 1931 was the beginning of Rabi's molecular-beam laboratory at Columbia University, from which came pioneering experimental results—hard, accurate, stubborn data—that were at the forefront of nuclear physics throughout the decade. From this laboratory came experimental results that altered the premises of nuclear physics and brought fresh insights to theoretical deliberations about the atomic nucleus. And from it came students and postdoctoral fellows who fulfilled Rabi's dream of greatness for American physics.

Victor W. Cohen was Rabi's first graduate student, his first molecular beamist who, coming at the beginning, helped in the design and construction of the original beam system. Late in 1931 the atoms of the alkali metals were streaming through Cohen's molecular-beam apparatus.

Still later in 1931, the first two papers from Rabi's laboratory were submitted for publication. The first paper was in collaboration with Gregory Breit. Soon after coming to Columbia, Rabi did the predictable: he, along with Breit, professor of physics from New York University, started a seminar group, a theoretical seminar that brought together faculty and students from the two institutions and from other nearby universities. In the context of this joint seminar, the conversations between Breit and Rabi ranged over the whole of physics; but they did come to one focus: the problem of determining nuclear magnetic properties by means of molecular beams. Their discussions on this topic resulted in a letter to *Physical Review* dated November 10, 1931.[5] In this first publication, they developed theoretical results that showed how the classic Stern-Gerlach experiment could be modified to reveal properties of the nucleus. This often-cited paper, whose contents are referred to simply as the "Breit-Rabi theory," was the foundation for the experimental molecular-beam work of the next seven years.

The second paper was the abstract, entitled "The Nuclear Spin of Cesium by the Method of Molecular Beams," of a paper presented by Rabi at the New Orleans meeting of the American Physical Society (APS) during December 29–30, 1931.[6] In the abstract, Rabi hedged, having obviously written it to meet the abstract deadline for the New Orleans meeting, before he had definitive results to report. Moreover, this early work on cesium was never published.

The reason for this failure lay in Rabi's very nature. Any observation by an experimental physicist—a reading from a voltmeter, a blip on the screen of an oscilloscope—is the end-product of a long chain of reasoning. An experiment is carefully designed to allow the physicist to question nature in a specific way. The observation is the answer to the question. Physical theory is involved both in getting to the observation and in getting from the bald observation to a result that has meaning. The dynamic of physics is this intercourse between experiment and theory. After spending one day in the laboratory taking data, an experimental physicist may spend two weeks at a desk doing the theoretical calculations necessary to get from the raw data to the desired end results. Data can be analyzed, they can be displayed in graphs, lines can be carefully fitted to the data points, information can be derived from the graphs themselves, statistical treatments of the data can be carried out, and so on. Such analyses are tedious and time consuming, and Rabi did not like to do them.

Not only did Rabi fail to publish the results of the earliest cesium work, on which he had reported at the December 1931 APS meeting; but he did not publish the results of the early deflection experiments he and Cohen did together on the sodium atom. In fact, it was not until March 1933, almost two years after Cohen started working, that the first experimental results—the nuclear spin of sodium—were published.[7]

Indeed, months and months of work were never communicated to the outside world:

> We had just experiment after experiment. We had experiments in different magnetic fields, different magnetic inhomogeneities [non-uniformities] giving rise to different deflections which we measured. Months of work. The deflection lines were diffuse, and one line would diffuse into another. From our results, along with an assumed value for the electron's magnetic moment, you could get out the various interaction constants such as the interaction of the nuclear spin with the electron spin, and you could get out the value of the nuclear spin itself. All you had to do was to sit down and just calculate it from the data points we had. That didn't please me, it seemed to me a tedious sort of thing. I never published it. I just couldn't get down to write that thing. It didn't grab me.

The dogged, brute-force approach to experimental physics did not suit Rabi's temperament. His laziness became an insurmountable barrier in the face of tedium: "[Fitting data to curves] and dull work like that is not my forte. If we had had computing machines—if that had happened —I would never have gotten my Nobel Prize."[8]

This is all reminiscent of Rabi's graduate school days, when for two years he grew crystals, unable to muster the resolve to do the work necessary to measure the magnetic susceptibility of his samples. Then he devised a new way to measure susceptibilities—a simple way, a way with style, a style reflecting his own personality; and the foot-dragging drudgery suddenly became ecstatic delight. A similar transformation occurred early in 1933. Burdened by tedium he could not stomach, Rabi said, "This is not for me. I'm going to do this my way. I'm going to know my answer by the end of the day."

A few weeks later, Cohen walked out of Pupin Hall into the darkness of early morning. After a long day at the laboratory, he should have been tired—but he was not. He walked with a light step across the campus and entered the subway station on the corner of 116th Street and Broadway. He was going home to sleep, but he was not sleepy. He had just finished an experiment with the equipment that he and Rabi had recently redesigned. The results were definitive. Cohen looked in the faces of those other passengers whose lot it was to be on a subway during the earliest morning hours. He had the rarest of feelings. "I know something that none of you know," thought Cohen. "I am the only one in the world who knows that the nuclear spin of sodium is $\frac{3}{2}$."[9]

With Cohen's definitive result, Rabi had his answer by the end of the day. Moreover, with that knowledge, Rabi moved nearer to God.

CHAPTER

6

The Resonance Method

> After the first experiment, everything was easy. Since you're doing experiments of that sort, there ought to be something aesthetic about them.
>
> —I. I. RABI

A FEW physicists, of whom Enrico Fermi is the archetype, stand astride the whole of physics and cannot be classified: they seem to know everything and are able to do everything. Next to Einstein, Rabi considers Fermi, the Italian Nobel laureate, to be the greatest physicist he has known. To an extent more limited than Fermi, Rabi was both a theoretical and an experimental physicist. He was more than able to do new theory and did so as he advanced his experiments toward the resonance method. To this day, he eschews being classified as theoretician, experimentalist, or nuclear physicist: "I am just your local physicist," he says, somewhat smugly.

The molecular-beam laboratory at Columbia University began in 1931 and continued without interruption until November 6, 1940. Except for the happy diversion provided by the birth of a second daughter, Margaret Joella, on Columbus Day, October 12, 1934, these years were, for Rabi, the most focused years of his life: every day, seven days a week, from morning until night, he did physics, its commanding joy forcing aside library browsing and opera. "Helen must have thought she was living with a different man than she married," said Rabi referring to this period.

It was an auspicious time, a time made to order for the likes of Rabi. First, there was quantum mechanics, which, though complete, was untried: an awesome formalism pregnant with potential, ready to be put to the test. An underlying theme of Rabi's physics throughout the 1930s was to challenge quantum mechanics, to coax it into a corner in order to see if its principles would be found wanting.

And then there was nuclear physics. Protons and neutrons combine in various ratios to form the nuclei of the chemical elements. While nuclear physics goes back to the discovery of the nucleus by Ernest Rutherford in 1911, the beginning of *modern* nuclear physics can be set in 1932 when James Chadwick, a British physicist, discovered the neutron. A second theme of Rabi's physics throughout the 1930s was the precise measurement of nuclear properties.

Superimposed on all of this and making it all happen were the people. Great students. Great postdoctoral fellows. Each student and each postdoctoral fellow made individual contributions without which the end product would not have existed. However, Rabi determined the shape and character of the product. With their individual talents, these students and postdocs could have pursued a whole range of questions, but, in so doing, would have broken the pattern; they would have broken the spell. It was Rabi's vision that kept them on the track. Targets of opportunity, however enticing, did not divert them from Rabi's questions of concern. This is the reason that one, looking back, can see a pattern to the work done in the molecular-beam laboratory at Columbia during the 1930s. This pattern is an exhibit of Rabi's taste in experimental physics and his style in science. Even more, much more, this pattern reveals Rabi's personality and his nature.

The magnetic resonance method was born in the fall of 1937; however, it was in the making for many years. We shall begin in 1931.

How is the feeble glimmer of a star measured against the lustrous brilliance of the sun? How is the sun's brightness kept from swamping the faint light of a star? These questions are analogous to the one that faced Rabi early in 1931. He wanted to measure the magnetic moment of a nucleus in the way that Stern had measured the magnetic moment of a silver atom. The problem was that an atom has a magnetic moment about 2,000 times larger than that of a nucleus. The question, How can the minute nuclear moment be measured in the face of the swamping effect of the large atomic moment? was answered by the Breit-Rabi theory in 1931.

In the Stern-Gerlach experiment, a strong magnetic field is used to deflect the moving beam particles. This *strong* field acts directly on both atomic and nuclear magnetic moments, and 99.95 percent of the resulting deflection is due to the large atomic moment. There is virtually no chance of identifying that 0.05 percent contributed by the nucleus. However, Breit and Rabi showed that if a *weak* magnetic field is used, the tiny nuclear moment is effectively joined with the large atomic moment so as to affect distinctively the pattern of the deflected beam. For example, a strong magnetic field, acting on the large atomic moment, would split a beam of hydrogen atoms into *two* subbeamlets; on the other hand, a weak magnetic field, acting on the atomic moment coupled with the nuclear moment, would split the beam into *four* subbeamlets. Thus, in a weak deflecting field, the nuclear magnetic moment exhibits itself in a definite way. It was on the basis of this theory that Rabi and Cohen began to design and to build a state-of-the-art molecular-beam system in 1931.

The physics department at Columbia was content with Rabi's return to molecular beams. No one hindered him, but neither was there robust support. Financial backing was meager. Anyone, however, interested in physical results rather than splashy equipment, and willing to work at taking data rather than demanding the latest piece of hardware to ease the burden, could do a lot of physics—especially in those days—on a shoestring. As in his high-school days when he built a radio station out of parts scavenged from the streets, alleys, and back lots of Brooklyn, Rabi and Cohen assembled a simple Stern-Gerlach deflection system. This was the first step in the evolution of the magnetic resonance method.

In the simple deflection method, a beam of atoms or molecules passes between the poles of one magnet. These poles are shaped in such a way as to produce a magnetic field stronger at one pole than at the other. This varying, or inhomogeneous, field exerts a force on the magnetic moment of a beam particle as it passes between the pole faces. The beam is long and narrow—a fraction of a millimeter in thickness. The magnetic deflecting force acts at right angles to the beam particle's velocity so as to add to its straight-ahead velocity a small sideways velocity. As a result, the beam particles strike the detector at a position that is slightly shifted, either to one side or the other, from the center position of the undeflected beam.

The principal difficulty with the simple deflection method is that the particles in the beam move with a whole range of velocities. The average velocity of the beam particles depends on the temperature of the source from which they emanate. Most particles have velocities that are near the average velocity; like any quantity of a statistical nature, however, other velocities can be smaller or larger than the average value. Since slow particles are deflected more than fast ones, the deflected beam is not a sharp replica of the undeflected beam, but is smeared out. To interpret the smeared-out deflection pattern, one must make theoretical and experimental assumptions and do extensive analysis—tasks that suited neither Rabi's disposition nor his taste.

A second difficulty with the simple deflection method is that the magnetic-field inhomogeneity must be known: that is, the magnetic-field strength must be calibrated point by point. Such calibrations are not only irksome but also impossible to do with great precision. Thus, there is an inherent uncertainty in the strength of the deflecting field, resulting in an inherent uncertainty in any deflection that is measured.

And, most important, the simple deflection method did not allow Rabi to have his answer "by the end of the day."

Rabi wondered what combination of forces could be exerted on the beam atoms so that they would reveal their secrets more directly. How could the featureless smear of the deflection pattern be transformed into a pattern with features that conveyed the nuclear spin of sodium just by looking? "My attitude towards physics . . . has always been profound faith and profound skepticism. Profound faith and skepticism. I really felt I wanted to be convinced of nuclear spin. It sounded all right, the theory [of quantum mechanics] explained a whole lot, but I knew enough about the history of physics to know that a good explanation is not necessarily so."

Rabi relied strongly on his intuition, which allowed him, in a manner of speaking, to put himself into the beam and, along with the other beam particles, experience the sudden jolts and subtle nudges as he streamed through the apparatus. As Polykarp Kusch has said, "He [Rabi] appears to ride around on the electrons within an atom or asks the question, 'If I were an electron, what would I do?' Possibly, through sheer force of character he gets the electron to do precisely that."[1]

So, Rabi rode the sodium atom, first by clinging to an electron, then by sitting on its nucleus. He could feel the beam split decisively into two beamlets by the force of a strong magnetic field acting directly on the large magnetic moment of the sodium atom's outermost electron. If he could now block out one of these beamlets and thus allow only one to continue on its way into a *weak* and *reversed* magnetic field—weak, so that the field would gently separate the beamlet into still smaller beamlets by acting on the combination of atomic and nuclear magnetic moments; and reversed so that the separated beamlets would be sharpened by collapsing the spread resulting from the difference in deflections between the fast and the slow atoms as they passed through the first field—then he would need another strong (and also reversed) field to bring the whole pattern of separated and sharpened beamlets back toward the center of the apparatus where the individual beamlets could be detected. If the nuclear spin were I, (2I + 1) beamlets should be detected.

Rabi discussed his ideas with Cohen, and the two men started to work on them. Additional deflection fields were added to the system: the first split the beam into two parts; the second subdivided the beam still further, depending on the value of the nuclear spin; the third shifted the spread-out beamlets back toward the center of the apparatus for detection. Between the first and second deflecting fields, a slit was added which allowed only one beamlet to continue through the apparatus.

Rabi's ideas were sound, but their implementation raised new problems. He and Cohen started with a beam containing a relatively few atoms, half of which were thrown away, and the remaining half further subdivided. How does one detect the rarefied presence of each little beamlet? A new detection system would have to be developed. One by one, solutions to other problems were found.

One morning Victor Cohen, unable to wait for the elevator to take him to the fifth floor of Pupin Hall, bounded up the steps two or three at a time. Earlier that morning, he had found the nuclear spin of sodium, and now he wanted to show the world. He went straight to the laboratory and threw the switches that brought life to his apparatus. As the source oven slowly heated to its operating temperature, Cohen checked the pressure gauges. The pressure readings were low, indicating a good working vacuum. By this time, a few other laboratory workers had wandered in, and soon Rabi made his appearance. The timing was perfect, and Cohen called them all over. A steady flow of sodium atoms left the hot oven; half of them wended their way through the three deflecting fields. Systematically, Bill Cohen slowly moved the detector wire across the beam: the signal first increased and then decreased—a signal peak—one beamlet. Cohen continued the slow movement of the detector wire. The signal increased again and fell again—a second beamlet. A third time, the detector signal increased and fell—evidence of a third beamlet. Still Cohen moved the detector wire, and a fourth time the signal increased and fell—a fourth beamlet. How long would this go on? Cohen steadily moved the detector wire as Rabi watched the signal monitor. Would there be another beamlet? Rabi watched. The monitor registered nothing—nothing—nothing. Cohen stopped. The drama was over, but the excitement was about to begin. There were four signal peaks, four beamlets, which meant that the nuclear spin of sodium is 3/2.*

To this day, the sodium result obtained with Cohen stands as one of Rabi's most satisfying experiments:

> The world was young and I was young and the experiment was beautiful. It satisfied everything I wanted to see. There was an artistry in it or whatever it is called. . . . It just charmed me. These atoms in spatially quantized states, analyze them in one field, turn your focus back, and there it is. Count them! It was wonderful. There I really, I really believed in the spin, there are the states, count them! Each one, I suppose, seeks God in his own way.

To manipulate a beam of atoms in such a finely controlled fashion as to bring the atoms in one distinct quantum state onto the detector was the first big step toward the resonance method. The importance of this step was twofold: first, it infused the members of Rabi's team with the confidence that they could control the motion of beam particles in subtle ways; second, this first step, though spectacular, was limited. Counting the peaks gave the size of the nuclear spin, but they wanted to measure other nuclear properties as well, properties such as magnetic moments.

One Saturday afternoon in May 1933, Rabi called into his office Sidney Millman, a graduate student who had just passed the departmental qualifying examination and was therefore about to begin his own dissertation research. Rabi invited Millman to join his molecular-beam group and suggested a thesis topic: the determination of the nuclear spin and the magnetic moment of potassium. Rabi talked to Millman about Cohen's work then in progress and suggested that the "zero-moment" method that Cohen was going to use for the study of cesium might also be applied to potassium. "This was all new to me and sounded quite exciting," Millman recalled later. "I agreed right there and then to start my research."[2] He was shown an area in Cohen's laboratory on the fifth floor of Pupin Hall and there began to build his own molecular-beam system.

*If the number of beamlets equals $(2I + 1)$ where I is the size of the nuclear spin, four beamlets requires I to equal $3/2$ since $2(3/2) + 1 = 4$.

By the time Millman started his dissertation research, the Rabi laboratory was a pulsating hive of activity. A second laboratory on the tenth floor of Pupin had been started with its own cast of young physicists— mostly postdoctoral fellows. At any time of the day or night, on any day of the week, the lights in the Rabi labs would be aglow and someone would be there working.

The zero-moment method was another experimental technique motivated by Rabi's need for simplicity, his desire for an immediate answer. It had style. The zero-moment method revealed properties of the atomic nucleus with an immediacy whose impressiveness was challenged only by its clarity. The method is based directly on Breit-Rabi theory which shows that, for specific values of the deflecting magnetic field, the *effective* magnetic moment is zero (the *actual* magnetic moment, a property of the nucleus itself, is not zero). This means that, for specific sizes of the deflecting field, all beam particles, regardless of their velocities, will be undeflected (because their effective moment is zero).

Millman could begin an experiment with the deflecting field turned off entirely, and line up the detector to receive the full strength of the undeflected beam. The detector signal would, of course, be strong. Then he would turn on the deflecting field and slowly increase its strength. As beam particles were deflected, the detector signal decreased. Then, as the strength of the deflecting field was slowly increased, the detector signal would rise and fall—a peak!—indicating that some particles were passing straight through the magnetic field without being deflected. The process was continued until no more peaks appeared. From the number of peaks, and from their relative spacing, the nuclear spin could be determined. For his dissertation, Millman studied the alkali metal lithium.

The zero-moment method provided not only nuclear spins but also nuclear magnetic moments. The rendering of these data, however, was neither experimentally nor theoretically straightforward. To begin with, one particular magnetic-field strength that allowed particles to pass through undeflected had to be known. In other words, one calibration was necessary (the field in homogeneity was *not* needed). Even this one calibration, however, proved unnecessary when a new method was developed to generate magnetic fields.

Jerrold Zacharias, a Rabi postdoctoral fellow, doubted that the field between the iron pole faces of a magnet could ever be accurately calibrated. The outcome of his skepticism was a different method for generating a deflecting magnetic field—namely, by electrical currents, which produce magnetic fields. From the geometry of a current, the magnetic field can be calculated directly, and the error-riddled calibration avoided altogether. The trick was to know the geometry accurately.

With Sam Cooey, Rabi's master machinist, the ideas and sketches were translated into hardware. With the smallest of tolerances, a jig was machined to hold two wires in a parallel configuration. The separation of the two wires was known precisely. When these two wires carried an electrical current of known magnitude, the properties of the deflecting field could be calculated directly. Millman, and other fifth-floor students, used the two-wire deflecting field and the zero-moment method to determine both the spins and the magnetic moments of several alkali metal nuclei.

The finances of most universities, including Columbia, were strained during the Depression years of the early 1930s, and Rabi got little financial support from the university for his research. When he really needed a piece of equipment, he would go to Dean Pegram and present a carefully reasoned explanation for what he wanted. About this time, however, Harold Urey received a grant of seventy-six hundred dollars from the Carnegie Foundation in honor of his discovery of deuterium. (Urey, a faculty colleague of Rabi's from the chemistry department, would win the 1934 Nobel Prize in chemistry.)

> Well [Rabi later recalled], Urey did one of the most extraordinary things imaginable. He gave me half of it. I had nothing to do with his discovery. What a greatness in Harold Urey—what a tremendous magnanimity to do something like that!
>
> He had a deep faith in me. . . . He told somebody, referring to me, "That man is going to win the Nobel Prize." I don't know what he saw in me. . . . But what a tremendous magnanimity! That money set me free. It made me independent of the Physics Department.[3]

While Rabi could "see" specific results or "feel" the outcome of an experiment, to explain in detail to Dean Pegram was very difficult: "Besides, Pegram was a wonderful guy, extremely intelligent, and he'd have ideas, too. Next thing I knew we were collaborating, and I wasn't interested in collaboration. All I wanted out of him was money, admiration, and encouragement. With Urey's money I was free. I was able to do things on my own."

And Rabi needed to be free. His laboratory was growing in people, flourishing in ideas, and expanding in experimental methods. A new method, however, did not necessarily render obsolete an older method.

A case in point is the refocusing method developed during 1935. The zero-moment method had one major drawback: it could not be applied to atoms whose nuclei had a spin of ½. The refocusing method could be applied to all atoms. There were advantages with both methods, and both methods continued to be used concurrently. As a consequence, it was not possible to cannibalize old equipment and use the parts in the new apparatus. For the refocusing method, new hardware was required, and new hardware required money. With Urey's money Rabi was free to expand his experimental base and to do so on his own.

Whether with sledgehammer techniques or with graceful, teasing subtlety, the experimentalist cannot get something from nature without a price. The refocusing method allowed the vexing problem of the beam-particle velocity distribution to be artfully sidestepped. The outcome of this method, as with the zero-moment method, did not depend on the speeds of the beam particles. The cost of this independence was that the researcher did need to know the magnetic field inhomogeneity.

In the refocusing method, two deflecting magnets were used. Atoms were deflected once, then once again in the opposite direction so that in the end they arrived where they would have arrived had there been no deflection at all. Slow beam atoms were deflected more than fast ones by each magnet; but in the end, all were refocused into the detector.

The experimental procedure was beautifully simple. Beam particles went through two deflecting fields in sequence—the first called the A-field which pushed them one way, then the B-field which pulled them the opposite way. With both deflecting fields turned off, the detector's location was adjusted so as to register a strong signal and thereby indicate that it was receiving the undeflected beam. Then the B-field was activated. The B-field split the beam into two major subbeams. One subbeam missed the detector to the right, while the other missed it to the left. The detector signal was essentially zero.

Next, the A-field was activated. Slowly the deflecting field was increased in strength from zero to ever larger values. Atoms in the quantum state identified with the largest effective magnetic moment were the first to be refocused into the detector. The detector signal rose, then fell. Quantum state by quantum state, beamlets of atoms were slowly swept over the detector as the attendant rise and fall of the detector level signaled their passing. From the number of peaks detected and from a knowledge of the magnetic field characteristics, both the nuclear spin and the magnetic moment of an atom could be determined.

Nuclei have intrinsic spins (angular momentum) and magnetic moments. The magnetic moment has both a magnitude and a sign. In 1935, the sign was missing. The sign of a magnetic moment can be either plus or minus: if the spin and the magnetic moment have the same space-quantized direction, the sign of the moment is plus; if these directions are opposed, the sign is minus. The signs of nuclear magnetic moments became important in the mid-1930s as a result of the work on the hydrogens being carried out in the tenth-floor laboratory by Rabi, Zacharias, and Jerome (Jerry) M. B. Kellogg, another postdoctoral fellow.

The effect of the signs on their data was subtle—so subtle, in fact, that there was no effect at all. As beamlets of a particular atom were refocused into the detector, the same pattern was observed regardless of whether the sign of the atom's moment was plus or minus. The problem of determining the signs was something like trying to determine whether someone's right hand or left hand is pushing the front-door buzzer.

In 1936, Rabi wrote a theoretical paper (one of the few he ever wrote by himself) in which he analyzed experiments that had been done in Stern's Hamburg laboratory in 1932 and 1933.[4] The purpose of Stern's experiment had been to answer a question that went back to the days of the old quantum theory, the days when the idea of space quantization strained credulity. The question was, Can an atom that is "clinging" to a magnetic field with some particular space-quantized orientation be shaken loose? Can an atom be made to change its orientation?

Putting the question to the potassium atom, Stern and his associates had sent atoms streaming through a magnetic field in which they would take on a specific spatial orientation. Then Stern played a trick: he arranged for the atoms to leave the magnetic field they were in, and suddenly enter another field—a field whose direction changed from the one the atoms were used to, to a new direction. The question could be asked, Would the atoms, upon entering the field with the new spatial direction, stubbornly maintain their original orientation, or would they follow the direction of the changing field?

The Stern group determined that, when the direction of the magnetic field is changed quickly enough, the atoms, on passing from one field to another, will reorient. It was in this reorientation process that Rabi saw the possibility of determining the signs of nuclear magnetic moments. He described this idea in his 1936 paper. The idea was Rabi's; the work to implement it fell to his students.

In their tenth-floor laboratory, Kellogg and Zacharias dismantled the molecular-beam apparatus, stretched it out a bit so that a new magnetic field—the "T-field"—could be inserted between the two deflecting fields. The T-field was a strange one, its configuration giving it a treelike appearance. The direction of the field went up the trunk and then fanned out to right and left like tree limbs. A beam particle entered the T-field moving *against* the field (from the tips of the limbs in toward the trunk of the tree); and, on departure, the particle moved *with* the field (from the trunk out toward the ends of the limbs). As a particle moved rapidly through the T-field, it "saw" a magnetic field change quickly from one direction to another; it "saw" a field that appeared to rotate.

Rabi recognized that if this apparent rotation was synchronized with the precession rate of the magnetic moment (the Larmor frequency), the T-field would exert a tipping force on the magnetic moment and make it flop from one orientation to another. These reorientations would open the way for determining the signs of nuclear magnetic moments.

Kellogg and Zacharias made another addition to the apparatus. They added a barrier between the first deflecting field and the T-field. With this barrier, one of the subbeams coming out of the first deflecting field was stopped before it entered the T-field. By observing the changes in the signal level of the detector as *preselected* beamlets were allowed to pass through the T-field, one could infer the signs of the magnetic moments. It all worked: the T-field did its job.

What Kellogg and Zacharias did on the tenth floor, Henry Torrey, another Rabi graduate student, did on the fifth: he built a refocusing system complete with T-field. There he, along with Millman and Zacharias, determined the signs of the nuclear magnetic moments for the alkali metals.

The T-field was the last significant modification made to Rabi's apparatus before the advent of the magnetic resonance method. The refocusing method together with the T-field provided a provocative experimental milieu. With deflecting magnets laid out along the flight paths of the beam atoms, Rabi and his crew learned how to exert a fine sense of control over beams of particles. They learned where and how barriers and gates could be set up to allow only select beamlets to pass on to the second deflection stage and, from there, to the detector. They learned detection techniques and the idiosyncrasies of various deflection systems. They learned how to make atoms flip from one space-quantized orientation to another and to detect a reorientation. The fingers playing over the controls of the apparatus had a feel for beams. Everything was poised for the next step.

Concern with experimental accuracy and precision occupied the thoughts of Rabi and his students during the 1930s. They had started with the simple Stern-Gerlach experiment with uncertainties of at least 10 percent. The zero-moment method was the best of all and, when it worked, it worked well. The refocusing method produced results with uncertainties of about 5 percent. The best of their experimental results prior to the resonance method carried uncertainties of about 3 percent.

The uncertainties associated with these results were not altogether due to the design of either the apparatus or the experiments. Limits were also established by physical theory. Neither the zero-moment method nor the refocusing method yielded the value of the magnetic moment directly; rather, the quantity directly measured is the energy difference between two quantum states. To get from this number to the value for the magnetic moment, one had to use theory—theory that was only approximate. The magnetic resonance method inaugurated a new era of precision: the experimental and theoretical difficulties that limited the precision of earlier results no longer existed.

The idea in Rabi's 1936 paper, the one that led to the determination of the signs of magnetic moments, came to him as he walked up the hill from his home on Riverside Drive toward the campus:

> One day I was walking up the hill on Claremont Avenue and I was thinking about it [the sign of the nuclear magnetic moment] kinesthetically with my body. Now, yes, I was thinking about this as follows: here's the moment and it's wobbling around in the direction of the field and [to find] the sign was to find out in which sense it was wobbling. To do this, I have to add another field which goes with it or against it. This is the idea, just concretely. The whole resonance method goes back to this.

His intuition was sound, and atoms did reorient in such a way that the signs of their magnetic moment could be determined. But Rabi's 1936 paper was essentially qualitative, and later that year he set out to extend his earlier ideas and to develop them into a quantitative theory of atomic reorientations. His theory was published in 1937.

This paper, entitled "Space Quantization in a Gyrating Magnetic Field," presented a theory that became the basis for the magnetic resonance method.[5] After the war, this was the paper cited independently by both the Harvard physicist Edward Purcell and the Stanford physicist Felix Bloch in their papers announcing the discovery of nuclear magnetic resonance (NMR) in bulk matter. Today, fifty years later, this paper is cited by laser physicists who use Rabi's "flopping formula," derived in the 1937 paper, thus showing how a great paper can be applicable far beyond the immediate intentions of its author.

In this paper, Rabi derived an expression that gives the probability that an atom will be reoriented by a magnetic field that changes direction (gyrates). By using the T-field, Kellogg, Millman, Zacharias, and other physicists had been observing these reorientations. Rabi wanted both to know more exactly the conditions conducive for reorientations and also to extend the range of applicability of the general method.

As an atom moves through the T-field, it experiences a changing magnetic field. More specifically, the atom "sees" a magnetic field—first in one direction, then in another. From the atom's point of view, the magnetic field appears to rotate. Rabi's 1937 paper showed that the critical factor is the frequency of this apparent rotation.

The frequency of the apparent rotation is significant because of a second frequency. When an atom with a magnetic moment is placed in a magnetic field, its motion is like that of a spinning toy top. The axis of a spinning top precesses (rotates) around the vertical direction. As the spinning top slows, the precessional circles get bigger and bigger until the top topples to the floor. Here the analogy breaks down because the spin of atoms is intrinsic and "never slows down." But the spin axis of an atom does precess around the direction defined by the magnetic field. Furthermore, this precession occurs with a specific frequency—the "Larmor frequency"—that depends on the magnetic moment of the particular atom and on the strength of the magnetic field. Hence, Rabi's result. As an atom goes through the T-field, it "sees" a rotating field—a field rotating with a specific frequency. If that frequency is equal to the atom's Larmor frequency, then the probability for reorientation is relatively large. On the other hand, if that frequency is either much below or much above the atom's Larmor frequency, the probability for reorientation is small.

Rabi's 1937 paper, completed in February and published in April, is the theoretical basis for the magnetic resonance method. The steps needed to implement the method were simple: the T-field had to be replaced with an oscillating magnetic field embedded in a uniform magnetic field. Zacharias remembers sitting in Rabi's office discussing the fact that "if you apply a radio frequency [that is, a magnetic field oscillating with a radio frequency], you can make it flop."[6] After the basic ideas for this method were in place, however, implementation of the resonance method did not begin for over seven months.

Several factors contributed to the delay. First, there was, in a sense, a backlog of work to finish: namely, determining the signs of the magnetic moments that had been determined earlier; for this task the T-field method was adequate. Second, the T-field method appealed to Rabi: "It had things in it—splitting the beam, counting peaks, getting the signs of moments." Third, there was no pressing reason to rush: "There was this very happy condition that nobody was competing with us. It was such a wonderful period."

Rabi's "happy condition" was challenged in September—a challenge answered by the implementation of the resonance method. The Columbia physics department and Rabi's laboratory were a natural stopping-off place for European physicists visiting the United States. In September 1937, C. J. Gorter from the University of Groningen in Holland was such a visitor. The previous year, he had unsuccessfully attempted to observe a magnetic resonance effect in a solid sample of lithium fluoride. When visiting Columbia, Gorter, according to Rabi, said, "Why aren't you doing it this way?" meaning, "Why aren't you using an oscillating field?" Rabi acknowledges that, "Gorter's visit was a stimulus. I knew about his work; in fact, he didn't tell us anything we didn't know. But he asked me, 'Why aren't you doing it this way?' Well, I liked what we were doing, but I saw that he might go after it and we might get some competition. So I said, 'Let's do it.' Gorter's visit stimulated me into saying, 'It's time to do it the other way.' "

Gorter visited on a Saturday. On Monday morning, two days later, the pulsating vacuum pumps connected to Millman's apparatus were shut down, and modifications were started.

The ranks of Rabi's corps of postdoctoral fellows was expanded in September of 1937 by the arrival of Polykarp Kusch and, on that Monday morning, he joined Millman (who by that time had received his Ph.D. degree) and Zacharias in an all-out effort to modify Millman's apparatus so that it could be used for the resonance method. They started with a basic refocusing molecular-beam system. Between the two deflecting magnets that provide the A- and B-deflecting fields, a third magnet was placed. The pole faces of this magnet were flat so that a uniform field, the C-field, was established between them. Embedded in the C-field was a wire loop shaped like a bent hairpin. The loop was connected to a radiofrequency oscillator that sent a radiofrequency current through it. As particles of the beam passed between the sides of the hairpin loop, they were subjected to an oscillating magnetic field—a field that could change the orientation of precessing atoms.

The modifications did not take a long time. With Rabi, Kusch, Zacharias, Kellogg, and other physicists looking on, Sidney Millman made a final adjustment to the collimating slits so that the detector registered the presence of an intense beam. Molecules of lithium chloride were streaming unmolested through the apparatus. Millman turned on the B-field which deflected the beam molecules out of the detector. The detector signal vanished. Millman turned on the A-field and slowly increased its deflecting strength. Everyone watched the detector, waiting for its signal to rise as molecules were refocused back into the mouth of the detector. Molecules left the first deflecting field with a particular spatial orientation. They left the second deflecting field with the *same* spatial orientation and were refocused into the detector. When the detector signal reached full-beam level, everything was ready.

This was the moment. There was no sound except for the pounding vacuum pumps. Millman set the frequency of the oscillator at 3.518 million cycles per second. His hand moved to the rheostat controlling the current in the electromagnet—the magnet that produced the C-field. Millman steadily turned the rheostat and watched the ammeter that registered the current in the windings of the electromagnet. The current read 110 amperes. The beam detector was recording a full-beam intensity.

Millman continued to increase the current—111 amperes—112 amperes. Rabi's eyes darted back and forth between the ammeter and the beam detector. The full beam was still arriving at the detector. 113 amperes—full beam. No one spoke. They no longer heard the rhythmic throb of the pumps. 114 amperes—level dropped a lot. 116 amperes—the bottom fell out of the signal level. Much of the beam was no longer being refocused into the detector. There were glints of anticipated excitement in all the eyes fixed on the detector. Millman, with steady hand, continued turning the rheostat. 117 amperes—the beam was returning to the detector, and the signal level jumped up dramatically. 118 amperes—jumped up some more. 119 amperes—back to full-beam strength. 120 amperes—no change. The watchers stirred restlessly, breaking the tension. 121 amperes—still no change. The tension broke entirely as cheers filled the lab and reverberated down the corridor.

"Rabi was beside himself," Kusch said later.[7] Backs were thumped and hands were shaken. For the first time ever, a nuclear magnetic resonance absorption had been recorded. The nucleus was lithium.

What happened as Millman increased the strength of the C-field? Recall that molecules left the first deflecting field with a particular space-quantized orientation. As they moved through the oscillating field, nothing happened until the current reached 115 amperes. This current produced a C-field in which the Larmor precession frequency of the lithium atoms almost matched the frequency of the oscillating field (3.518 million cycles per second); thus, some of the lithium atoms flopped to a new orientation and were not refocused into the detector by the second deflecting magnet. At a current of 116 amperes, the match was almost exact, and many, many lithium atoms flopped from one orientation to another and missed the detector. It was at this point that the bottom fell out of the signal level. At 119 and 120 amperes, the Larmor frequency was no longer in resonance with the frequency of the oscillating field, and the probability was slight for a reorientation; hence, they were all refocused into the detector, and the signal was once again large.

Helen and Rabi threw a party that night, and graduate students and postdoctoral fellows came to celebrate. Everyone was exuberant, especially Rabi who circulated in high excitement among the members of his team. Rising above the noise of many simultaneous conversations, a frequent sound could be heard: Rabi's high-pitched laugh.

Although even at that time, January 1938, it was likely that the events of the day might be crowned with a Nobel Prize, no one could have foreseen how important the magnetic-resonance method would prove to be—for not only physics but also chemistry, biology, medicine, and the whole of science.

When the celebrations were over, Millman, Kusch, and Zacharias, with all dispatch, applied the new resonance method to some alkali metals. The results were stunning: the uncertainties were less than 1 percent. In the meantime, on the tenth floor, Rabi's attention, as well as Zacharias's, was shifting back to the hydrogens. The equipment in that laboratory was being modified so that they could make their first assault on the hydrogens with the new resonance method. For over five years, Rabi, Kellogg, and Zacharias had been hard at work on the hydrogens. Now, with the resonance method, they hoped to get the precision that would enable them to resolve some of the questions that had hovered over their work. They got the precision, and they answered the questions. In the process lurked a major surprise.

7

The Hydrogens: 1933-40

> You felt if you were measuring the properties of hydrogen, the most fundamental nucleus, you just measure it and do it as well as you can. It was bound to fit into some or other scheme. And, if it didn't, it was significant. Here you have a system that you could understand. There were no complications. Anything I couldn't understand was because there was something to be discovered.
>
> —I. I. RABI

HYDROGEN has a special appeal to physicists. It is the simplest atom with one electron revolving around the simplest nucleus—a single proton. Physicists are drawn to simple systems because they offer the most basic kind of understanding. Physics, a quantitative science, requires a generous use of mathematics. While the mathematical equations for simple systems are tractable, they are intractable for complex ones: for example, the Schrödinger equation for the hydrogen atom can be solved *exactly,* in contrast to the Schrödinger equation for the helium atom, the next simplest atom, which can be solved only approximately.

Deuterium, the isotope of hydrogen discovered by Urey in 1932, is sometimes called heavy hydrogen. (Water whose molecules contain deuterium instead of hydrogen is called heavy water.) Deuterium is chemically identical to hydrogen, but it is physically different, being twice as massive: the nucleus of deuterium, called the "deuteron," contains one proton and one neutron. The deuteron is the simplest compound nucleus in nature and, as such, is a favorite system for nuclear theorists.

From an extension of their momentous experiment, Stern and Gerlach had been able to show that the magnetic moment of the electron is essentially equal to 1 Bohr magneton*—a finding in agreement both with the expectations at the time and, later, with Dirac's theory of the electron. In 1932, Stern decided to try and measure the magnetic moment of the proton. Not only was he well aware that the experiment would be difficult, but he, along with everyone else, thought it would merely confirm what he, and everyone else, thought they already knew. (Pauli, the great theorist, told his former colleague, "If you enjoy doing difficult experiments, you can do them, but it is a waste of time and effort because the result is already known.")[1] All physicists assumed that the magnetic moment of the proton would have a value consistent with Dirac's theory: namely, that it would be about two thousand times smaller than the electron's magnetic moment.† It was this fact, the small size of the proton's magnetic moment, that made the experiment such a *tour de force.* Stern and Otto Frisch designed their first experiment based on the predictions of the theorists.

The Stern-Frisch experiment was a simple deflection experiment: that is, a sideways force acted directly on the magnetic moment of the proton, and the proton itself was deflected from its straight-ahead course. So that the much larger moment of the electron would not totally obscure the small effects due to the proton, Stern used a beam of molecular hydrogen for his experiment.

A molecule of hydrogen consists of two hydrogen atoms bound together chemically. Unless the molecule is subjected to extreme conditions, the two atoms of hydrogen are bound together in such a way that the magnetic moments of the two electrons are oppositely directed and cancel each other out—entirely. With molecular hydrogen, the large moment of the electron did not present a problem. There were, however, other problems.

First, ordinary hydrogen is really a mixture. When two hydrogen atoms come together to form the molecule, the magnetic moments of the two *protons* can be directed either oppositely (in which case, it is called parahydrogen) or in parallel (orthohydrogen). In an ordinary sample of hydrogen gas, three out of four molecules are in the ortho

*The Bohr magneton is the quantum unit for an electron's magnetic moment.

†Or, precisely, the magnetic moment of the proton was expected to be smaller by the ratio of the masses of the electron to the proton—by a factor of 1,836.

form. The deflection pattern that Stern and Frisch could expect would be complicated by the presence of these two forms of the hydrogen molecule.

Second, as a molecule of hydrogen moves around in a container—or through Stern's apparatus—it rotates or tumbles. This tumbling motion creates an additional magnetic motion called, appropriately, the rotational moment. Moreover, this rotational moment was unknown: it had never been measured. Furthermore, and still more complicating, the faster the molecule rotates, the bigger the resulting rotational moment.* As a result, the deflection pattern would be even more complicated.

Third, the proton's moment is minute. In order to produce a measurable deflection, Stern and Frisch would have to push the beam method to its limit. Magnetic fields and magnetic field inhomogeneities many, many times larger than those previously used would have to be generated in order to deflect hydrogen molecules by a measurable amount.† Strong fields are more difficult both to generate and to regulate.

In summary, Stern's objective was to measure the magnetic moment of the proton. Stern and Frisch planned to send hydrogen molecules between the iron poles of an electromagnet and to measure exactly how far the molecules were deflected out of their original trajectory. Unfortunately, each molecule was deflected by an amount proportional to its *total* magnetic moment, which was the sum of two unknown parts.

Stern and Frisch began by accepting the conventional wisdom: that is, they assumed the magnetic moment of the proton to be equal to 1 nuclear magneton,‡ and designed their apparatus accordingly. They calibrated the deflecting field—a process plagued with uncertainties in spite of the care taken. For the part of the magnetic moment due to rotation, they used a value that had been calculated by Hans Bethe on the assumption that the hydrogen molecule rotates as a rigid structure. With Bethe's value for the rotational magnetic moment, the early results of the Stern-Frisch experiment fell into the expected range. It looked as

*Rotational motion is another property that is quantized. Only discrete rotational rates are allowed; there is, however, a vast array of these allowed rotational states, and any given molecule can be in any one of them. The rotational magnetic moment is different for each rotational state.

†In the Stern-Gerlach experiment, the magnetic field and field inhomogeneity had measured about 1,000 gauss and 10,000 gauss per centimeter, respectively. By contrast, in the first proton experiment, Stern employed magnetic fields in excess of 10,000 gauss and field inhomogeneities in the range from 150,000 to 200,000 gauss per centimeter.

‡The nuclear magneton is the unit used to express nuclear magnetic moments. The Bohr magneton, the unit for electronic magnetic moments, is 1,836 times larger than the nuclear magneton. Other than their relative sizes, the two units are the same.

though the theorists were right: the magnetic moment of the proton seemed to be about 1 nuclear magneton.

Then Stern learned of a way to measure *independently* the rotational part of the total magnetic moment. The result of this measurement was much, much smaller than the value calculated by Bethe. Immediately, the experiment took on new and tremendous significance. With the rotational part smaller, the proton's contribution to the total magnetic moment would have to be larger than 1 nuclear magneton.

Stern asked Enrico Fermi whether the small value he and Frisch had measured for the rotational magnetic moment was reasonable. The Italian physicist questioned Bethe's assumption that the hydrogen molecule rotates as a rigid entity. Would not the rigidity be lost because the wispy electrons lag behind the rotating nuclei? With a nonrigid model, a new calculation was done that gave, for the rotational value, a magnetic moment very near to Stern's measured result.

The conclusion was clear: the Stern-Frisch experiment gave a value for the proton's magnetic moment that was much larger than expected.

At the end of a seminar about the experiment, presented while it was still in progress, Stern had concluded by asking the physicists in attendance to write their predicted value for the proton's magnetic moment on a slip of paper and to sign it. The value predicted by each physicist was, in accord with Dirac theory, 1 nuclear magneton. The Frisch-Stern result was in the range of 2 to 3 nuclear magnetons—two to three times larger!

Stern immediately began a new experiment, this time with Immanuel Estermann. On the basis of the proton's magnetic moment being two to three times larger than anticipated, they redesigned the experiment, trading the strength of the deflecting force for greater precision. In fact, they did the experiment in two different ways, both of which forced them to the same conclusion: the magnetic moment of the proton is in the range 2.25 to 2.75 nuclear magnetons.

The result was a major discovery. Frisch has recalled the experiments: "Stern was sure he was confirming the magnetic moment of the proton as given by Dirac theory; he was very much put out when we got a different value. . . . He certainly tried very hard to find an error in our interpretation. Finally he rather reluctantly admitted that he had discovered something which he didn't mean to discover."[2] This discovery was specifically cited when Otto Stern won the Nobel Prize in physics in 1943.

The Stern-Frisch and the Stern-Estermann papers were published together in *Zeitschrift für Physik* in 1933.[3] A short time later, the editors of the same journal received another paper by Estermann and Stern, on the magnetic moment of the deuteron (then called the deuton).[4] Whereas the proton papers were long, detailed, and quantitative, the deuteron paper was short, sketchy, and qualitative. There were two reasons for this dramatic difference, as Estermann and Stern explained in their second paper. First, they had very little heavy hydrogen (Urey had discovered deuterium only the previous year, in 1932). They had received a small glass capsule containing 0.1 gram of water (about 85 percent was heavy water), from Gilbert Lewis, a chemist at the University of California, Berkeley, and this small sample was all they had to work with. The second reason was vague: "Due to the short time we had at our disposition for these experiments . . . ," they wrote.[5] The "external causes" they also mentioned were an oblique reference to the upheaval then going on in Germany. In January 1933, Adolf Hitler had been elected Chancellor of Germany. The following June, just as the proton experiments were completed, Estermann (a Jew) was notified that his tenure with the University of Hamburg would be terminated on September 30. Stern, also a Jew, tendered his resignation.* Since, however, the nazification of Hamburg was proceeding at a much slower rate than in other parts of Germany, Stern and Estermann gambled on being able to work a few months longer. The deuteron experiments "were carried out with the sword of Nazism hanging over our heads," wrote Estermann many years later.[6] The two physicists worked late into the night, but there was not enough time to get the detailed data they wanted. The best they could do was to establish that the magnetic moment of the deuteron was considerably smaller than that of the proton.

After the experiments had been brought to a premature conclusion, both Estermann and Stern left Germany for the United States. Stern became a professor of physics at the Carnegie Institute of Technology in Pittsburgh. Shortly after he left Hamburg, the Nazis dismantled his laboratory.

After reading of Stern's unexpected finding in the August 29, 1933, issue of *Zeitschrift für Physik,* Rabi decided that it was imperative to remeasure the proton's magnetic moment. The Stern result needed verification—which Rabi could provide, and do so by a fundamentally different method based on Breit-Rabi theory. Where Stern used molecular hydrogen and very strong deflecting fields which exerted strong forces directly on the tiny moment of the proton, Rabi could use atomic

*Since Stern had fought for Germany in the First World War, he had not yet received his termination notice.

hydrogen and weak deflecting fields and thus avoid some of the major difficulties Stern had faced.

It was at this time that Kellogg and Zacharias were beginning work in Rabi's laboratory. The former, having just finished his Ph.D. program at the University of Iowa, came to Columbia University as an instructor in the physics department and chose to work in Rabi's laboratory. As for Zacharias, he had recently completed his Ph.D. (under Professor Quimby at Columbia University) and had tried unsuccessfully to get a job at Columbia; as he recalled later, "I couldn't get one because I was Jewish."[7] In this same connection, as Zacharias has said, Rabi was different:

> Rabi was an unusual case in that Heisenberg had buffaloed Dean Pegram to hire him. And Rabi was the only Jew and was an unusual guy. They [Columbia University administrators] were willing to have [Jews as] graduate students, but not to have [Jews as] faculty. And this was true of Bell Labs and all other universities. And Hunter College too; Hunter College needed an exhibit Jew. That's not why Columbia hired Rabi, not as an exhibit. The blatant anti-Semitism in the universities lasted until World War II.[8]

Thus, unable to get a paying job at Columbia, Zacharias worked there as an unpaid associate from thirty to forty hours a week while also teaching full time at Hunter College.

Zacharias, too, had read the papers of the Stern group and did not believe the result. He doubted the reliability of Stern and Estermann's measurement because he doubted that they could calibrate their magnetic fields with sufficient accuracy. "So I went to Rabi," said Zacharias later, "and said, 'Rabi, I'll work with you if you'll work on atomic hydrogen. Atomic hydrogen is as complicated a beast as I am willing to get involved in.' "[9] Second, Zacharias proposed that magnetic-field inhomogeneities be created by electric currents rather than by iron magnets. "I won't measure magnetic gradients" is how Zacharias put it to Rabi: "And Rabi was bold enough to say, 'O.K.' "[10] For the next seven years Zacharias worked in Rabi's laboratory.

Rabi, Kellogg, and Zacharias began their adventures with the hydrogens late in 1933. Of course, it was Kellogg and Zacharias, along with another postdoctoral fellow, Carl Frische, who began the work of building apparatus. Rabi set Frische loose on building a discharge system to generate atomic hydrogen. Kellogg began building the vacuum system, and Zacharias worked on the two-wire deflecting magnets. Rabi supplied them with ideas, whittled on pieces of wood, and entertained them with his rendition of favorite operatic arias. Quimby remembers, "He [Rabi] had ideas, but he just didn't like to push a screwdriver or a soldering iron."[11]

In their first experiment on the hydrogens, started early in 1934, they used the simple Stern-Gerlach deflection method. The experiment was crude, with all the maladies of the simple deflection method. The team had to assume the temperature of the beam. With this assumed value, they could calculate the range of velocities possessed by the beam atoms provided they assumed the kinetic theory of Maxwell. The deflection pattern was smeared out because fast atoms were deflected less while slow atoms were deflected more.

The crudest feature of all was the way they detected the beam of hydrogen atoms—by means of a chemical reaction. A glass plate coated with a yellow chemical (molybdenum oxide) was the detector. At those points where the beam impinged on the glass plate, the yellow oxide was reduced to a blue oxide. The whole experiment hinged on the subjective interpretation of the observed deflection pattern: two fuzzy blue fringes against the background of yellow. The center of each fringe was a darker blue; the edges of each fringe were obscure as blue merged and blended into the yellow background. The experimenters selected points on the sides of one fringe which appeared to have the same shade of blue; thus, the value obtained for the magnetic moment of the proton depended on subjective color judgment.

With a beam of deuterium atoms, the magnetic moment of the deuteron was determined by the same procedure.

In announcing experimental results throughout the 1930s, Rabi followed a pattern: first, he, or one of his students, presented a research result at a meeting of the American Physical Society; then a paper was published in the *Physical Review*. Behind this procedure lay Rabi's eagerness for attention: he wanted his work to be recognized. Since his dissertation experience had taught him that a published paper will not necessarily be seen or recognized, he presented papers at meetings where he discussed his results with physicists from around the country and whetted their appetite for the published accounts.

Accordingly, the results of the first experiments on the hydrogens were announced in preliminary form at the April 1934 meeting of the American Physical Society in Washington, D.C., and were published in final form six weeks later in *Physical Review:* the magnetic moment for the proton was in the range 2.93 to 3.58 nuclear magnetons; and that for the deuteron, 0.57 to 0.97 nuclear magneton.[12]

These results from Rabi's laboratory not only enhanced the surprise element of Stern's results—namely, the large size of the proton's moment—but also raised new questions. Why didn't the magnetic moments of the proton, as reported by Stern and Rabi, agree with each other? The largest value consistent with the Stern measurement was 2.75 nuclear magnetons; the smallest value compatible with Rabi's experiment was 2.93 nuclear magnetons. Since the two experimental methods were fundamentally different, the question was raised whether some physical effect was causing the discrepancy. The deuteron results were in basic agreement. (After Stern arrived in Pittsburgh, he published a brief note reporting the value of 0.7 nuclear magneton for the magnetic moment of the deuteron.)[13]

The difference between Stern's and Rabi's results was troubling; but, as Rabi, Kellogg, and Zacharias wrote in the conclusion of their paper, "the substantially fair agreement of the two results must be regarded as more important."[14] As, indeed, it was. The magnetic moment of the proton was about three times larger than anyone had predicted. It was also about three times larger than was consistent with Dirac's theory, which showed that the proton could not be considered an elementary particle in the same sense as the electron could be.

The deuteron result was also a surprise because of its implications. In the deuteron, which consists of just two particles—a proton and a neutron—bound together, nuclear forces are displayed the most vividly and the most simply. In 1934, however, the deuteron was important for another reason: it provided the only means for inferring certain physical properties of the newly discovered neutron. From their results, the magnetic moments of the proton and deuteron, the Rabi group concluded that the magnetic moment of the neutron could have any one of four values: +4, −4, +2.5, or −2.5 nuclear magnetons. The ambiguity in their conclusion derived from two unknowns. First, magnetic moments can be positive or negative; in 1934, the signs of the magnetic moments (+ or −) were unknown. Second, it was not known whether the two moments within the deuteron—the proton's and the deuteron's—were aligned in a parallel or an antiparallel configuration. Whichever of the four possible values for the neutron was correct, the experimental result contradicted the theoretical prediction that the magnetic moment of the neutron should be zero.

The first experiments on the hydrogens by the Stern and the Rabi groups raised more questions than they answered. Why was the proton's moment so anomalously large? Why were different results obtained in the two experiments for the proton's moment? Why was the neutron's moment non-zero? Besides these questions, there was an uncertainty of at least 10 percent in both the Stern and the Rabi results. The importance of both the proton and the deuteron demanded that their properties be known more precisely. Clearly, there was every reason to think about new and better experiments.

The second round of experiments started in 1935 at Columbia University with Rabi, Kellogg, and Zacharias. In this round, two particularly irksome sources of error that had been present in the first Columbia experiment were eliminated. To begin with, there was no more squinting at fuzzy blue fringes: a gauge was added to the apparatus so that the arrival of hydrogen atoms could be detected objectively. Second, there was no more guessing about the velocities of the beam particles: the refocusing method eliminated the distinction between fast and slow particles.

The refocusing method, discussed earlier, was developed in the tenth-floor laboratory in the context of the hydrogen experiments. The idea was typically Rabi, and he loved it: "The experiments were beautiful. There are the tricks you can play . . . it has tremendous charm."[15] With either Kellogg or Zacharias at the controls, hydrogen or deuterium atoms were sent through the collimating slits and into the deflecting fields. The B-field was held constant while the strength of the A-field was slowly increased. The researchers could watch the detector respond as the atoms ended their sinuous trip through the evacuated chamber.

Another addition, besides the gauge detector and the refocusing magnet, was made to the 1935 apparatus—not to get better, but to get new, results. As described earlier, the T-field was inserted between the two refocusing magnets in order to determine the sign of both the proton's and the deuteron's magnetic moment. Since the size of the proton's magnetic moment was anomalous, the question of its sign was particularly significant. Would it be positive or negative? "I had people to bet either way," said Rabi later.

He got maximum coverage for the results of the new experiment. At a meeting of the American Physical Society in St. Louis during January, the sign of the proton's magnetic moment was announced: it was positive. The next month, the sign of the deuteron's magnetic moment was made public at a meeting in New York City: this sign, too, was positive. The newest value for the deuteron's magnetic moment was presented to an audience in Washington, D.C., in May; and, finally, the newest value for the proton's magnetic moment was given at a meeting across the country, in Seattle, during June. The full-length paper giving details and results of the Rabi group's second experiment on the hydrogens was published in the September issue of *Physical Review*.[16] They reported the proton's magnetic moment to be in the range +2.70 to +3.00 nuclear magnetons, and the deuteron's magnetic moment as between +0.82 and +0.88 nuclear magneton. The uncertainty in these 1936 results had been narrowed considerably over the 1934 results: from 10 percent to 5 percent.

With these new data, the magnetic moment of the neutron could, for the first time, be deduced: it was given as −2 nuclear magnetons—a mysterious result.

Although the results of Rabi's second experiment were in agreement with the results of Stern's first experiment, both Stern and Rabi were still challenged by hydrogen. In Pittsburgh, Stern, along with Estermann and Simpson, began a new experiment in 1936 to measure more accurately the magnetic moment of the proton. In this second experiment, Stern's group responded to both of the two principal sources of error in the 1933 Hamburg experiment: the uncertainties in the strength of the magnetic field, and the uncertainties about the way velocities were distributed among the hydrogen molecules in their beam.

First, the group developed a new method for calibrating the strength of the deflecting field and, with this new technique, measured the field on a point-by-point basis. They claimed that the uncertainty in their field calibration had been reduced to less than 2 percent. Next, with hydrogen molecules streaming through their evacuated chamber, they recorded the reading of their beam detector for several extremely low chamber pressures. On the basis of these data, they could say what the reading of their beam detector would be if the chamber pressure were actually zero. This extrapolation back to zero pressure gave them a better account of both the fast and the slow molecules as well as of the velocities between.

Apart from these improvements, the Pittsburgh experiment was the same as the one done in Hamburg. In July 1937, the researchers sent to the editor of *Physical Review* a paper describing their experiment and giving their results.[17] For the magnetic moment of the proton, the Stern group reported a value in the range of 2.39 to 2.53 nuclear magnetons.

Expressed another way, their result was 2.46 ± 0.07 nuclear magnetons —an uncertainty of 3 percent.

Once again the results of Stern and Rabi were at odds. The largest value of the proton's magnetic moment compatible with the Stern experiment was 2.53 nuclear magnetons, while the smallest value consistent with the Rabi experiment was 2.7 nuclear magnetons. Whether this difference was real was an open question.

One fact was absolutely clear: the magnetic moment of the proton was almost three times larger than expected. With an anomaly on their hands, physicists were forced to recognize that neither the proton nor the neutron could be understood in terms of Dirac theory. Further, the fact that Dirac theory *did* explain the properties of the electron meant that there were fundamental differences between electrons and protons. The proton was a mystery.

As long as a question hovered over their results, and their experimental uncertainties could be reduced still further, Rabi would not abandon the hydrogens: "I want to make sure I've cleaned up in the phenomena I've seen. I don't want anybody to make a great discovery in the field I'm working in. So, my idea was to do this as accurately as possible and to see if we could get this fitted together and know the reasons behind it."

When the magnetic-resonance method burst upon the scene late in the year of 1937, the next step with the hydrogens was obvious. While the resonance method took its initial form in the fifth-floor laboratory, there was overlap in personnel between Rabi's fifth- and tenth-floor laboratories, and there was, quite literally, direct contact between them.

Running down the side of Pupin Hall from a window on the tenth floor to one on the fifth was a busbar—a strip of copper about 1 inch wide and ¼-inch thick—providing direct electrical contact between the two laboratories. The electric currents activating the deflecting magnets in their molecular-beam systems were supplied by huge submarine batteries filled with lead and acid. These batteries, about 5 feet tall, sat on strong wooden supports and, like all batteries, ran down and had to be recharged. The generator for charging the submarine batteries was on the tenth floor but, by means of the busbar, was also able to charge those in the fifth-floor laboratory.

The work of Cohen, Millman, Kusch, the graduate student Don Hamilton, and others was carried out primarily on the fifth floor where the systems were designed to generate and to detect beams of the alkali metals and other nongaseous atomic elements. The gas systems, designed for the hydrogen work, were on the tenth floor where Kellogg and Zacharias carried out their daily and nightly work.

Early in 1938, the ranks of the tenth-floor crew were reinforced by the addition of a new graduate student—Norman F. Ramsey, Jr. Ramsey was an unusual student with a strong theoretical inclination and a mathematical adeptness to complement his interest in experimentation. He brought new strength to the Rabi team, a strength Rabi would soon use to the full. Ramsey, like Zacharias, did experiments on both floors.

This human contact between the fifth- and tenth-floor laboratories was further enhanced by the need to share equipment. Rabi did not splurge money on equipment. There was not much money to begin with, and he was loath to spend what he had. Much to the chagrin of the Carnegie Institution, he was still clinging to some of the money Urey had given him five years earlier: "The Carnegie people kept writing me letters saying, 'You're not spending money. It's bollixing up our books.' "[18] He would respond, "We're trying to be careful with the money." To him, that money was security, and he would not give away his independence. So the research was carried out on a shoestring. Often one piece of equipment, vital to the needs of both groups, had to be shared between the two laboratories, five floors apart.

When it became apparent that the resonance method offered unprecedented accuracy, the tenth-floor group began the modifications necessary to transform their refocusing apparatus into a magnetic resonance system. It did not take long. By the summer of 1938, the third experiment on the hydrogens was under way, with Kellogg, Ramsey, and Zacharias taking the data.

For the third experiment, molecular hydrogen was used in place of atomic hydrogen. Beams of ordinary hydrogen (H_2), heavy hydrogen (D_2), and mixed hydrogen (HD) could be used and could provide a kind of internal cross-check. The magnetic moment of the proton could be determined from beams of both H_2 and HD, while the deuteron's magnetic moment could be measured with beams of D_2 and HD. Everything looked great—except the data.

Data taking began in July 1938. From the very first, the resonance data for H_2 looked distinctly different from the resonance data taken on the fifth floor. On the other hand, the data for D_2 looked more or less correct, while that for HD looked quite correct. As the C-field was slowly varied, it was expected that the detector signal would remain constant until the resonance condition was satisfied; at that point, the detector signal would first decrease and then return to its original level.

All their expectations were satisfied with the molecule HD. As predicted, two strong resonances were observed when HD was sent from the source, through the pushing, flopping, and the pulling magnetic fields, and on to the detector. One of the resonances was associated with the proton; the other, with the deuteron. There was, however, a subtle difference between these two resonance absorptions: the one due to the proton was sharp and narrow, while the deuteron's resonance absorption was broader. The difference was small and, in the early stages of the investigation, not disturbing.

These two resonance absorptions were sufficient to determine the magnetic moments of both the proton and the deuteron. It was a satisfying moment when, at the Washington, D.C., meeting of the American Physical Society, held in late December 1938, they were able to announce their preliminary results: the proton moment was in the range 2.76 to 2.80 nuclear magnetons, and the deuteron moment was in the range 0.846 to 0.860 nuclear magneton. The uncertainty in these results was only 0.7 percent.

While the Rabi group was pleased with the precision of the new result, they were thoroughly intrigued with the fascinating new information coming from the hydrogens. Where the HD molecule had been straightforward, the molecules H_2 and D_2 were presenting a challenge. For the molecule H_2, the Rabi group expected to observe a single, strong, narrow resonance absorption; they saw instead a pattern of six absorptions. For D_2, their expectations were the same. And they did see a strong, single absorption, but one significantly broader than expected. Furthermore, the strong absorption was bracketed on each side with three smaller resonances. These puzzling features, which had emerged in July and August, prompted new design features in the molecular beam apparatus. By early October the newly designed apparatus was operating smoothly. The improved data revealed more clearly the details of the curious resonance patterns of H_2 and D_2.

The unexpected complexities in the data of both H_2 and D_2 had, in part, the same origin. In H_2, for example, there are two protons, each with its magnetic moment. Each moment is "aware" of the other one: that is, there is an interaction between them. Furthermore, each proton moment interacts with the magnetic moment that arises from the rotation of the molecule (the rotational magnetic moment discussed earlier). These two interactions have the effect of splitting one major resonance absorption into six smaller ones. These interactions explained two things: first, the six resonance absorptions observed in H_2; second, the

111

three small resonance absorptions seen on each side of the principal resonance of D_2.

Something was wrong, however. The same theory that, by late December, seemed to give an adequate account of the six resonances in H_2 failed in the case of D_2. Specifically, the six small resonances of D_2 were more widely separated than allowed by the theory. It was Rabi who first realized that this mismatch between theory and data might be due to an unsuspected property of the deuteron. Everyone knew that the deuteron has a magnetic moment. Suppose it has another moment? Suppose it has a quadrupole moment?* If the deuteron was a perfect little sphere, it would have no quadrupole moment; on the other hand, if the spinning deuteron bulged at its equator, it would have one.

When the effect of a quadrupole moment was included in the theoretical analysis, the mismatch between theory and data disappeared. From their early data, Rabi's workers were able to extract a number—a preliminary one, to be sure—representing the size of the deuteron's quadrupole moment. In a letter dated January 15, 1939, and signed by Kellogg, Rabi, Ramsey, and Zacharias, the announcement of their discovery was sent to the editors of *Physical Review*.[19]

The discovery of the quadrupole moment of the deuteron was not only totally unexpected but also of major significance, requiring nuclear physicists to discard a fundamental assumption on which all theories of nuclear forces had up to then been based. The gravitational force between two celestial objects as the sun and the earth is a "central" force: that is, it acts along the imaginary line connecting their centers. It had always been assumed that the forces acting between the particles inside a nucleus were also central forces. Thus, for example, the force between the proton and the neutron inside the deuteron would act along a line connecting their centers. On this assumption, however, the deuteron would be spherical and would have no quadrupole moment. Throughout 1938, many papers—including one by Julian Schwinger,[20] another illustrious graduate student of Rabi's—were published on the theoretical implications of Rabi's celebrated quadrupole moment: that is, that the nucleus is not so simple; that, inside it, unexpectedly complex forces are at work.

The analysis of the data inherent in the six resonances of H_2 and in the quadrupole moment of the deuteron required, for the first time in

---

*A magnetic moment is a "dipole" moment. The next higher moments are a quadrupole moment, an octapole moment, and so on. The higher the order of the moment, the weaker is its influence.

Rabi's mother, Sheindel, around 1930.

ABOVE: Rabi's wireless telegraph station and (BELOW) Rabi, in his early teens (around 1912), at the controls.

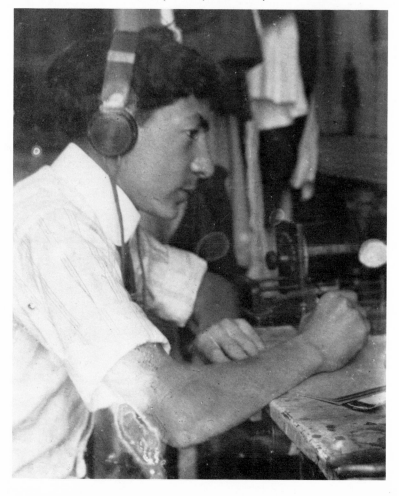

At the same time Rabi was interested in telegraphy, he was also interested in gardening and photography. Here Rabi is in his garden ready to photograph the photographer.

During the summer of 1916, the summer before he entered Cornell University, Rabi worked as a clerk at Macy's Department Store. Here is Rabi behind the counter at Macy's.

Some of the graduate students at Columbia University who worked together during 1923–1926 to learn the quantum theory. From left to right: S. C. Wang, Ralph de Kronig, Myron Schwarzschild, Mark Zemansky, and Rabi.

The Hamburg group in 1928: from left to right sitting, Otto Stern and John Taylor; standing, Herr Knauer, Otto Brill, Ronald Fraser, Rabi, and Immanual Estermann.

A 1929 photo of (left to right) J. Robert Oppenheimer, Rabi, Lewis Mott-Smith, and Wolfgang Pauli on the lake in Zurich.

Rabi at Columbia University during the early 1930s.

From 1940 to 1945, Rabi was at the MIT Radiation Laboratory. This is Rabi, Associate Director of the Rad Lab, during the war years.

Rabi just after the war, 1947, in Cotuit, Massachusetts.

Rabi and Enrico Fermi around 1950.

From left to right, Niels Bohr, James Franck, Einstein, and Rabi around 1952.

Rabi and Helen at Woods Hole in August 1957.

A group of Nobel laureates at the 1960 Rochester Conference. From left to right, Emilio Segrè, C. N. Yang, Owen Chamberlain, T. D. Lee, Edwin McMillan, C. D. Anderson, Rabi, and Werner Heisenberg.

Rabi's retirement from Columbia University in 1968 was an opportunity for some of his former students and friends to come together. From left, Norman Ramsey, Jerrold Zacharias, Charles Townes, Rabi, V. W. Hughes, Julian Schwinger, Edward Purcell, William Nierenberg, and Gregory Breit.

Rabi, 1984.

Rabi's laboratory, the full mathematical apparatus of quantum mechanics. The theory had to be adapted to their particular situation, and then long and onerous calculations were required to show that the six resonances observed for H_2 could in fact be accounted for exactly by interactions within the hydrogen molecule. Herein lay the importance to the Rabi team of Norman Ramsey, a physicist particularly adept at applying complex theory to the end of calculating predicted results.

By July 1939, Rabi's group was ready to submit for publication their full-length paper on the magnetic moments of the hydrogens, as determined by the resonance method; this paper was published in October.[21] In the meantime, the calculations associated with the deuteron's quadrupole moment were still going on. The paper on this topic, submitted in February 1940, was published in April,[22] a few months before Rabi and many of his team left their tenth- and fifth-floor academic laboratories for other laboratories geared to the demands of war (see chapter 9).

Spanning the period from 1933 until 1940, the experiments on the hydrogens started in Hamburg, Germany, and ended in New York City. They started with a stunning surprise: the magnetic moment of the proton was three times larger than expected. After the first round of these experiments, it was clear that the magnetic moment of the proton was larger than expected, but the best that could be said was that it was somewhere between 2.25 and 3.58 nuclear magnetons. With the development of ingenious experimental methods, and the refinement of experimental procedures, the uncertainties in the results grew increasingly smaller. At the end of the experiments, Rabi could say with confidence that the moment of the proton was in the range of 2.765 to 2.805 nuclear magnetons.

The proton's magnetic moment was an anomaly and could not be explained in detail. Today, the proton is still shrouded in mystery—in striking contrast to the electron whose magnetic moment is understood with exactitude: that is, measured (in Bohr magnetons), the electron's magnetic moment is 1.001 159 652 38; while, in theory, it is 1.001 159 652 41.

The experiments ended as they began—with a surprising discovery. Thirty years after the discovery of the deuteron's quadrupole moment, Hans Bethe identified three important events during the formative years of nuclear physics: first, the detailed description of nuclear forces; second, the use of the Yukawa potential; third, "and perhaps this is even more important—the quadrupole moment of the deuteron was discovered."[23] This discovery could in no way have been made with Stern's technique or with the methods Rabi used in 1934 and 1936. Only the precision inherent in the magnetic resonance method was sufficient to reveal one of Nature's long-kept secrets.

At the end of these experiments, Rabi could say, "The power of the mathematical methods [that is, the theory] used to explain these results is not up to the precision of the experimental methods."[24] What Rabi said then remains still true today.

CHAPTER

8

The Human Side of Physics: The Birth of Radiofrequency Spectroscopy

> I love to see a concrete thing. That's because of my nature. I like philosophical expression, but to be scientifically important it has to be precise and, you see, I'm very happy if I can give something precisely. I can say, "Here, I've done this, and this is the number. There's no question about it; you can build on it."
>
> —I. I. RABI

PHYSICS, like any science, is built on an empirical foundation. Take, for example, the magnetic moment of the proton. All the physicists thought they knew that it was 1.0 nuclear magneton, but all were wrong—as Rabi's 1939 value of 2.785 $\pm$ 0.02 nuclear magnetons demonstrated. When a number is determined by a carefully executed experiment, an experiment that can be repeated at will, the datum cannot be ignored. As Rabi has said, "You have to walk around it." Still today, physicists must walk around some of Rabi's data because their theories fail to adequately account for them.

While physics is the paragon of exactitude, the ultimate in objective rigor, it is also a human activity. Rabi brought to his physics both his pluses and minuses. The same man who saw great physics as a way to touch God saw it also as a way closed to women. Rabi thought most women temperamentally unsuited for great physics: "I'm afraid there's no use quarreling with it, that's the way it is."[1] He never had a woman postdoctoral or graduate student; he typically did not support the candidacy of women for faculty positions in his department.

As for the men of Rabi's group, there was harmony when it came to physics, or experiments, or equipment. Rabi's penurious ways regarding equipment made sharing a necessity: "There was not once any controversy," Kusch has recalled. "It's your turn or mine. No difficulty, absolutely no difficulty."[2] Of course, they did not necessarily all like each other. "Somehow or other I didn't get along with Zacharias. I don't know why," says Kusch.[3] Zacharias concurs: "I didn't get along very well with Kusch. He and I would scrap."[4] Jerry Kellogg, on the other hand, endeared himself to everyone.

The postdoctoral fellows and students in Rabi's group were variously talented. Some enjoyed building things and seeing pieces of metal transformed into a precision device. Some enjoyed designing apparatus and using it. Rabi acknowledges, for example, that when Kellogg, or Millman, or Zacharias built equipment to their standards, he was unable to operate it. "We wouldn't let him touch the apparatus," Zacharias has said.[5]

Nor did Rabi want to touch the apparatus. When the apparatus on the tenth floor was malfunctioning, he was on the fifth floor, and vice versa—as Ramsey remembers it:

Rabi was very active on the ideas for the experiments, but he was completely uninterested in details. In other words, he really was the stimulating and guiding force. When things were going well and you were getting interesting data, he was right there on top of the experiment helping in the interpretation. But when there were leaks in the apparatus, he just disappeared. In fact, during construction he did virtually no work himself in the form of building the apparatus.

Whenever we were taking interesting data, Rabi would come in and sit down. He liked to whittle, and he used to whittle on the [wooden] supports of the submarine batteries. We were afraid they would collapse, so . . . one of the jobs of the experiment was having nice pieces of whittling wood on hand to keep Rabi entertained while the experiments proceeded. So, while he didn't contribute to the manual work . . . or the detailed design or construction of the apparatus, he contributed very importantly to the concepts of the experiment, and the concepts of the apparatus, and the interpretation of the results.[6]

But, the human side of physics includes much more than the interplay of personalities and the blending of talents. The great physicists have an inner rhythm that infuses both their labors and the products of their labors with a distinctive identity—that is, with style. And a physicist's style is shaped by background and upbringing, by philosophical commitments, by preconceptions about the nature of things, by the disposition of intellect, by a *modus operandi*—as surely as is the style of a great artist or composer.

Rabi used the metaphor of religion to convey his deeper feelings about physics. It was an active metaphor. Since doing good physics was "walking the path of God," Rabi had to be selective in the physics he pursued. It would be sacrilegious to litter God's path with mundane trivialities. Many were aware of Rabi's ability to "hit the jackpot" in his physics; but for him, it was merely a matter of having lofty standards: "I think that 'God' is a very good heuristic principle—a standard by which you can judge things."[7]

Rabi *needed* high standards: he was lazy, bored, and irresponsible in the face of routine. He floundered in his dissertation research until he found a clever way to outflank the onerous chores associated with the standard brute-force method. He floundered in his solid-state research for the lack of sharp ideas to cut through his boredom. He dallied in his earliest molecular-beam research out of his unwillingness to carry out the arduous analysis and lengthy calculations necessary to transform his raw deflection data into numbers with meaning. With tedium he is indolent. "Life is too hard to do an experiment just to do an experiment. It has to have meaning to you, a rather profound meaning."

Rabi's desire to have answers by sundown reflected more than laziness: motivating this desire were the convictions and biases he brought to physics in general and to the physics of the 1930s in particular. In Rabi's judgment, the driving force of physics is the experimentalist:

"Look at the discovery of America. The theory told Columbus he would land in India, but he discovered America. Unexpected. And what made the discovery possible? The instrumentalities of the ship: the keel, the rudder, the compass, stellar navigation." Devices such as the vacuum pump and the triode of deForrest; techniques such as the magnetic resonance method; and discoveries such as that of the electron, radioactivity, and X rays are the hinge points of physics. "I love to see concrete things," Rabi has said. "That's because of my nature. I like philosophical expression, but to be scientifically important it has to be precise and, you see, I'm very happy if I can give something precisely." Concreteness, precision, numbers—the primacy of experimental results. How are all these brought together? By counting peaks at the end of the day. By knowing without doubt that the spin of sodium is $3/2$.

The physics of the 1930s further influenced Rabi's desire for clean, crisp, immediate answers. Quantum mechanics was new, its ideas were astounding, and its mathematical formalism was awesome:

> I was skeptical about quantum mechanics and about nuclear orientations. I was very skeptical about it. I could use it and I knew it, but I was skeptical. Quantum mechanics is a *strange* theory. It's very hard to think of it except mathematically. I had to satisfy myself. It's hard for me to describe the pleasure and joy we had in these experiments . . . half philosophy, half craftsmanship. It just charmed me. Analyze the beam in one field, then another field, turn your focus back and there it is. Count them! Four peaks. It was wonderful. I really believed in the spin.

Rabi was adept at playing tricks with nuclear spins, and derived great personal satisfaction from doing so. Furthermore, the conceptual framework associated with the precessing magnetic moment was tremendously appealing. So much so, in fact, that the resonance method was delayed for a brief time and the development, in his laboratory, of radiofrequency spectroscopy was—for Rabi at least—less than fully welcomed.

Consider a nuclear magnetic moment as a tiny bar magnet. If this little nuclear magnet is placed in a magnetic field directed along the vertical, it orients itself at some angle with respect to the field.* The essence of space quantization is that a nuclear magnetic moment can take only

*The magnetic moment cannot align itself exactly along the magnetic field without violating Heisenberg's uncertainty principle.

118

certain orientations with respect to an externally applied magnetic field. The number of orientations depends on the size of the nuclear spin. If the spin is ½, only two orientations are allowed; if the spin is 1, three orientations; and for a spin of ³⁄₂, four orientations. So it goes. Whichever allowed orientation a nuclear magnetic moment happens to find itself in, the moment precesses around the field direction with the same frequency—the Larmor frequency (see page 95). However, with magnetic fields suitably applied, nuclear magnetic moments can be forced to alter their space-quantized orientation: that is, they can be made to "flop" from one orientation to another; and these "flops" can be detected experimentally. To think of forces causing magnetic moments to "flop" from one orientation to another is to think in dynamical terms.

There is a second way to conceptualize nuclear magnetic moments in a magnetic field: that is, the spectroscopic way, which is couched in the formalism of quantum mechanics. In the quantum mechanical view, discrete magnetic energy states are accessible to the nucleus. Subject to certain rules, spectroscopic transitions between these energy states can occur, and can be detected experimentally.

The dynamical mode of conceptualization uses space-quantized orientations, whereas the spectroscopic mode of conceptualization uses energy levels. The dynamical mode uses "flops" while the spectroscopic mode uses transitions. A close parallel can be drawn between these two ways of looking at magnetic moments in a magnetic field; in psychological terms, however, these two conceptualizations are very different. The dynamical mode involves images that can be visualized: all of the words used—*orientation, precession, flops, reorientation*—bring to mind clear images. By contrast, the spectroscopic mode is mathematical and abstract. A transition between two quantum states cannot be visualized.

Either conceptual framework, the dynamical or the spectroscopic, would have been adequate for Rabi's purposes in the middle 1930s. He could have used either; the choice was his—and in the choice he would reveal something about himself.

It was the work of Stern and his group that brought the "flopping" magnetic moment to Rabi's attention. For a man whose kinesthetic intuition prompted him to say of himself, "I think with my body," the precessing and flopping magnetic moment was a delight. The dynamical mode was Rabi's choice. Like a pillar of fire, the precessing and flopping moment guided him with surety through a series of experiments during the mid-1930s. Then came the time when the dynamical scheme slowed his progress slightly and, still later, stalled it. The more flexible spectro-

119

scopic scheme with the power of quantum mechanics behind it had to be used to make sense out of what appeared to be nonsense. Following the failure of the precessing-flopping moment to provide an adequate conceptual framework for the observations of Rabi's team, they adopted the spectroscopic framework—a transformation that, aided mightily by the younger physicists in Rabi's laboratory such as Norman Ramsey, took place quickly. When the conceptual transformation was complete, a new research field was born. This part of Rabi's story began in late 1935.

The problem facing him that year was to find a way to determine the signs of nuclear magnetic moments. He imagined beam particles moving through the refocusing system. If some of the particles could be made to flop from one orientation to another as they passed through the region between the two deflecting magnets, they would not be refocused into the detector. The change in the detector reading could open the way to infer the signs of nuclear moments. This line of thinking had led Rabi to the idea of the T-field.

The T-field did its job. For the next twenty-one months, Rabi took great delight as he watched Kellogg, Millman, Zacharias, and others "controlling the flop." Atoms with their nuclear spins merrily precessing around the field direction would move through the first deflecting field. Then they hit the T-field; and a few atoms, only a select few, would be flopped into a new space-quantized orientation. This select group of atoms would be culled out of the huge atomic flock by the second deflecting magnet.

Rabi was having so much fun doing these experiments that he did not quickly follow through on the implications of his 1937 paper. Nor did he follow through on the obvious implications of those discussions he carried on with Zacharias: "I liked what we were doing. It satisfied something deep within me." Rabi, whose physics was motivated by his intuition, by his kinesthetic sense, liked both the vivid image of the precessing-flopping moment and the T-field method. As we have seen, the spell was broken by C. J. Gorter's visit and the threat of competition: "We really had a charmed life, nobody pressed us, just having a great time in the lab. I guess it was between us and nature, sort of a private thing . . . but when I saw that he [Gorter] might go after it and we might get some competition, I said, 'Well, let's do it.' " Less than four months afterward, he saw the first magnetic resonance curve.

The early experiments in measuring the magnetic moments of nuclei with the new resonance method were regarded as a very precise method of measuring precessional frequency. In other words, they continued to conceptualize their experiments in dynamical terms—in terms of pre-cessing-flopping moments. Everything was fine so long as the atoms or molecules being studied had a single magnetic moment.

This state of affairs changed in July 1938 when, in the tenth-floor laboratory, Norman Ramsey was taking data. The beam particles were molecular hydrogen (H_2), and the observed data conflicted with expec-tations; as he has recalled:

> At the time we did the experiments, our dominant thoughts, ... our expectations, all our discussions were as if we were measur-ing a nuclear magnetic moment. The model was a precessing top within a magnetic field and since the proton had a single magnetic moment, we were very much expecting to see a single sharp reso-nance. . . . We were very upset by our first H_2 result. We had gotten this great experiment going and all we had to do was to get one beautiful resonance, . . . and all we saw was a bunch of junk.[8]

What these physicists saw looked like a "bunch of junk" because it did not conform to their expectations. Also, their molecular-beam sys-tem, as then designed, did not display the data in the clearest form. Recognizing that modifications to their apparatus were necessary, they tore their beam system apart and reassembled it around a modified design. The data from the new apparatus were definitive, there being not the one sharp resonance they expected, but six sharp resonances.

The dynamical conceptual scheme with its precessing and flopping magnetic moments could not provide a quantitative account of the six sharp peaks. The reason resides in the fact that the hydrogen molecule contains not one, but two magnetic moments: the two protons in the nuclei of the two hydrogen atoms making up the molecule. A new con-ceptual scheme was necessary to account precisely for the way these two magnetic moments influenced each other within the molecule and, in that mutual interaction, destroyed the inherent simplicity of the one-moment system. The new conceptual scheme, the spectroscopic, brought with it the full abstract formalism of quantum mechanics.

During the academic year 1938–39, Rabi was a visiting professor at the Institute of Advanced Study in Princeton, New Jersey. It made abso-lutely no sense for him to be there. His laboratories in Pupin Hall at Columbia were charged with excitement. The resonance method was new, and data with unprecedented precision were being obtained daily.

The quadrupole moment of the deuteron had just been discovered. Rabi was riding the crest of a wave. As a result, his activities at the institute were nominal; in fact, he had a long commute to Columbia.

The final paper in the Rabi series on the hydrogens, a paper in which the first magnetic-resonance measurements on the proton and the deuteron were reported, was written by Rabi and Ramsey in Princeton at the institute—after months of long and arduous calculations by Ramsey, Kellogg, and Zacharias applying the theory of quantum mechanics to the hydrogen molecule. They showed that the theory accounted exactly for the six peaks.[9]

Writing the paper went smoothly until they came to the title. For Ramsey, who had done the measurements in the laboratory, the six peaks had become spectral lines; for Ramsey, who had worked for months calculating energy states between which quantum transitions occurred, the hydrogen data had become spectroscopic data. He wanted the phrase "radiofrequency spectroscopy" in the title. Rabi, who was always more interested in a physical result than in a method, argued against it. Besides, he was still charmed by the images of precessing magnetic moments flopping from one orientation to another. Finally, they compromised. In July 1939 they sent to the editorial offices of *Physical Review* a manuscript with the title "The Magnetic Moments of the Proton and the Deuteron," thereby emphasizing the results of the experiment. But there was also an auspicious subtitle, "The Radiofrequency Spectrum of H_2 in Various Magnetic Fields."[10]

This paper is, from a conceptual point of view, a mixed bag. The results from the molecules HD and D_2 were described and displayed in terms of reorientations (flops). The graphs showing the data from these molecules were called "resonance curves." By contrast, the molecule H_2 was treated with the abstract formalism of quantum mechanics. The graphs displaying the H_2 data were called, not resonance curves, but rather "radiofrequency spectra." The precessing-flopping moment was losing conceptual territory.

In the meantime, Kusch and Millman were hard at work on the fifth floor of Pupin. If, they reasoned, the magnetic-resonance method can be used to do radiofrequency spectroscopy on the hydrogen molecule, it can also be used to do radiofrequency spectroscopy on atoms. The only difference: atoms would require a higher radiofrequency. Soon Kusch and Millman were doing spectroscopic studies on atoms of lithium and potassium. The precision of their results was on the order of 0.01 percent. Of course, when data was coming out, Rabi was there.

Six months after the paper on the hydrogens was submitted for publication, Kusch, Millman, and Rabi sent to *Physical Review* another paper entitled "The Radiofrequency Spectra of Atoms."[11] The subtitle of six months earlier was now the primary title. Moreover, this was a different paper. There was no mention of precessing moments, no mention of the Larmor precession frequency, no mention of reorientations. Kusch and Millman were no longer measuring magnetic moments; they were doing spectroscopy.

In going from the "floppy" method to the spectroscopic method, they neither moved to a new laboratory nor constructed new apparatus. They did change, however, their experimental procedure. When they considered themselves to be reorienting magnetic moments, they *fixed* the radiofrequency at one value and *varied* the magnetic field through the resonance value. As spectroscopists, they *fixed* the magnetic field at one value and *varied* the radiofrequency. In one sense, a slight change; in another sense, a dramatic testimony to the conceptual transformation, to the birth of radiofrequency spectroscopy. With the aid of new devices that would be developed during the Second World War, a wealth of detailed information about the structure of matter would be the progeny of that birth.

In 1940, Rabi gave a paper, entitled "Radio Frequency Spectra of Atoms and Molecules," at the annual meeting of the American Association for the Advancement of Science. For this paper the AAAS awarded him a prize of one thousand dollars, stating in the citation that, in his research, he had "extended[ed] the range of scientific knowledge regarding atoms in a very significant way." (The full citation is given in appendix A, page 265.)

Rabi publicly welcomed the new radiofrequency spectroscopy and reveled in the spectroscopic mode of thinking, and was the author of thoroughly spectroscopic papers. Privately, however, the situation was different. When asked the point at which he switched from thinking in terms of flopping moments to thinking in terms of quantum transitions, his answer was immediate and direct: "Never switched. My thinking of this is, always has been, physical." Rabi was deeply drawn to the dynamical system of magnetic moments flopping in various magnetic-field configurations. With his physical and kinesthetic intuition, he, so to speak, saw the nucleus from the inside—as Kusch once observed (page 86). Given Rabi's style of thinking—physical rather than mathematical—it is not surprising that he "never switched." Such styles of mind enlighten the human side of physics.

CHAPTER
9

Rabi Goes to War

I took the war personally.

—I. I. RABI

AMERICAN physicists had an inside view of the tragedy that was developing during the years before the Second World War. Physics transcends nationalism, and physicists come together as colleagues regardless of the language they speak. Einstein attracted world attention when he immigrated to the United States to escape the anti-Semitic oppression of the Nazis. His arrival during 1933 stirred concern; but he was one man and, for much of the public, a special case—a celebrity. But during 1933, the physics grapevine carried tales of Nazi tyranny, personal accounts of painful uprooting, dramatic narratives of hastily planned departures, and inquiries—sometimes desperate—about the availability of faculty positions outside of Germany.

Otto Stern, in whose laboratory Rabi worked during his year in Hamburg, came to the United States in 1933. Stern was Jewish. In June 1933, John von Neumann visited Berlin and Göttingen and saw the situation there. He wrote a letter on June 19 to his Princeton colleague, Oswald Veblen, listing German physicists who would soon be required to leave their positions in German universities. Felix Bloch came in 1934. He was Jewish. Hans Bethe, whom Rabi had met during his brief stay in Munich, came in 1935. With a Jewish mother, Bethe was an undesirable. Enrico Fermi left Rome in December 1938 to go to Stockholm where he received the 1938 Nobel Prize in physics. By prearrangement, he did not return

124

to Italy but went from Stockholm to the United States, where he became a colleague of Rabi's at Columbia University. Laura Fermi, Enrico's wife, was Jewish. There were many more.

Each new arrival brought fresh descriptions of Nazi activities, a living testimony and, for some, a daily reminder of the awful reality of Hitler's Germany. As the end of the 1930s approached, the sense of despair felt by many physicists was growing in its intensity.

In 1937, Bethe went to Germany and wrote to Rabi on his return: "Heisenberg wants to stick it out in Germany as far as I could find out. Stark [a pro-Nazi physicist] has made another great attack on him and Sommerfeld and Heisenberg want to go on strike until Stark apologizes. This will bring him either into a concentration camp or to America. Germany was terrible."[1] In August 1938, P. P. Ewald wrote to Rabi: "Things are getting worse and worse in Germany. I received word yesterday that Lise Meitner [a Jewish physicist] had been 'eloped'— because otherwise she would not have been able to leave. A warning was added for me not to attempt to return."[2] D. A. Jackson, a friend of Rabi's who was independently wealthy and a gentleman physicist, wrote from England in October of 1940 and described how his life had been changed by the war. As a new pilot in the RAF, he pledged to Rabi that the British would not give in to Hitler and he asked Rabi to get up a collection at Columbia for a fighter plane or a bomber.

In a 1940 letter to a German physicist, Ed Condon, Rabi's close friend, expressed his feelings in the most direct fashion and, in so doing, expressed the feelings of many American physicists:

> You imply that our press does not deal fairly with Germany. It is hard for me to understand your basis for thinking so. . . .
>
> I am not concerned with the truth or untruth of any particular daily news story. You cannot deny that America is flooded with refugees from Germany, Austria, Czecho-Slovakia and Poland, for I know many of the high-type scientific people who are here because of German barbarism. I have one Czech refugee living in my own house. Professor Mott of Bristol, England, has two refugee girls from Prague in his home. I know of many people who are called on to assist in overcoming in small measure the hurt done to thousands of human beings by Germany. I know people who saw the synagogues burn in Germany. I know Czech professors who are cast out of their position in their own country. . . . I know a distinguished Polish professor of physics here who suffered months of anguish

because of the uncertain fate of his three-year-old daughter in Warsaw. Even if I believed nothing of what the newspapers print I could not help being shocked and embittered by what I know of recent happenings from close personal friends.

... I am sure that millions of Americans feel as I do, that life in a world under victorious Germany would be simply intolerable. They hope that Britain and France are equal to the dirty job of stopping German rapacity, but if they are not equal to it, we will come in, as we did before, to make sure that liberal political principles are not crushed from the earth.

My friend, if you find physics so absorbing as not to know these things, I excuse you, but please do not count on me for any kind of support for the German cause. Quite the opposite! I shall help the cause of democracy by every means I can.[3]

But France was not "equal to the dirty job." Two months after Condon's letter, armored Panzer divisions of the German army rumbled around the Maginot Line and across the French countryside. In June 1940, the nation of France fell to the Nazis. The situation was desperate. Jerrold Zacharias remembered a troubled conversation he had with Rabi while they stood on the corner of Broadway and 116th Street. It was summertime, and they were talking about the war. "My Lord in Heaven, what will we do?" Zacharias asked Rabi. "I don't know," answered Rabi, "I don't know."[4] Rabi was deeply disturbed:

The German people were, at that time, so morally corrupt [he said later]. It is one of the most mysterious of things. There was no question of the German pre-eminence, the depth of their education. They had the best music, they had the best physics, they had wonderful theater, great literature. They were efficient, great at manufacturing ... everything. Yet the Hitler anti-Semitism was a tremendously motivational power for them. This great anti-Semitic feeling was endemic, it had built up over a century or so. It was deep, it was persuasive, and it was in part what allowed Hitler to rise. This whole country was motivated by anti-Semitism. I don't understand it and I have never run into anyone who could explain it satisfactorily.

These people [the Germans] were destroying Western civilization. My highest aspiration is for the scientific culture to spread and become universal, and they were destroying it in its essence. They had no regard for anything except their crazy pan-Germanic ideas. These Hitler ideas are very powerful. They energize an element of mankind that always exists; it appeals to something that is always present. It could be in this country too. It is part of our human nature. You realize how thin civilization is. There has always been a terrible fight to establish a culture in which science could live. So when France fell, my God, it made the protection of England and the United States profoundly important. Once civilization is destroyed, once a culture in which science can live is broken down, it might not be re-established for thousands of years because this is a habit, this grows. It doesn't lie in precepts, it lies in people, their habits, their customs.

On top of everything was the anxiety of not knowing what the German scientists were doing to advance the Axis war effort. However ill advised or immoral were German scientists in their apparent willingness to participate in the Hitler regime, their scientific and technical prowess was no less potent. It was recognized clearly and generally that German science, if marshaled for the purposes of war, would be formidably effective. As a measure of this concern, a censorship committee was set up in the spring of 1940 by the National Research Council. This committee, originally proposed by Rabi's earlier collaborator Gregory Breit, was to control information published in American scientific journals—especially information about uranium fission.

The scientists may have seen more clearly than did the general public the dimensions of the war as it unfolded during its early months: they sensed the likelihood of the United States's eventual involvement. By contrast, most of the general public, many members of Congress, and perhaps even President Franklin D. Roosevelt himself saw the role of the United States as one of supplying material goods to England and France. It was not our war. The minds of some people may have changed in June 1940 when Italy entered the war, when Germany occupied Paris, and when the British army was almost trapped on the Continent with its back against the North Sea. By the slightest of margins, the British troops were evacuated at Dunkirk. On June 27, 1940, ten days after the fall of France, twenty-four days after the Dunkirk evacuation was complete, President Roosevelt approved the order establishing the National Defense Research Committee (NDRC).

The formal establishment of the NDRC did two things instantaneously: it made official a group of men already working and planning; and it opened the door for federal dollars to implement research and development. The chairman of the committee and the man whose handiwork led to the committee itself was Vannevar Bush. Bush, an engineer who in earlier years was associated with the Massachusetts Institute of Technology, was in 1940 president of the Carnegie Institution of Washington. The other members of the committee, already given major responsibilities, were Roger Adams, head of the chemistry department, University of Illinois; C. P. Coe, of the U.S. Commission of Patents; K. T. Compton, president of the Massachusetts Institute of Technology; James B. Conant, president of Harvard University; J. A. Furer, rear admiral in the United States Navy; F. B. Jewett, president of the National Academy of Sciences; Irwin Stewart, executive secretary of the Office of Scientific Research and Development; and R. C. Tolman, dean of the graduate school at the California Institute of Technology. One of the first jobs of the new NDRC was to canvass colleges and universities throughout the country to get an inventory of facilities that might be used for specific research projects and to obtain a thumbnail sketch of the talents and specialties of American scientists.

The first suggestion made by the armed services came from the air corps, which was interested in the possibility of carrying out bombing missions even when target areas were obscured by clouds. Thus, the air corps requested the NDRC to do basic research at ultra-high frequencies and investigations of pulse transmission. Compton, under whose jurisdiction this activity fell, immediately organized a group to study the applications of microwaves—radiowaves with a very short wavelength, 10 centimeters or less. This group, called the Microwave Committee and later Division 14 of the NDRC, was headed by Alfred L. Loomis, a New York lawyer who had pioneered in the study of microwaves.

Since the charge to the NDRC was to coordinate, to supervise, and to conduct research on problems relating to the conduct of warfare, the first task of the Microwave Committee was to assess the radar work already going on in both the U.S. Army and the U.S. Navy. As scientists, they found the secrecy between the armed services unacceptable: it made no sense for the U.S. Army to struggle with a question whose answer the U.S. Navy might already have. It was just such a problem the NDRC was supposed to eliminate. The Loomis Microwave Committee also found that the radar systems then in use employed long radiowaves, of 150 centimeters (or even longer).

The advantages of microwaves are many. In the application of radar, a beam of radiowaves is sent out in search of a target. The beam spreads out as it moves farther from the transmitting source. When the spreading beam strikes a bomber, the periscope of a submarine, or an artillery shell from an enemy cannon, a tiny fraction of the original beam is reflected back toward the transmitting source. The reflected beam also spreads out as it moves farther and farther from the reflecting object. A tiny fraction of the reflected wave arrives back at the starting point —the radar system—and there must be detected. The more effective the radar, the longer is its range; the longer its range, the smaller the returning echo. The problem barring the advance to shorter wavelength microwaves was, in the summer of 1940, the lack of a transmitting source of microwaves powerful enough to give rise to a detectable echo. At summer's end, the Microwave Committee was ready to write a report —"a sign," said one of its members, "that we didn't know what to do next."[5]

Then, in September 1940, the situation changed. What has been called "the most valuable cargo ever brought to our shores" arrived from England.[6] The cargo could be held in one's hand. It was an odd-looking little thing—a disk sandwiched between two smaller disks. From each disk emerged a tube, first of metal (the metal tubes were soldered to the disks), then merging into glass. Inside the tubes, leading from outside to the inside of the device, were wires. The glass ends of the tubes had been heated to the point that the glass had melted down around the wires, allowing a vacuum to be maintained inside the device. This was a cavity magnetron, and was, so to speak, hot off the laboratory bench.

Radar, in 1940, was top priority to the British, separated as they were by only a few miles of water from the airfields of the German Luftwaffe. As early as mid-1938, curious wooden towers, 200 to 300 feet tall, dotted the southern and eastern shores of Britain. Atop these towers were radar antennas which were part of the radar systems monitoring the approaches to the English Channel. This radar network, called the Chain Home, employed radiowaves 10 meters long.

It was in all likelihood the Chain Home that, primitive though it was, saved England. In August 1940, the Battle of Britain began. With the Chain Home radar network detecting German bombers before they were halfway across the North Sea, the RAF could get its fighters into the air to meet the enemy head on. On September 15, the Nazis lost 185 planes out of a total of 500 attackers. Without radar, the Battle of Britain would have been lost, and the British Isles would have been laid open for invasion.

However effective the 10-meter waves of Chain Home, they were not as potentially useful as shorter waves—for several reasons. First, very large reflectors are required to keep long wavelengths from spreading out so as to severely limit their range for radar detection. By contrast, short wavelengths can be contained in a narrower beam that focuses more power on the target and, in turn, gives rise to a stronger echo. In short, the physical dimensions of the equipment associated with radar systems is proportional to the wavelengths employed: the shorter the wavelength, the smaller much of the necessary equipment. Hence the push to shorter wavelengths; and by the summer of 1939, Edward "Taffy" Bowen had succeeded in generating radiowaves 1.5 meters long —a major advance over 10-meter waves.

The ultimate goal of 10-centimeter wavelengths was reached on the morning of February 21, 1940, in a physics laboratory at the University of Birmingham. There, John Randall and Harry Boot developed the cavity magnetron and it was there, on that day, that they activated their first prototype—an extraordinary improvement, as was immediately apparent. Cigarettes could be lit by the beam of microwaves that came from the magnetron; far-off car headlights could be made to glow by its radiation. At this first trial, the magnetron was beaming out 400 watts of power at a wavelength of 9.8 centimeters. By the summer of 1940, this prototype model of the magnetron had been improved to the point where it generated 10,000 watts of power at a 10-centimeter wavelength.

This powerful new magnetron was the precious cargo carried by the British Technical Mission when its members disembarked from the vessel *Duchess of Richmond* in Halifax, Nova Scotia, on September 7, 1940. Headed by Sir Henry Tizard, they met first with representatives of the U.S. Army and Navy to provide the latest information on the developments of airborne radar that were taking place in Britain. Then the members of the Tizard group met with members of the NDRC for extended discussions over the period September 28–30. During these discussions, Bowen unveiled their prize exhibit—the cavity magnetron. The Tizard mission hoped, with the magnetron as incentive, to solicit the help of American physicists in the development of microwave radar.

The magnetron was taken to the Bell Telephone Laboratories where, on Sunday, October 6, 1940, it was operated in this country for the first time. The demonstration had a profound effect on the members of the NDRC. At this time when Hitler's forces had reduced the free world to a teetering England, its far-off dominions of Canada, Australia, New Zealand, and India, and an indifferent, but stirring, United States, a new truth settled over the members of the NDRC as they recognized that the principal barrier to a full-scale development of microwave radar systems had been removed. Now, based on the cavity magnetron, the resources of United States science could be organized to carry out the research and development needed to realize the benefits of microwave radar. Some members were optimistic about the outcome; others guarded—but after October 6, the pace of events dramatically accelerated.

On the following weekend, October 12–13, the Microwave Committee decided to establish a central laboratory to develop microwave radar. (There had been proponents of a plan to divide the effort among university laboratories around the country.) The laboratory was to be staffed with physicists from universities. Furthermore, this as-yet-unformed laboratory would concentrate on three projects: Project I, of the highest priority, to build an airborne 10-centimeter radar system that could be used by a pilot to detect other aircraft; Project II, to design a precision gunlaying radar—a system that would track on a target and aim artillery; and Project III, the development of a long-range navigational device.

On October 18, the decision was made to locate the central laboratory on the campus of the Massachusetts Institute of Technology. Compton agreed. On October 25, the NDRC approved the decisions that had been made by the Microwave Committee.

Before the decisions of the Microwave Committee had been officially approved, before MIT had been chosen as a site for the new venture, the hoped-for laboratory had a director. On October 15, Lee A. DuBridge, chairman of the physics department and dean of the faculty of arts and sciences of the University of Rochester, received a telephone call from Ernest Lawrence, who was with Alfred Loomis in the latter's New York City apartment. The ensuing conversation was typical of many in the weeks ahead: "Look," said Lawrence, "we have an important job having to do with National Defense coming up. I can't tell you about it, but I assure you it's very important."[7] The next morning DuBridge was on a train headed for the city and later that day he accepted the directorship of the new laboratory.

During this same day, October 16, DuBridge, Loomis, and Lawrence came up with a plan to get those physicists who could form the core of the microwave project together in one place at one time. It was a clandestine scheme. A conference on Applied Nuclear Physics was coming up on October 28–31 at, of all places, MIT. DuBridge and Lawrence called a select group of physicists and "invited" them to this conference.

Most of the six hundred physicists who came to this conference did so to give papers on their recent work, to learn about the work of others, to talk physics in corridors and around lunch tables, and to see their friends. A few came for another reason: they had gotten the telephone call. Except for subtleties, it was an ordinary conference. A perceptive conferee might have wondered about the hastily called, secretive sessions or about the theme of microwaves that seemed to be the common denominator of some of the last-minute sessions. Or about the luncheon meetings.

The Algonquin Club of Boston was the "home away from home" for the British radar specialists (a secret entrance to the club had been arranged for their use), and it was here that a luncheon meeting brought together a select group of American physicists and the radar people from Britain. Rabi was there, as were F. Wheeler Loomis and Ed Condon, and John Slater, A. J. Allen, and E. M. Lyman, among others. At this meeting the proposal for a microwave laboratory was revealed and the nature of the overall problem was identified. Now the anxiety and the worry that had been gnawing at many physicists had a focus, a purpose. The answer, "I don't know," given by Rabi to Zacharias's troubled question asked only a few weeks earlier, was no longer accurate. "The war in Europe was going so badly," said Rabi later, "I was dying to get into something. When I heard of this [the radar project], I said, 'I want to be in on it.'"

The MIT conference concluded on October 30. Seven days later, the day after Election Day, Rabi left his graduate students, his postdoctoral fellows, his laboratories, his family, New York City, and headed for Cambridge. It did not matter that he knew neither the time that would elapse nor the events that would transpire before he could return to his beloved city, his home university, and his happy laboratories. He was going to war.

10

The MIT Rad Lab

> When someone approached me with an idea, I'd look at him coldly and say, "How many Germans will it kill?" Our objective was to win the war.
>
> —I. I. RABI

NOW Rabi did something he had previously shunned: he went on the lecture tour for Sigma Psi, an honorary society for scientists:

I went around the country giving Sigma Psi lectures and used the opportunity to recruit for the laboratory. I'd go to some place, give my lecture, and ask to speak to some of the young people there. I'd tell them, "We have this laboratory; it's not a very good laboratory, conditions are difficult, and we are working on a project about which I can't tell you. Now I'd like to have you there in two weeks." And they came.

And they came quickly. As if a trap door opened under them, young scientists dropped out of one life into another. Ernest C. Pollard, a nuclear physicist from Yale University, was recruited informally by Ernest Lawrence. A short time later he received a telegram from Lee DuBridge asking for his services. Pollard put the telegram into the pocket of his lab coat, hung the coat on a hook in his Yale laboratory, and walked out of the lab. Five years later, after the war was over, he returned to find the lab coat hanging on the same hook, the telegram tucked into the same pocket.[1]

Ironically, Rabi was one of the earliest arrivals—an irony arising from the fact that, in 1940, some authorities regarded New York to be full of radicals and Communist sympathizers and were, as a consequence, somewhat uneasy about putting New Yorkers into high-security positions. Hence, when Rabi went to DuBridge to volunteer his services, DuBridge "was a bit reluctant . . . but I persuaded him."[2] When Rabi got the "green light," he left immediately for Cambridge: "I didn't have my affairs [in New York] in order. I just left. I wanted to get into this thing."

Sometime during those first, early days, the new undertaking became known as the Radiation Laboratory or, more simply, the Rad Lab. It was an accurate name: the Rad Lab physicists were involved in developing systems to generate and to detect microwave radiation. It was also a deceptive name: since the Berkeley Radiation Laboratory was a world-famous center where cyclotrons were designed, built, and then used to study the atomic nucleus, an outsider had every reason to believe that the MIT Rad Lab was another center for nuclear research. This assumption was further supported by the many nuclear physicists who were seen coming and going. In November 1940, nuclear physics was still an innocent subject, far removed from matters of practical significance.

The first meeting of the Rad Lab staff was held on Monday, November 11, Armistice Day. The objectives of this first meeting were serious indeed, but its style was informal. Only a few physicists were there and they all knew each other. Furthermore, mutual respect gave each of them a sense of confidence and freedom. As Rabi has quipped, "We all came from the same bar."

The informal organizational structure influenced the way responsibilities were assigned, as Rabi has described: "We chose up just like a baseball team. We chose up sides. What would we take? Well, I took the magnetron. I had no idea how it worked." Kenneth T. Bainbridge took pulse modulators; A. J. "Ajax" Allen, antennas; L. A. Turner, receivers. And so it went.

The informality did not apply to security; the restrictions around MIT's Building 6 were rigid. The magnetron was kept in a safe; the windows of the laboratory were painted black so that no one could look in; a guard at the door restricted access. Inside the building, however, the restrictions were nonexistent. Members of one group would work with those of another group. Ideas were welcomed from any source.

Later in November, a crude structure was erected on top of Building 6. This shack would house the radar prototype systems still to come.

By mid-December, there were about thirty-five people working at the

Rad Lab: thirty were physicists, and most of these were nuclear physicists fresh from their university laboratories. They knew little to nothing about the microwave electronics that would be needed to translate the British 10-centimeter magnetron into a working radar system. But the Rad Lab physicists were not alone: no one knew much about microwave electronics. It was a new field, a new technology. With confidence bordering on naïveté, they plunged into their work.

The early weeks of the Rad Lab were, according to Lee DuBridge, "a blitz."[3] The feasibility of microwave radar had to be established quickly if the project was to survive. On December 16, one month after the effort was initiated, a schedule of target dates was adopted. The goals were ambitious:

Goal 1: By January 6, 1941 (three weeks), there was to be a microwave system working in the rooftop shack.

Goal 2: By February 1, there was to be a system mounted and working in the B-18 bomber that had been supplied to the laboratory by the U.S. Army.

Goal 3: By March 1, there was to be a system adapted for and working in an A-20-A airplane, the fighter plane most likely to be used for night combat.

On January 4, two days ahead of the scheduled target date, a radar beam was sent out from the rooftop lab, and echoes from the buildings in Boston across the Charles River were detected. In less than two months after they had walked into the Rad Lab, a group of physicists, with no previous knowledge about microwave electronics, had put together a prototype radar system. It was crude, but it worked.

The jubilation over this early success was brief. There were problems. First, it was not good enough to pick up signals from buildings; they had to be picked up from an aircraft in flight. Second, there was the transmit/receive (T/R) problem. Any system to be used in a fighter plane had to be compact; therefore, it was absolutely necessary to use the same antenna for both transmitting a radar signal and for receiving the return echo. Unfortunately, the outgoing signal is a million million million times stronger than the incoming echo. The problem was thus how to use the antenna and transmission line that pours out the powerful radar beam at the same time to detect the feeble echo that bounces off a target and returns in less than one millionth of a second. It is rather like trying to detect a mote of mist while standing under the great falls of Niagara.

The problem was solved, however crudely, by the first T/R equipment. On January 10, 1941, Lee DuBridge, who was in Washington, D.C., received a telegram that read: "Have succeeded with one eye." From the top of Building 6, the physicists had successfully detected the radar echo with the same dish antenna they had used to transmit the radar beam.

The transmit/receive problem is a good example of how the Rad Lab physicists were able to confront entirely novel situations, yet were able to apply the principles of their discipline in a systematic fashion to effect a solution. On numerous occasions the success of the radar project came to depend on their ability to solve a crucial problem such as the T/R box question. Sensitive detectors could not be used until a surefire method was developed to isolate the minute incoming echo signal from the monstrous outgoing radar beam. The eventual perfection of the T/R box by James L. Lawson did this and cleared the way for ongoing development.

Within twenty-five days of setting up target dates, they had bounced radar signals off Boston buildings and detected the echo with "one eye." But there was no time for celebrating their successes. The tension and concern created by the war were exacerbated by the skepticism of some governmental officials who questioned whether academic physicists could successfully carry out a project such as the development of microwave radar. If they failed, who would answer for the wasted taxpayers' money? On February 7, DuBridge was back in Washington confronting the testy members of the Microwave Committee. Since no radar signal had been detected from a flying aircraft, there was talk of junking the whole project. DuBridge fidgeted.

Back on the rooftop in Cambridge, the activity was frantic. One physicist peered through a crude telescope sight while another held an antenna. In the distance, a plane was taking off from East Boston Airport (now Logan International Airport). All other eyes were on the monitor. A blip appeared on the screen. The airplane, gaining steadily in altitude, was successfully tracked. One of the physicists—no one remembers who—skittered down the narrow spiral staircase from the roof and raced to a telephone. DuBridge took the call in the Washington meeting room. The room grew quiet. DuBridge recalls that exciting moment: "I answered it right there in the meeting and I guess probably everybody realized what was up. . . . Whoever it was that called me said, 'We've detected an airplane at two miles.' So I held up two fingers [indicating two–mile detection] and they all said, 'O.K., let's go!' And we went from there."[4]

The first four months of the Rad Lab's existence was "the blitz" period: the staff was small and the emphasis was on quick, definitive results to build confidence in the minds of skeptics. Consequently, the major efforts were concentrated in two areas: component development and the airborne 10-centimeter radar system. The gunlaying radar (Project II) and the navigational radar (Project III) had, during these early weeks, a lower priority.

The development of key components—the T/R box, for example— was, of course, a necessary precursor to any tactically useful system. The magnetron, the heart of the radar system, was another component that demanded and received its share of attention. In spite of the fact that, early on, there was no adequate account of how the magnetron really worked,* Rabi and the physicists in his group were quickly able to make improvements on the device. They flew, so to speak, by the seat of their pants using informed intuition, clever hunches, and just trial and error as their guides. They developed power-measuring techniques and frequency analyzers to assess more precisely just how the magnetron was performing. This knowledge enabled them to get more power out of the device than the British had thought possible.

From the very earliest days, Rabi recognized the importance of pushing magnetron technology down to shorter wavelengths. There were reasons explaining the reduction of radar wavelengths from 1,000 centimeters to 150 centimeters and on down to 10 centimeters. In addition to compactness and sharpness of focus, short wavelengths provide more detailed information. If you throw a big beach ball at a picket fence, the ball bounces back as if it hit a wall, but gives no information about the detailed structure of the fence. If, on the other hand, you project small marbles at the picket fence, some will get through altogether, while others will bounce back through a range of reflection angles. By studying the way marbles bounce off a picket fence, one can learn detailed information about the fence. In similar fashion, short wavelengths bouncing off a target can resolve finer features and give more detailed information about the target itself than can long wavelengths. For these reasons, Rabi wanted to develop 3-centimeter cavity magnetrons—and by the spring of 1941, barely five months after the Rad Lab project was started, Rabi's group had a working model of such a magnetron.

The path from 150-centimeter waves to 10-centimeter waves to 3-

---

*In *The Physicists,* Kevles relates the story of how Rabi told the theoretical physicists standing around the disassembled parts of the magnetron, "It's simple. It's just a kind of whistle." Ed Condon was quick with a response, "Okay, Rabi, how does a whistle work?"[5]

centimeter waves is not simply a matter of changing a few wires. Entirely new techniques, most of them unknown at that time, had to be learned, developed, and applied. Electrical power is delivered to a pop-up toaster (and other appliances) by a simple two-wire cord. Wires will not work for microwaves. Hollow, metal conduits, called waveguides, are required; and waveguide components had to be invented in order to shuttle microwave power from one part of the radar system to another. All these techniques were new, and creative minds were a necessity. At the same time that the Rad Lab personnel were learning the peculiarities of working with 10-centimeter microwaves, Rabi was pushing on to the 3-centimeter region, thereby setting the stage for even more challenging demands on their technical talents.

While the vision of Rabi and the other physicists who saw the need to work toward shorter wavelengths was commendable, the wisdom and tolerance of the decision makers, whose approval Rabi needed in order to proceed, was indeed extraordinary. To military officers, the 3-centimeter project must have looked like a waste of valuable time and effort. It already seemed presumptuous to be developing 10-centimeter radar systems when the 150-centimeter units were just appearing and were still unproven. To those policy makers in charge of the Rad Lab, it must have appeared ludicrous to hear physicists who had just launched into the entirely unknown 10-centimeter region begin to stress the need to push the frontier to still shorter wavelengths. That the 3-centimeter project was allowed to happen is miraculous—so also was the fact that the 3-centimeter project succeeded beyond all expectations.

March 1941 was both an end and a beginning for the Rad Lab: the blitz was over, and, as DuBridge said, they could settle down to work. The number of personnel had grown to 140—90 of whom were either physicists or engineers. Throughout the month of March, a lone B-18 army bomber could be seen flying sorties off the coast of New England. Inside the aircraft, physicists were testing the first experimental airborne 10-centimeter radar system. On March 27, they were flying over the water at an altitude of 2,000 feet. Nine miles away, a 10,000-ton ship was headed for port. To the surprise of everyone, the radar echoes from the ship were observed with a clarity totally unanticipated. The Rad Lab physicists were so excited that they asked the B-18 pilot to head for New London, Connecticut, a submarine base. There, in the waters near the base, a submerged submarine was detected from a distance of 3 miles and an altitude of 1,000 feet.

The sightings of the ship and the submarine were the first evidence that radar performed well over water. These sightings also brought to an end the concentration on airborne radar systems. With only minor modifications, the airborne system could be transformed into a new tactical device: aircraft-to-surface vessel (ASV) radar. The navy wanted a trial system immediately, and the British requested two sets as quickly as possible. Other tactical devices were envisioned, and the Rad Lab physicists began to diversify.

Research for war requires speed. Project II, gunlaying radar, had as its objective a wholly automatic system that, when an enemy aircraft was picked up on the radar screen, would lock on that target, track it, and feed the necessary information into an anti-aircraft gun and automatically aim the gun. In a low-key fashion, this project was initiated in January 1941. By cribbing parts that had been developed for the high-priority airborne system, the physicists were able to get a gunlaying radar system into operation on the roof of Building 6 during the month of February and, on the last day of May, they demonstrated the system's ability to track automatically on an airplane. In December, a truck-mounted system was demonstrated at Fort Hancock for the benefit of the U.S. Army. This gunlaying radar system, the SCR-584 (*S*ignal-*C*orps *R*adio Set), was used in essentially unchanged form throughout the duration of the war.

Project III, the long-range navigational system, was also started in a low-key fashion: waiting for parts, waiting for manpower, and improvising. Nonetheless, the basic development of LOREN, as it came to be known, was complete by September 1941. Field tests carried out in December and January 1942 were so impressive that the army and the navy were immediately eager to have the system operational.

On December 7, 1941, the Japanese attacked Pearl Harbor. Four days later, both Germany and Italy declared war on the United States. By this time, the MIT Radiation Laboratory had been operating for a little over one year and had an impressive array of prototype systems in operation. The original concentration on the 10-centimeter airborne interceptor system had spawned many offspring: aircraft-to-surface vessel search radar; airborne fire-control radar; blind-bombing radar. Furthermore, the basic research and much of the development of 3-centimeter radar had been completed. When the United States entered the war, not one 10-centimeter microwave radar system was in combat use anywhere in the war; however, the basic thinking had been done, the crucial breakthroughs had been achieved, field tests had been carried out, and microwave radar was poised to emerge from the laboratory.

Pearl Harbor marked the second turning point of the Rad Lab. Du-

Bridge, Rabi, and the other "old-timers" who had come to Cambridge for a few months now realized that the life of the project would be measured in years; hence, the laboratory grew at a hectic rate over the first six months of 1942. The increased size of the laboratory, the increased number of projects, and the increased involvement with the military services led to the recognition that the organization of the laboratory needed to be formalized. A divisional structure was adopted with ten divisions (later, two more were added). A steering committee, made up in part of the heads of each division, established policy for the laboratory. Rabi was the head of Division 4, the Research Division; and somewhere along the way—there seems to be no record of when it actually happened—he became an associate director under Lee DuBridge.

> It quickly became evident [said DuBridge later] that Rabi's talents were too widespread to confine him to a particular piece of the lab.... Rabi's self-appointed interest, with our enthusiastic support, was to make sure that all the groups in the laboratory were looking beyond tomorrow.... He's the one who said, "We got to get a group started working on 3-centimeter radar," and then, later on, 1-centimeter radar.... So he was the forward-looking general director of research. He was invaluable.[6]

As an organization, the Rad Lab worked intimately with three other organizations: the British radar organization; the armed services of both the United States and Great Britain; and American industry. Much of the success of the Rad Lab was a direct by-product of the enlightened way these working relationships were established. The importance of the British contribution to radar development cannot be overemphasized. It was, after all, the British who developed the 10-centimeter cavity magnetron. Throughout the war there was very close collaboration between British and American scientists, successes on one side of the Atlantic being shared with the physicists on the other side. "We learned so much from the British," Rabi has said. "They saved us a year at least. They'd been in the business. Not only the tricks of the trade, but the meaning of radar, the tactics of how it's used, what the whole philosophy is, which they had brilliantly worked out."

The happy working relationship that developed between the civilian scientists and the military officers almost defies logic. The scientific and military traditions could hardly be more different: the scientific terrain is constantly changing, and scientists live with change; military principles are old and time-honored. The key word in the military lexicon is authority; in science, authority resides primarily in evidence garnered from nature. Scientists question; soldiers obey.

At the outset, the admirals and generals were horrified at the absence of a chain of command, at the freewheeling structure of the Rad Lab, and skeptical about the likelihood of physics professors producing anything useful. A common attitude among many military thinkers was that production, testing, and training should be based on known techniques and established models. Many saw no need for research.

The military were reluctant to divulge tactics, to reveal proposed uses for radar equipment. Their wariness showed. In one of the earliest exchanges, a group from the navy came to talk with Rabi, who was in charge of advanced development, and described some devices they wanted. As Rabi recalls the incident:

> I asked, "What are they for? What is their purpose?" This naval officer looked me in the eye and said, "We prefer to talk about that in our swivel chairs in Washington." I didn't answer, but I didn't do anything either. Then they came back; again they had a problem. This time I said, "Now look, you bring your man who understands radar, you bring your man who understands the navy, who understands aircraft, you bring your man who understands tactics, and then we'll talk about your needs." That was a pretty hard thing for them to swallow, but they did it. We developed a wonderful relationship. They were worried about snooper planes following the fleet, and they wanted to shoot them down. We developed a height-finding radar to be used on the ship, a radar to be used in conjunction with airborne radar. This started a relationship with the navy that was very important to us. When we got to know one another, when they learned we were trying to help them and that we respected them, when they discovered we didn't want any of the glory, we came to be friends with great mutual respect.

The insight and understanding that the physicists developed for the tactical needs of both the army and the navy were responsible for the immediate success of the radar systems when they were used in arenas of combat.

The relationship between the Rad Lab and industry developed through stages, but in its final form it was the most effective. The pattern throughout the war was more or less the same: the Rad Lab staff did the basic research, the basic development, and built a prototype system. When the tests of a new system proved satisfactory, it was demonstrated for one of the armed services; and, upon their approval, the system was turned over to a private corporation for engineering refinements and production. The separation of the roles, however, was never quite so clean. The novelty of microwave radar coupled with the inadequacy of appropriate facilities and personnel made it necessary for the Rad Lab to play an overseer's role. This, of course, brought charges from industry of governmental encroachment on private industry.

The scale of the industrial operation was staggering. Literally hundreds of manufacturers, subcontractors, and vendors were involved. Rad Lab personnel had to be in close contact with each of them— explaining the job to be done, training engineers in the intricacies of the new systems, and identifying the test equipment necessary to carry out the assignment. The result was that Rad Lab research physicists followed their creations through the manufacturing design step, through production, out into the field, and even into combat. By the same token, a policy was adopted to bring industrial engineers into the act during the early stages of development. This helped to facilitate the transition from the prototype to the production models. Later, Karl Compton referred to the Rad Lab as the "greatest cooperative research establishment in the history of the world."[7]

From the time the United States became an active participant in the war, radar played a role. Within a few weeks after the declarations of war were signed, German U-boats were controlling the waters off the eastern coast of the United States. An indication of our total lack of preparedness is the fact that during the month of February 1942 alone, eighty-two U.S. merchant ships were sunk by German submarines. During the same early weeks, Rad Lab scientists were modifying the airborne interceptor units for use as aircraft-to-surface vessel search. On the night of April 6, a radar-equipped B-18 bomber on its first night patrol spotted a German U-boat from a range of 11 miles and an altitude of 300 feet. The B-18 gave chase and sank the submarine. A week later, another radar sighting was made, and this time the U.S.S. *Roper* gave chase and sank the German submarine U-85 into the waters off Cape Hatteras. (I further discuss the use of radar in the war in chapter 12.)

There were fewer than five hundred Rad Lab employees at the beginning of 1942; at the end of the year, there were almost two thousand Rad Lab badge wearers. There was also a dramatic increase in the diversity of the projects being pursued—a total of fifty projects in all. The earlier radar systems that had been developed were in widespread use in all the theaters of the war. In Cambridge, the long view was still inspiring the Rad Lab physicists.

Earlier ideas, presumptuous as they might have seemed at first, had reaped bountiful harvests. The 3-centimeter microwave radar systems, for example, were in rapid development and production for both airborne and shipboard use. This success, and others like it, encouraged everyone to be imaginative.

Good ideas, of themselves, were not sufficient. New ideas were funneled into Rabi's Advanced Development Division. Once they were there, it was he who established the context in which they were considered. No basic research idea was pursued unless its proponents could demonstrate its potential usefulness in war. On this Rabi was adamant. As the official historian of the Radiation Laboratory, H. E. Guerlac, has written: "It is significant that this [approach] to a considerable extent reflected the opinion and influence of the head of the research division [Rabi], who, though the Laboratory's most celebrated physicist, was one of the most forceful and insistent advocates of the policy of getting new radar systems into the field."[8]

And the war-winning ideas, with their resulting new radar systems, came. They included a system that would allow precision bombing to be carried out even in heavily overcast conditions; the ground-control-approach system that would guide bombers to a landing in soupy fog; the microwave early warning system for long-range detection (or control) of aircraft.

The first satellite Rad Lab was established in March 1942. Its purpose was to develop a magnetron to produce 1-centimeter microwaves. For this undertaking, a new team was recruited to begin the basic research and a new satellite lab was located at Columbia University. Rabi was given the responsibility for this new venture. Apart from his obvious delight in bringing such an important project to his home campus, Rabi's reason for suggesting Columbia as a site was the fact that many of his old team were still there and could provide the nucleus of a strong staff. Rabi was named nonresident director, and J. M. B. Kellogg associate director. Kusch and Millman were original members of a staff that eventually grew to seventy-four people. By June, only three months after it was created, the Columbia Rad Lab physicists had built four 1-centimeter magnetrons and were testing them.*

*The Columbia Rad Lab eventually occupied the laboratories where Rabi's molecular-beam experiments had been carried on. The original magnetic resonance system was taken apart and discarded. Even Rabi's office was occupied; thus, most of his pre-1940 papers were destroyed and/or lost.

The early radar systems for high-altitude bombing used 10-centimeter microwaves. Since, with these units, it was difficult to identify specific targets, it was decided, in January 1943, to switch to 3-centimeter units. Here the advantages of short wavelengths were graphically demonstrated: the high-altitude systems using 3-centimeter microwaves showed coastline features in such detail that the Army Air Force demanded that the Rad Lab deliver 20 sets by September 1. The first bombing mission using 3-centimeter microwaves took place on November 3, 1943. These 3-centimeter systems were so successful that production was turned over to private industry: by the end of the war, the Philco Company had produced 7,835 of these 3-centimeter systems, and Western Electric had delivered 10,995.

From the beginning, Rabi's research group at the Rad Lab was busy developing basic ideas and solving new technical problems. By 1943, however, when most of the basic ideas were understood, the primary task became one of transformation: the transformation of the basic ideas into field-practical applications. Also, the reports coming in from the fields of combat provided detailed information about the 6,000 radar systems that had already been delivered to the army and navy. With this information, modifications could be made to improve performance.

One of the most ambitious projects undertaken by the Rad Lab, Project Cadillac, was proposed in February of 1944 and was ordered by the navy in April. The goal of this project was to obviate the principal weakness of shipboard radar: namely, its inability to see beyond the horizon. Enemy aircraft flying over the water's surface at very low altitudes—a technique used by Japan's kamikaze pilots—could not be detected by shipboard radar until it was too late to mount an effective counterattack. Project Cadillac required the elaborate electronic integration of shipboard systems with airborne systems. As such, it was the most complex system produced by the Rad Lab. At the height of its development, 20 percent of the Lab's technical staff were committed to it. With masterful administration, the system was taken from development to production in only thirteen months.

The Allies were on the offensive in 1944, and the eventual outcome of the war became more clearly predictable with each passing week. The research and development activities slowed to a halt, and the Rad Lab personnel became occupied with field service. In September 1944, Lee DuBridge received a bulletin from Vannevar Bush saying the preparations should begin to bring the laboratory to an end.

In 1944, the Rad Lab was big, employing almost four thousand people;

the cost of operation had reached $125,000 per day. Around the world, in all theaters of war, thousands of radar sets were enabling admirals, generals, and fighting men and women to push back the Axis forces.

Meanwhile, far to the west, another project, vital in its own way to the war effort, had begun in April 1943. While he never worked formally for this project, Rabi often gave it the benefit of his advice and, when summoned, would slip quietly away from Cambridge and head out to a mesa in New Mexico.

11

Los Alamos Advisor

I was asked by Oppenheimer to join it [the Los Alamos Lab] and be the deputy director—take charge of the experimental work. I refused because I was serious about the war. . . . I never went on the payroll at Los Alamos. I refused to. I wanted to have my lines of communication clear. I was not a member of any of their important committees, or anything of the sort, but just Oppenheimer's advisor.

—I. I. RABI

IN a formal sense, the Manhattan Project began in the spring of 1943. The physicists who gathered in Los Alamos were an anxious lot, their anxiety fired by uncertainty.

With the discovery of nuclear fission by the Austrians Lise Meitner and Otto Frisch in January 1939, physicists recognized almost immediately that the atomic nucleus was a potential source of energy. The energy invested in bringing protons and neutrons together to form the core of an atom is immense. A fraction of this energy can be withdrawn by cleaving the uranium nucleus into two equal parts. A small sphere of uranium can overwhelm the electromagnetic forces that hold together the physical and biological structures of our world.

Whether the potential of nuclear energy could be realized depended on the details of the fission process. Fission occurs when a uranium nucleus absorbs a neutron and thus becomes unstable—an instability the nucleus resolves by splitting into two nearly equal parts. The question then was, Were any other neutrons emitted in the fission process?

146

And, if there were, How many? Might there be a self-sustained nuclear reaction? And if a chain reaction, would it build up quickly enough to create an effective explosion? (A slow buildup would release sufficient nuclear energy to blow the bomb itself apart, thereby stopping the fission reaction prematurely.) Could the fissionable isotope of uranium, U-235, be separated in pure form on a large scale? (In naturally occurring uranium, only 1 out of 140 uranium atoms is the crucial isotope U-235.) Could practical methods be envisioned to surmount the many technical problems? Answers to such questions had to be found before an organized effort to build a military weapon could be justified.

Nuclear fission was the topic of conversation among physicists during January 1939. Bohr, on his way to the United States, heard about the discovery of fission during a stopover in England and, on the day he arrived in the United States (January 16), announced the discovery and discussed its implications in a lecture he gave at Princeton University. Fermi learned of the fission discovery as a result of this lecture. Ten days later, he and Rabi were in Washington, D.C., for a conference on theoretical physics where they met with Bohr to discuss the subject of nuclear fission.

After the Washington meeting, Leo Szilard, a refugee physicist from Hungary, wanted to talk with Fermi and to get his thoughts on the details of the fission process. In his recollections of this period, Szilard has recalled the conversation:

> Fermi was not in, so I told Rabi to please talk with Fermi and say that these things ought to be kept secret because it's very likely that neutrons are emitted, this may lead to a chain reaction, and this may lead to the construction of bombs. So Rabi said he would. . . . A few days later . . . I again went to see Rabi, and I said to him, "Did you talk to Fermi?" Rabi said, "Yes, I did." I said, "What did Fermi say?" Rabi said, "Fermi said 'Nuts!' " So I said, "Why did he say 'Nuts!'?" and Rabi said, "Well, I don't know, but he is in and we can ask him." So we went over to Fermi's office, and Rabi said to Fermi, "Look, Fermi, I told you what Szilard thought and you said 'Nuts!' and Szilard wants to know why you said 'Nuts!' " So Fermi said, "Well . . . there is a remote possibility that neutrons may be emitted in the fission of uranium and then of course perhaps a chain reaction can be made." Rabi said, "What do you mean by 'remote possibility'?" and Fermi said, "Well, ten per cent." Rabi said, "Ten per cent is not a remote possibility if it means that we may die of it. If I have pneumonia and the doctor tells me that there is a remote

possibility that I might die, and it's ten per cent, I get excited about it."[1]

By the end of 1941, three years after its discovery, enough knowledge about the fission process had accumulated to warrant stepping up the scale of the effort. In January 1942, all uranium work was consolidated at the University of Chicago in the newly formed Metallurgical Laboratory. The director was Arthur H. Compton, the brother of Karl Compton. During that summer a group was organized at the University of California, Berkeley, under the leadership of J. Robert Oppenheimer to study more specifically the possibility of a fast chain reaction and the feasibility of an atomic bomb.

Throughout these early years, uncertainty about what was happening in Germany with regard to nuclear fission haunted physicists and motivated their efforts. The British were particularly worried. On May 5, 1942, Kenneth Bainbridge returned from England and duly informed the Uranium Committee, a committee established by President Roosevelt, that it was the consensus in Britain that the Germans were ahead in the fission-bomb work. Such rumors, which came all too often, were frightening and only intensified the "overriding concern" expressed by Vannevar Bush: "I had great respect for German science. If a bomb were possible, if it turned out to have enormous power, the result in the hands of Hitler might indeed enable him to enslave the world. It was essential to get there first."[2]

As the technical questions were embraced with greater understanding, organizational issues began to assert themselves. After the appointment, in September 1942, of General Leslie R. Groves as head of the Manhattan District,* the pace of events quickened. He visited the various sites across the country where uranium work was in progress. The early visits were somewhat strained as the general and the physicists sized each other up; however, when he got to Berkeley and first met Oppenheimer on October 8, something clicked. Oppenheimer became *de facto* scientific director of the Los Alamos project months before he was officially so designated† and months before the laboratory itself existed.

By this time, Rabi had been at the MIT Radiation Laboratory for

*The Manhattan Engineering District, established on August 13, 1942, became the administrative structure under which the atomic bomb was developed. The first head of this administrative structure, Colonel James Marshall, had established his offices in New York City; hence, the name Manhattan District.

†There seems to be no agreement or a definite record of when Oppenheimer became scientific director.

almost two years. It was natural that Oppenheimer would seek his advice: natural, because there was an affinity between the two men—an affinity that had grown and developed since their 1929 meeting in Leipzig; natural, because Rabi, as the associate director of the Radiation Laboratory, had two years of experience in the administration of a large (and growing) laboratory, had been working directly with the military during that time, and, further, had valuable experience dealing with agencies in Washington, D.C. Oppenheimer lacked this kind of experience.

During the formative stages of the Manhattan Project, Rabi's practical advice to Oppenheimer was of the greatest importance.

> Without Rabi [Hans Bethe has said], it would have been a mess because Oppie did not want to have an organization. Rabi and DuBridge came to Oppie and said, "You have to have an organization. The laboratory has to be organized in divisions and the divisions into groups. Otherwise, nothing will ever come of it." And, Oppie, well, that was all new to him. Rabi made Oppie more practical. He talked Oppie out of putting on a uniform.[3]

Uniforms or civvies? Military or civilian? After the decision was made to have a centralized laboratory and after that eventful site visit on November 16, 1942, to the Los Alamos Ranch School—a small school perched on the cone of a large extinct volcano rimmed by the Jemez Mountains—several secret meetings were held at the Biltmore Hotel in New York City. Five men attended these meetings: General Groves, Dana Mitchell, Robert Bacher, Oppenheimer, and Rabi.* Of the various practical considerations discussed, one topic in particular sparked heated differences of opinion: Should the laboratory be militarized? This question was not answered immediately; but, from the very first, Rabi and Bacher's position was firm: they were adamantly opposed to the induction of scientists into the army.

The proposed militarization of the laboratory was the principal concern that brought Rabi to a meeting in Washington, D.C., on January 30, 1943. Oppenheimer and Rad Lab physicists Bacher, Luis Alvarez, and Edwin M. McMillan were also there. Oppenheimer had already agreed that, when the laboratory began to function, he would become a lieutenant colonel; in fact, he had already ordered his army uniforms. General Groves had persuaded Oppenheimer to run the laboratory as a military

*Dana Mitchell was from Columbia University, and Robert Bacher from Cornell University.

installation. As Bacher said later, "Rabi and I took an extremely dim view of this and we talked to him [Oppenheimer] in no uncertain terms about it. We pointed out to him that lieutenant colonels didn't have anything to say, and that if he tried to establish a scientific laboratory [with] a hierarchy that was composed of military people, that it just plain wouldn't work."[4] "We *knew* the military," said Rabi. "We'd been engaged in making military things, had the military around us. We knew it wouldn't work. In the first place, none of us would come."

Two days after the Washington meeting, Oppenheimer wrote the following letter to James Conant, the OSRD (Office of Scientific Research and Development) member who was coordinating many aspects of the uranium project.

Washington, D.C.
February 1, 1943

Dear Dr. Conant:

The discussion of which you were a witness in the early stages with Rabi, McMillan, Bacher, and Alvarez continued all Saturday. Rabi, with the full concurrence of the other three men, formulated the following indispensable conditions for the success of the project: (1) That the Laboratory must demilitarize: the arguments here were first that a divided personnel would inevitably lead to friction, and to a collapse of Laboratory morale, complicated in our case by social cleavage, and, more important, that in any issue in which we were instructed by our military superiors, the whole Laboratory would be forced to follow their instructions and thus in effect lose its scientific autonomy. My efforts to persuade the men that such a situation would not arise were unsuccessful.

(2) That the execution of the security and secrecy measures should be in the hands of the military, but that the decision as to what measures should be applied must be in the hands of the Laboratory.

After laying down two further conditions, Oppenheimer expressed his uncertainty about how General Groves might respond to the "indispensable" conditions, and then concluded:

Dr. Rabi will be in town this week, and I have suggested that he come to discuss these matters with you. I shall be in Berkeley from

Thursday on, and shall be glad to come back as soon as I can be helpful.

It seems to me that with some sacrifice and considerable delay we might have been able to make a Laboratory go, more or less, without fulfilling the conditions listed above. I believe that a real delay in our work would, however, have been inevitable. At the present time I believe that the solidarity of physicists is such that if these conditions are not met, we shall not only fail to have the men from M.I.T. with us, but that many men who have already planned to join the new Laboratory will reconsider their commitments or come with such misgivings as to reduce their usefulness. I therefore regard the fulfillment of these conditions as necessary if we are to carry on the work with anything like the speed that is required.[5]

A compromise was effected on the military issue, a compromise communicated by Conant* to Oppenheimer and Groves on February 25: during the early experimental stages of the work, the laboratory would be run under civilian administration. Later, but not before January 1, 1944, the scientists and engineers would become commissioned officers and take their orders from military superiors. Bacher's response to the compromise was to submit *one* letter both accepting an appointment on the staff of Los Alamos and resigning from it. His announced resignation would be effective the day the laboratory was put under military control.

Bacher never resigned because the transition to military control never occurred—an outcome that was, for Rabi, a personal triumph: "I think the greatest contribution I made to the war effort in Los Alamos was to help persuade Oppenheimer to keep the laboratory civilian."

One of the most ticklish problems facing Oppenheimer was the recruitment of a staff. Many of the most able physicists were already holding responsible positions in the Radiation Laboratory at MIT. As early as November 30, 1942, Oppenheimer had written to James B. Conant: "In view of . . . the very large number of men of the first rank who are now working on that project, I am inclined not to take too seriously the no's with which we shall be greeted. . . . The job we have to do will not be possible without personnel substantially greater than that which we now have available."[6]

---

*Conant himself took some persuading. He had been a chemical officer in the First World War and was comfortable with the idea of a militarized laboratory.

151

In mid-December, Oppenheimer went to Cambridge where he began his raid on the Rad Lab physicists. He talked with Rabi, whose experience and know-how he was eager to get—so eager, in fact, that he offered Rabi the associate directorship of the laboratory and applied the pressure of personal friendship. But Rabi refused to be moved by Oppenheimer's wiles; and finally, after two months, the latter bowed to Rabi's decision: "I know that you have good personal reasons for not wanting to join the project, and I am not asking you to do so. Like Toscanini's violinist, you do not like music."[7]

Rabi *did* have personal reasons for rejecting Oppenheimer's offers; in fact, he gave Oppenheimer four: First, there was his family. Helen did not want to go ("That's no place to raise children")[8]; and, further, they did not want to take the children out of their schools. Second, he thought the chance of success for the Los Alamos project—the development of a fission bomb—was fifty-fifty at best. Third, he did not like the whole idea:

> I was *strongly* opposed to bombing ever since 1931 when I saw those pictures of the Japanese bombing that suburb of Shanghai. You drop a bomb and it falls on the just and the unjust. There is no escape from it. The prudent man can't escape, [nor] the honest man. . . . During the war with Germany, we [in the Rad Lab] certainly helped to develop devices for bombing, . . . but this was a real enemy and a serious matter. But atomic bombing just carried the principle one step further and I didn't like it then and I don't now. I think it's terrible.

There was a fourth reason behind Rabi's refusal of the associate directorship of the Manhattan Project. That reason was the war itself:

> I was thoroughly involved *in* the war. After all I was associate director of the Radiation Laboratory and I felt we could lose the war because of the lack of radar. As far as the fission bomb was concerned, it was very iffy. I simply did not feel that I could leave the Radiation Laboratory as I was important to Lee DuBridge in helping to form policy in connection with Washington, the military, and the war. All of these reasons were combined. I wouldn't know how to weight them, but I would say that the chief thing was the war.

Rabi was not alone in his view about the importance of radar work. Felix Bloch, for example, was actually at Los Alamos for a short period before he quit to join the Harvard project involved in the development of radar countermeasures. "I quit for many reasons," said Bloch, "but one of the reasons was that I didn't think it [the bomb project] was going to decide the war against Germany. I could have been wrong, but fortunately I was right."[9] Robert Bacher has recalled that "people at the Radiation Laboratory thought that this was just absolutely crazy to take people off radar and put them on this fool's project out there."[10]

While resigned to Rabi's decision to stay at the Rad Lab, Oppenheimer did not cease to call upon Rabi for help and advice. On February 26, 1943, Oppenheimer wrote to Rabi:

I am asking two things of you, within the limits set by your own conscience.

(1) I hope that we can have a conference on the physics ahead of us in April, perhaps from the 10th to the 30th, at Los Alamos. The theoretical people I should like to have there at that time, and some of the experimental ones will be there too, though they may be busy with installation. I should like to have you come to that to talk over the physics, and to give us the benefit of your advice at a critical time. This is not a method of tricking you into the project, and it is not for the purpose of talking politics. It is just for the physics, and such relatively simple arrangements as we have to make at that time to see that the physics gets done.

(2) There are two men whom I should be more than reluctant not to have on the project: Bethe and Bacher. I think that you know the reasons in each case, and agree with them. You have a great deal of influence with these two men, and they in turn on many others who are involved in the project. I am asking that you use that influence to persuade them to come rather than to stay away.[11]

Rabi complied with both of Oppenheimer's requests—and more. Some of the Rad Lab's ablest physicists left Cambridge and headed west to join the new project. Not only did Oppenheimer get Bethe and Bacher, but also men such as Luis Alvarez, Kenneth Bainbridge, and Norman Ramsey. They all left with the blessings of DuBridge and Rabi.

Thus, though never on the payroll of the Manhattan District, Rabi's counsel was important to Oppenheimer; and, through that counsel, his influence on the project itself was, at specific times and on specific issues, prominent.

Rabi and Bacher went to Oppenheimer's April meeting together. "We just disappeared from Boston," said Bacher. "We traveled under assumed names. . . . We stopped in Chicago and talked with Wigner [a physicist from Princeton]. We made contact with him in a very complicated way, met him at the train station while we changed trains."[12] The meeting brought together thirty individuals who listened to the accounts of the latest experimental data and the most recent theoretical calculations. With this information in hand, the participants at the April conference planned the work programs for each of the newly defined divisions of the laboratory.

The April 1943 conference marked the beginning of the Los Alamos project. From its beginning until its end, Rabi appeared on the mesa when needed. As Bethe has said, "Rabi was the fatherly advisor to Oppie."[13] And Rabi went, as he has said, "chiefly as a troubleshooter for Oppenheimer. He'd get into trouble with the central Europeans and some of the other people. Oppenheimer had decisions to make which he wanted to talk over with a friend. . . . Of course, Oppenheimer and I had known each other since our days with Heisenberg and Pauli, and we had kept up our friendship."[14]

In the summer of 1944, two fissionable isotopes were *slowly* being accumulated: the isotope U-235, by a gaseous diffusion method being carried out on a massive scale in Oak Ridge, Tennessee; and the isotope of plutonium, P-239, being produced by a nuclear pile in Hanford, Washington. The trick of an atomic bomb is to bring together, with lightning swiftness, two subcritical masses of a fissionable isotope. The gun method that had been devised for the uranium bomb could not be used for the plutonium bomb; thus, unless a new method could be found to activate a plutonium bomb, the accumulated P-239 would be useless. An implosion method had been proposed, but the technical difficulties loomed so large that summer as to deeply discourage not only Oppenheimer and his Los Alamos physicists, but also Bush and his OSRD members.

The urgency of getting the implosion method to work prompted other questions, as Rabi has recalled:

I was there in New Mexico, seated in the room with some of the top scientists there. The question was asked: Should the laboratory be extended? The big problem was: Where was the enemy in this field of work? We went over the history of the discovery, from 1939, when the first announcement of uranium was made.

What did the Nazis have? Who were the Nazi scientists? We knew them all. Where were they? What were they doing? What means did they have at their command? How could a nation like Germany, then engaged in a life-and-death struggle with Russia, spare the resources for this sort of development? We went over the whole thing again, and looked at the history of our own development and tried to see where they could have been cleverer, where they might have had better judgment and avoided this error or that error.

What then?

We finally arrived at the conclusion that they could be exactly up to us, or perhaps further. We felt very solemn.

One didn't know what the enemy had. One didn't want to lose a single day, a single week. And certainly, a month would be a calamity.[15]

This concern prompted a reorganization of the laboratory. Oppenheimer abolished the governing board and created a new technical board to grapple *only* with the issues of physics and technique. Rabi was named to the technical board and he, along with Niels Bohr, was named a senior consultant to the director, Oppenheimer.

Encouraging developments on the implosion method greeted the new year 1945. With this advance, however, came competing methods of initiating a chain reaction. There was no sure bet, no clear-cut choice. Some argued that since the laboratory did not have the resources to pursue all avenues simultaneously, a particular method should be selected and all efforts concentrated upon it. Otherwise, the July 4 target date would come and go with no test. There was a counterargument: if the method chosen for development failed, months would be lost. Oppenheimer opted to develop together the two methods deemed most promising.

As the activities leading up to the test intensified, the pressures on the director intensified as well. General Groves, recognizing the tension that was building in Oppenheimer, sent for his brother, Frank, and Rabi. Both men came; and each in his own way exerted a calming influence on Robert Oppenheimer. Everyone was tense. An element of levity, a betting pool, helped to ease the strain. The betting was on how big the explosion would be, and the bets ranged from zero (no explosion) to the theoretical maximum. Rabi bet the theoretical maximum.

Kenneth T. Bainbridge, a Rad Lab alumnus, was responsible for the July test of the implosion device. The site selected for the test was Jornado del Muerto, a barren desert near Alamogordo, New Mexico. In the early morning hours of July 16, 1945, America's greatest physicists lay sprawled on the sands of that desert: Rabi, lying between Norman Ramsey and Kenneth Greiser; Fermi, next in line. Other groups were scattered about. They all wore welder's goggles. They waited.

Rabi remembers the final moments of waiting:

Nine miles away from where we were, there was a tower about one hundred feet high. On the top of that tower was a little shack about ten by ten. In that shack was a bomb. . . . At first, the announcer said: "Thirty seconds"—"Ten seconds"—and we were lying there, very tense, in the early dawn, and there were just a few streaks of gold in the east; you could see your neighbor very dimly. Those ten seconds were the longest ten seconds that I ever experienced. Suddenly, there was an enormous flash of light, the brightest light I have ever seen or that I think anyone else has ever seen. It blasted; it pounced; it bored its way into you. It was a vision which was seen with more than the eye. It was seen to last forever. You would wish it would stop; altogether it lasted about two seconds. Finally it was over, diminishing, and we looked toward the place where the bomb had been; there was an enormous ball of fire which grew and grew and it rolled as it grew; it went up into the air, in yellow flashes and into scarlet and green. It looked menacing. It seemed to come toward one.

A new thing had just been born; a new control; a new understanding of man, which man had acquired over nature.

That was the scientific opening of the atomic age.*

The atomic age opened with a nuclear blast yielding the maximum energy and Rabi won the betting pool.

---

*These remarks were part of a speech given by Rabi on January 3, 1946—less than five months after the Alamogordo test—at the opening session of the Boston Institute for Religious and Social Studies. Sharing the stage with him at that meeting were Professor Howard Mumford Jones, Dr. Louis Finkelstein, and then Archbishop Richard Cushing.[16]

CHAPTER

12

Radar and the Bomb in War and in Peace

> Radar was an art, a very broad art. Actually, radar was for the benefit of civilians. . . . Their thing [the bomb] was a war thing and the beginning of misery.
>
> —I. I. RABI

THE Radiation Laboratory at MIT and the Manhattan Project at Los Alamos demonstrate the great achievement possible when high purpose is combined with great talent.

Both laboratories were communities of physicists: academic physicists, mostly young (Rabi, in his early to middle forties, was a "senior citizen") and, overwhelmingly, American. They came from universities where they had pursued their own independent research in their own individual ways in their own quiet laboratories. Then, often on short notice and with sparse information, they were asked to come. And they did: they hung up their lab coats and left their campuses and their homes, for an altogether different environment. No longer was one lord of his own agenda and the master of his own time; rather, each man was part of a massive project with interlocking parts and with interdependent schedules. Leaving the pursuit of basic knowledge, these physicists had now to apply their skills to the immediate and practical ends of war —a task each lab accomplished with dispatch.

The gathering of a group of individualists—many with first-rate minds, many of them experienced prima donnas—to work together as members of a team is in itself a considerable accomplishment. Both labs were run by physicists, for physicists.

The Rad Lab was run by three men: Lee DuBridge, F. Wheeler Loomis, and Rabi. Each was a good scientist, and they respected each other. They also respected the physicists working in the laboratory and were, consequently, receptive to everyone's ideas. Each of them was a willing listener although, as Ernest C. Pollard—one of the earliest to arrive at the Rad Lab and later a member of its steering committee—has pointed out, they listened differently.

> DuBridge and Loomis really didn't like being center stage: they were both superb pros at it when it was their turn, but it wasn't something they had a slight craving for. Rabi, I think, did relish center stage. So with DuBridge and Loomis one came rapidly, almost instantly, to the process of describing the tension of the moment and the only requirement was clarity and some urgency on your part. You had their attention and it was full. With Rabi there was a need to have an approach. The kind of problem you brought to Rabi was important and you would be wise to be selective. ... Once you had begun in the right way there was no problem with the rest: a keen intellect, full of sharp interest, [he] was with you on your problem. If you made the wrong selection, then maybe you weren't taking him with you. It was quite easy to learn this and Rabi's office would be open a day later no matter what.[1]

Pollard, as a member of the Rad Lab's steering committee, watched Rabi closely over five years:

> [Rabi] was unquestionably original: he did not fit any standard pattern at all. . . .
> He played an extraordinarily important role in the lab. He was resolutely and relentlessly in favor of winning the war; he had no question of the value of his giving up his extremely productive research work for that end. . . .
> He had a fair number of faults as all of us do and he sometimes made errors of judgment. . . . I remember that although he was open, friendly and approachable I never really felt quite comfortable with

him. This had nothing to do with his personal approach, but it did have to do with his obvious attainments.[2]

DuBridge and Oppenheimer were very different men and directed their laboratories, according to Rabi, in very different styles: "I think DuBridge was an *excellent* director. He was not flamboyant; he was an extremely modest man. Part of his success was his ability to convince people how happy he was to be the director of such a wonderful group of people, people he admired." By contrast, Oppenheimer was flamboyant; he had the ability and the charisma to be the leader of the Los Alamos project.

Almost from the beginning of the Second World War, months before the United States actually entered the conflict, the Rad Lab was *in* the war. Liaisons from the navy and the army had offices at MIT, and the Rad Lab leaders had offices in Washington. Radar systems were designed to meet specific tactical needs of the military, and new military strategies were developed to exploit the use of oncoming radar systems.

Rabi had an office in Washington. He was the man responsible for the Rad Lab's advanced development; accordingly, he took it upon himself to understand the war and to anticipate the type of radar that should be developed to meet its needs. Rabi's intuition, acute in his molecular-beam laboratory at Columbia, was a faithful guide during the war as well. Once, to a group of admirals and generals in Washington, he made a presentation in which he developed a scenario relating the war's unfolding with the needs for radar systems. "Doctor, where did you get this information?" asked the officers. Rabi had no answer except to say that he had thought very carefully about what he had been able to read.*

On Sunday, December 7, 1941, the war came to the Rad Lab's very doorstep. And soon after Pearl Harbor, Rabi and Edward M. Purcell went to England to confer with their opposite numbers in the British radar program. There, Purcell has recalled seeing a map, "the big map

*Karl T. Compton tells of one "claim to fame" of the U.S. Joint Chiefs of Staff's Committee on Radar, for which Rabi was the chief analyst: "In early 194[2] [the committee] selected, as a means of focussing its thoughts on practical issues, the conception of a landing operation carried across the Atlantic Ocean from the United States to the north coast of Africa, making a landing and establishing a beach-head, and later a base, in Africa, then moving armies across North Africa with parallel fleet movements in the Mediterranean, and finally crossing the Mediterranean to Italy and working up through Italy into the backdoor of Germany."[3] At each step along the way they attempted to analyze how radar could be used. Of course, their hypothetical exercise turned out to be exactly what happened: in November 1942, Allied forces invaded North Africa.

of the Atlantic with a pin stuck in for every sunken ship. Along the coast of the United States, from Maine down to Florida . . . there was scarcely room for another pin."[4] Each pin seemed to vindicate the boastful claim made by German Admiral Karl Doenitz in 1940: "I will show that the U-boat alone can win this war. Nothing is impossible to us."[5]

German U-boats roamed at will up and down the eastern seaboard of the United States throughout much of 1942. In February alone, eighty-two U.S. merchant ships were sunk by German submarines; and during the year, eleven hundred U.S. flagships were sunk. On February 11, 1943, addressing the British Parliament, Prime Minister Winston Churchill said, "The defeat of the U-boat is the prelude to all offensive operations."[6] By the middle of 1943, the sweeping eye of microwave radar had put the German U-boats on the run. During that summer, Admiral Doenitz was forced to admit that "the methods of radio-location [radar] which the Allies have introduced have conquered the U-boat menace."[7] And later, on December 11, 1943, he wrote:

> For some months past, the enemy has rendered the U-boat ineffective. He has achieved this objective, not through superior tactics or strategy, but through his superiority in the field of science; this finds its expression in the modern battle weapon—detection. By this means he has torn our sole offensive weapon in the war against the Anglo-Saxons from our hands. It is essential to victory that we make good our scientific disparity and thereby restore to the U-boat its fighting qualities.[8]

Airborne and shipboard radar had broken the back of the German submarine offensive.

Once they had gained control over the Atlantic, the Allies could look ahead. The offensive in Europe proper began in the summer of 1943. On the night of July 9–10, the U.S. Seventh Army and the British Eighth Army invaded Sicily. Five weeks later, at a cost of sixteen thousand casualties, Sicily was conquered. On September 3, General Bernard L. Montgomery's Eighth Army stepped on the toe of the Italian boot; six days later, General Mark Clark's U.S. Fifth Army invaded Italy at Salerno. The Allies fought their way north on the Italian peninsula and, in November, reached the Gustav Line (a line along the Garigliano and Rapido rivers, over the central mountains, north of the Sangro River, and east to the Adriatic Sea). Here the German defense held. To break the deadlock, a diversionary attack by the British forces on the Gustav

Line was planned to precede the landing at Anzio by the American forces. The purpose of the Anzio landing was to cut German communications and supply lines from the north.

On January 22, 1944, the American amphibious force landed on the beach at Anzio where some of the toughest fighting of the war took place. Onto that beach came artillery accompanied by one SCR-584 gunlaying radar system. They dug the radar system deep into the sand so that only the antenna was visible. With this one Rad Lab radar system guiding the artillery, fifty German planes were shot down and the beachhead at Anzio was successfully established. Later in the war, the SCR-584 radar system would guide artillery to the destruction of 85 percent of the German V-1 rockets before they struck their British targets.

Throughout the winter of 1943 to 1944, at the very time U.S. soldiers were wading ashore at Anzio, the British and the U.S. Army Air Forces were carrying out extensive bombing missions over the heartland of Germany. The Rad Lab delivered the first blind-bombing radar system to the U.S. Army Air Force in September; the system was first used in a blind-bombing mission over Germany on November 3, 1943. This system, known as the H_2X system, employed 3-centimeter microwaves. Rabi's earlier resolve to push the state of the art down to shorter wavelengths paid large dividends now: a bombardier flying high above thick banks of clouds could see, on his radar screen, a detailed image of ground features. For the remaining months of the war, the H_2X radar systems were used against both the Germans and the Japanese.

The bombing of Germany during the early months of 1944 was preparing the way for Operation Overlord, the Allied invasion of the European heartland. The 9th Air Force was called upon to destroy the German air-fighter strength. For this objective, airfields and landing strips in northern France, Belgium, and Holland became the prime targets. During these radar-guided missions, strange "construction sites" were discovered which were soon identified as launch sites for a "rocket bomb." This discovery caused great concern and anxiety among scientists and military leaders, who feared that these rocket bombs might be the vehicle for a new uranium bomb. Fortunately, the speculation turned out to be false: the launch sites were being constructed for the new V-1 rockets that the Germans had been developing.

On June 6, 1944, the largest amphibious invasion force in the history of warfare hit the beaches at Normandy. In the D-Day invasion itself, Rad Lab radar systems were used in three ways: first, radar was used in spectacular fashion during the pre-assault bombardment against the French beach from the Orne River at Caen in the north to the Vire estuary at Isigny in the south. The coastal defenses were to be neutralized, the German troops demoralized, and the communications destroyed. (These objectives were only partly realized.) The timing was tight, and there was no margin for error. Only five minutes were allowed between the last wave of bombers and the first swarm of assault troops. With H_2X radar systems, 2,698 bombers took part in the D-Day bombings, and not one single Allied soldier was killed by misdirected bombs.

The second use of radar was in the control of the landing itself. The LLCs (Landing Craft Control) that led the invasion force ashore were loaded with radar equipment, whose purpose was to provide precise navigation. With their radar systems, these LLCs had to direct the initial wave of amphibious assault troops to a specific point on the beach—specific within two hundred yards—at a precise time—with an error not greater than one minute.

The third use of radar was with the Troop Carrier Command. Coordinated with the beach landings was a parachute drop of the 82nd and the 101st Airborne Divisions behind the German coastal defenses. Specific drop zones were targeted, and radar beacons guided the parachute troops and the glider-borne infantry to their prearranged locations behind Utah Beach. Finally, the Microwave Early Warning (MEW) radar system was set up across the channel in Devon, England, to maintain control of the Thunderbolt fighters flying from the Brest peninsula, to guide bombers over specific targets, and to aid in the rescue of pilots downed in the English Channel. The MEW control room was a front-and-center seat for watching the aerial assault on the Normandy beachhead.

By the end of June 6, the Atlantic wall had been breached: the Allies had landed 120,000 men with supplies on the French shores. A beachhead was established. From this time on, the days of the Nazi *Wehrmacht* were numbered.

The Allied strategy, agreed upon immediately after the United States had officially entered the conflict in 1941, was to defeat Germany first —thus, in a sense, putting the Pacific war on the back burner. As the United States's productive capacity proved itself capable of responding to all challenges, the back burner got hotter and hotter. By January 1944, the Americans were on the offensive in the Pacific.

The war in the Pacific was very different from the one in Europe. The principal weapon in the Pacific was the carrier task force—a synchronous system of ships, planes, and men. The nerve center of the task force was the Combat Information Center (CIC). It was the radar systems in the CIC that gave the Officer in Tactical Command an instant overview of his own armada as well as the positions of the enemy; it was radar that could direct aircraft and control anti-aircraft fire.

Long-wave radar had already been used in the mighty naval engagements of 1942: the Battle of Coral Sea and the Battle of Midway. After Midway, the Japanese began installing radar equipment in their naval vessels, but their late start in radar development and application was a deficiency they could not overcome. In testimony after the war, Japanese Vice Admiral Guzawa identified the greatest strength of our forces: the ability to direct fighters by radar.

It is a demanding and difficult task to control a large task force zigzagging at high speed in the black of night with every running light extinguished; and, further, traffic control during a major amphibious assault is mandatory. In the Marianas operation, over 400 ships were involved; and in the Philippines landing, over 1,200 ships. These armadas functioned like a single organism, deftly coordinated, sweeping the enemy before them. In one single day at the height of the Battle of the Philippine Sea, the Americans shot down 402 Japanese planes and lost only 17. It was, they said, a "turkey shoot." Operations of these magnitudes could not have been carried out with such stunning success without the guiding control of radar systems. After the Battle of the Philippine Sea, Admiral Marc Mitscher said, "The long and costly efforts in research training and practical applications of radar have not been in vain."[9]

Guam, the Marianas, the Philippines, Iwo Jima, and Okinawa. The American forces steamed ever northward until, from Iwo Jima and Okinawa, they could launch strikes directly at the Japanese mainland. In the spring of 1942, the Japanese dominated the western Pacific from their own islands to the continent of Australia. By mid-1945 they had been pushed back to their starting position. And, for the Japanese, there was chaos. Their home islands were blockaded, and B-29 bombers were raining death and destruction upon their cities. The war with Japan was, in actuality, over before it was over.

From the theater of the Atlantic to that of the Pacific—on the land, in the air, and upon the seas—from an assault landing on the dusty shores of North Africa, to the return of aircraft from an assault on Iwo Jima—from guiding a parachutist through the dark to a drop zone in the south of France, to guiding a task force over the dark waters of the South Pacific—from directing the fire of artillery to directing the release of bombs: in every aspect of the war, the radar systems of the MIT Radiation Laboratory played a vital role.

Throughout the war, the activities of the Rad Lab were secret, DuBridge and Rabi impressing upon all its personnel that to talk to anyone about their work was a violation of a trust. Helen Rabi never knew what her husband was doing during their five years in Cambridge. After V-E day, as V-J day seemed imminent, a news release was prepared to tell the citizens of the United States about the radar project, and *Time* magazine planned a cover story for its August 20, 1945, issue.

Then, in quick succession, two bombs were dropped and two Japanese cities were destroyed. The war in the Pacific had ended precipitately. The radar story, scheduled for *Time*'s cover, was bumped to page 78, and the new cover celebrated V-J day, linked it to the work of the Los Alamos physicists. Oppenheimer became a celebrity. DuBridge remained virtually unknown. Scores of books would be written about the bomb and the people who built it; the radar story would remain in the archives at MIT.

It was Lee DuBridge who first remarked, "The bomb ended the war, but radar won the war."[10] For Rabi, the issue is settled: "There's no question in my mind. Radar kept the Germans from subduing England. Without it, the war would have been over. There we would have been with nothing we could do. Mount an invasion of Europe by ourselves? Out of the question. My appreciation for the British is just boundless for what they did during the war."

The two projects, the Rad Lab and the Manhattan Project, were different not only in war but also in peace.

In the fall of 1944, Rabi came to a momentus conclusion:

In the summer of '44, it was clear to me that the war was over in the sense of our developing new radar equipment. Yet I realized that we had amassed so much knowledge that unless we put it down in the form of books, then, after the war, there would only be one group who would know all this technology—the Bell Telephone Laboratories. Furthermore, remembering the First World War, there would be Senate investigations on how we spent all this money. With the books, we'd have something to show for it.

The Radiation Laboratory Series, of twenty-eight volumes, was, according to Lee DuBridge, "born in the mind of I. I. Rabi,"[11] "and was, according to Rabi himself, "the biggest thing since the Septuagint." Of course, he did not join the many physicists who wrote the series, being no more inclined to write a book than he had ever been to carry out a tedious experiment: you cannot write a book "by the end of the day."

The writing began in the fall of 1944. To some of the Rad Lab physicists, as DuBridge has recounted, it was an intrusion on their time to be asked to write a book-length report: "We were working like the dickens to get some radar out to the Pacific, and a number of people said, 'We can't be bothered with writing reports.' But Rabi insisted, bless his soul."[12] Then came December with the Germans' last frantic offensive: the Battle of the Bulge. "People came to me," said Rabi later, "and were saying 'You son of a bitch. You've got us working writing books and over there the boys are dying.' It was sort of traitorous and the heat was on. So I thought the best thing was to go to Los Alamos for a while and join Oppenheimer. I was always welcome there."

The Radiation Laboratory Series was published by McGraw-Hill Publishing Company under the general editorship of L. N. Ridenour (Rabi being, in his own words, "not much of an organizer"). These books went all over the world, teaching a generation of physicists and engineers microwave electronics. The postwar American electronics industry was, to a considerable extent, based upon the Rad Lab Series. "It was one of the greatest things we did for the country," Rabi has said with justified conviction.

In the summer of 1944, Rabi was looking ahead: thus, the Rad Lab Series; thus, the seminar series. When the war ended, all the physicists would be returning to their university positions. For the years of the war, the attention of the Rad Lab physicists was focused entirely on microwave radar. Although Edward Purcell, for example, passed within yards of his Harvard office each day on his way to and from home to MIT, he was so caught up with his duties at the Rad Lab that, for months at a stretch, it never occurred to him to drop in at Harvard. For these men, physics, in the general sense, had stopped in 1940.

In order to help the Rad Lab physicists get ready for the resumption of their academic research, Rabi started a series of biweekly seminars to be given by Pauli (then at the Institute for Advanced Study in Princeton), who would survey recent developments in physics. The seminars started with a crowded room, but attendance quickly dwindled. "At the first lecture," Purcell has recalled with amusement, "an enormous room was packed with people to hear Pauli. It was almost totally un-understandable to most people, including me. At Pauli's next lecture, attendance had shrunk by about a factor of four. As we still didn't get much

165

out of it . . . Rabi had the great idea to get Julian Schwinger to lecture in the weeks in between [Pauli's]. Julian was there . . . all of twenty-seven years old. . . . Julian began to lecture. And that was just marvelous. He reviewed the recent developments, where things had gone, what were the puzzles. . . . So gradually the attendance at Julian's lecture went up and Pauli's went down."[13]

When the Rad Lab physicists left Cambridge, they were more than ready to pick up their academic research, having acquired new understanding of a whole range of new techniques and new instruments that could be used to probe matter in a variety of new ways. They were ready, too, in a deeper sense. The wartime laboratories at Los Alamos as well as those at MIT provided the young physicists an unusual apprenticeship in their profession—an apprenticeship of unexcelled effectiveness as they sat in on discussions with Bohr, Fermi, Oppenheimer, Bethe, Rabi, and other great scientists. Beyond the friendships they made, and the mutual respect established, there developed in these physicists a corporal sense. When the war ended, that brotherhood of physics, vitalized by the war experience, became nationwide with each homeward-bound physicist.

Rabi is proud of the Radiation Laboratory and the job that was done there, and is also quick to point out that he was never on the payroll at Los Alamos. One can challenge Rabi's position on bombing, radar, and the atomic bomb. He turned down Oppenheimer's offer of the associate directorship of Los Alamos in part because of his revulsion against bombing; yet, "when we made this radar and it went into those bombers . . . I guess I thought that was fine. I didn't mind so much bombing Germans because they were Nazis." Further, while Rabi believed that the atomic bomb carried the bombing principle even beyond what he already did not like, he has said:

I didn't mind then and I don't now, the [atom] bombing of Japan. I say, didn't mind. That's wrong. I'll put it this way, it's a complicated thing. The Japanese were licked—there's no question in my mind—let's say in January 1945. There was no reason to continue the war. They were licked. But I'm not the United States. I am a citizen of the United States. And the Army, the Navy, and the Air Corps, the President, and the Senate didn't feel that way. So we were mobilizing everything. In the meantime, Europe was liberated and they were starving. The Japanese were licked and they wouldn't admit it. Wouldn't stop. And the Americans, I think they were so blind, they went right ahead and were prepared to sacrifice maybe a million people in landings [on the Japanese mainland]. So what are you going to do under the circumstances? We dropped the bomb. That's what we did, and I have part of the blame, like every other American. But, realistically looking at the situation, I felt we should do something to stop this [the war] quickly.

Rabi is a wise man, a man of principle—qualities so much a part of him that the physicist Arthur Roberts, whose clever songs had enlivened many a Rad Lab gathering, wrote a song about Rabi. The title of Roberts's song, "It Ain't the Money; It's the Principle of the Thing," has become part of Rabi folklore:

> When Rabi was a youngster on the sidewalks of New York,
> He didn't trip fantastics with a maiden named O'Rourke;
> He palled around with junk men goes the story that we hear
> And got himself equipment at a price that wasn't dear.
>   It ain't the money; it's the principle of the thing.
>   It ain't the money; there's things that money can't buy.
>   It ain't the money that makes the nucleus go round,
>   It's the philosophical, ethical principle of the thing.
>
> He took himself to Germany to spend a year or two
> With twinkling Otto Stern around to tell his troubles to.
> The catalogues were thinner then, but ceiling wax and string
> Were plentiful and popular, so dope didn't mean a thing.
>   It ain't the money; it's the principle of the thing.
>   It ain't the money; there's things that money can't buy.
>   It ain't the money that makes the nucleus go round,
>   It's the philosophical, ethical principle of the thing.[14]

The six other verses all end with the same refrain: "It's the philosophical, ethical principle of the thing."

The war changed the world, the Rad Lab and Los Alamos changed men, and the combination brought physics into a new era. Rabi had occupied center stage at the Rad Lab, and he liked doing so. When he won the Nobel Prize in the fall of 1944, the stage encompassed more than the boundaries of the Radiation Laboratory. Rabi was on his way to becoming a world figure.

13

The Part-Time Physicist

It [the Nobel Prize] changes your whole life because you become a public person. The prestige
is fantastic—although, it represents only a selection of the Royal Swedish Academy of
Sciences. There are other academies as great.
But the Nobel Prize does have this strong public
appeal.

—I. I. RABI

I wanted to go back to my own groove. Then I
found when I got back, the groove was gone.

—I. I. RABI

NO prize, national or international, compares with the Nobel in glam-
our, in esteem, in consequences. In 1944, I. I. Rabi won the Nobel Prize
for physics, in recognition of "his resonance method for recording the
magnetic properties of atomic nuclei."

Long before the Swedish Academy brought world fame to Rabi, he
had attracted attention. First, Heisenberg had recommended him to
Columbia University, and then Urey had generously given him the
thirty-five hundred dollars that enabled him to pursue his molecular-
beam work independently. The advocacy of a Heisenberg or a Urey
provides a measure of a person and flags him or her as someone worth
watching.

Few Nobel-laureates-to-be are totally surprised by the telephone call
that officially informs them of their award. The selection procedure

includes the solicitation by the Swedish Academy of nominations from former laureates and from other scientists. Guessing goes on throughout the scientific community, and rumors begin to circulate. Some likely laureates have even had celebration parties under way—only never to have the telephone ring.

Journalists can initiate or strengthen a rumor. On the day before Rabi's prize was announced, he received a call at the Rad Lab from a newspaperman. The conversation was simple:

REPORTER: Hello, I am Mr. Johnson. I represent a Swedish newspaper.
RABI: Yes, Mr. Johnson?
REPORTER: I suppose you can guess what I'm calling you about?
RABI: Yes, Mr. Johnson.
REPORTER: Have you heard anything?
RABI: No, Mr. Johnson.
REPORTER: Neither have I.

"I was pretty jittery about it," said Rabi. "I certainly wasn't telling anybody."

Rabi's 1944 Nobel Prize broke the five-year respite owing to the war; no prizes were awarded from 1940 until 1944. The Swedish Academy made up part of the loss by naming the 1943 winners along with those for 1944. The 1943 prize for physics went to Rabi's Hamburg mentor Otto Stern. ("He should have won it immediately after the Stern-Gerlach experiment," said Rabi later.) This news only added to the pleasure of Rabi's day:

It was an enormous pleasure and an excuse for many parties, in different parts of the country—the Radiation Laboratory and Los Alamos. . . I had a great time, and I can say, with only slight exaggeration, that I didn't draw a sober breath for six weeks. I couldn't go to Sweden—after all, the war was still on—but there was a sort of ersatz ceremony in New York, at the Waldorf-Astoria. There was a big dinner, and there were a few guests from the Scandinavian nobility. My medal was presented to me at Columbia by Nicholas Murray Butler [president of Columbia University]. Poor fellow, he was eighty-two years old and was really pretty far gone —he was then blind. But he had a good, resonant voice, and he made a few appropriate comments, during which he referred to me as "Fermi."[1]

The Rabis gave a party at their Avon Hill Street home in Cambridge. Physicists from both the Rad Lab and the Radio Research Laboratory at Harvard came and joined in the celebration. Edward Purcell remembers the refrain of a little ditty that was sung at the party by George Uhlenbeck and Felix Bloch:

> Twinkle, twinkle Otto Stern;
> How did Rabi so much learn?*

"There was general rejoicing in the Radiation Lab," DuBridge has recalled. Three weeks after the announcement of Rabi's prize, the steering committee of the Rad Lab was in session pondering the fact that Los Alamos had taken away some of their top people. Ivan Getting [a young physicist from Harvard University] said, "Look, we're short of top talent. Los Alamos has all those Nobel Prize winners out there." At this DuBridge remarked, "We have one Nobel Prize winner"—to which Getting responded, "Yeah, but we've only had him for three weeks!" "It brought the house down," said DuBridge.[2]

No honor or award compares with the Nobel Prize in its ability to draw its recipient from a position of relative obscurity into one of celebrity status—as Rabi himself has remarked. "There is some romance attached to it. . . . It puts the winner on a sort of pedestal, because of the great public attention and prestige and also the prestige among one's colleagues."[3] Three months after he won the prize, Rabi's Richtmyer Lecture was featured in the *New York Times*.

The Sunday, January 21, 1945, edition of the newspaper carried a story with the headline, " 'Cosmic Pendulum' for Clock Planned." There followed three lesser headlines: first, "Radio Frequencies in Hearts of Atoms Would Be Used in Most Accurate Timepieces"; second, "Design Termed Feasible"; and third, "Prof. I. I. Rabi, 1944 Nobel Prize Winner, Tells of Newest Developments." The story was written by science reporter William L. Laurence. Rabi, the fourth Richtmyer Lecturer, a lecture sponsored by the American Association of Physics Teachers in honor of F. K. Richtmyer, chose as his tribute to the former Cornell University physicist "a straight scientific talk. Therefore," reads Rabi's prepared lecture, "I am going to speak to you on 'Radiofrequency Spectroscopy.' I am very sorry that I will have very little that is new to

*Private communication to author from Edward M. Purcell.

contribute which has not already appeared in the *Physical Review* or the *American Journal of Physics*. The war has taken care of that, but it may not be remiss to review a subject if only as a sop to our nostalgia for our peacetime physics."[4]

The war was still on when Rabi delivered this lecture, and it is clear that he had neither the time nor the inclination to write out his speech completely: there are only three typed pages followed by a few hand-written notes. In these notes Rabi identifies four directions for future research. The third entry in his list contains two words: "atomic clocks." He proposed to his audience a clock that would provide the most accurate method of time keeping imaginable. He based the atomic-clock idea on the radiofrequency methods that he and his students had developed before the war interrupted their work.

Rabi must have spent the greater part of his lecture talking about the potential of an atomic clock for that is what he remembers, that is what caught the attention of the reporter Laurence, and that is the topic that brought responses from clock manufacturers and other industrial laboratories. "This exotic form of publication [in the *New York Times*] prevented access to patent protection," said Rabi later, "but it did not stop Jerrold Zacharias from actually building an atomic clock—the cesium clock which became widely used. Later, Norman Ramsey made a still more perfect atomic clock."[5]

When the war ended, Rabi himself could have built the first atomic clock. The Waltham Watch Company as well as Bulova expressed interest: "It was clear that I could do that other [build an atomic clock], but instead of that, what we did was to discover the intrinsic moment of the electron. And to me, there's no question." Rabi seems to imply that he chose to make a major discovery rather than to build an atomic clock. But one does not choose to make a discovery; rather, one chooses to pursue basic questions that might lead to unexpected answers. With two graduate students, John Nafe and Edward Nelson, Rabi pursued such a question.

In 1947, two experimental results held the attention of many physicists throughout the world. One of these results, the Nafe-Nelson result, came from Rabi's laboratory in the physics department at Columbia University. Once again, he was on a roll. Before the war he had discovered the quadrupole moment of the deuteron. It looked as though he was going to pick up his physics with the same abruptness as, five years earlier, he had dropped it. He was certainly demonstrating that the war had not dulled his acute sense of what should be measured. He still knew where to direct his attention.

While the war years had not altered Rabi's keen physical intuition, they did bring profound changes to the world. With the war's end had come the atomic bomb, with its potential for massive destruction, and Rabi was one of those helping to chart a course in the new world that atomic energy had created. This was one reason why he never again gave physics his full attention. But this was not the only reason: "I wanted to go back to my groove. Then I found when I got back, the groove was gone." Rabi's laboratories on the fifth and tenth floors of Pupin Hall had gone to war as well. When the Columbia Radiation Laboratory began in 1943 to develop 1-centimeter magnetrons for radar, laboratory space was needed—and part of it was provided by the molecular-beam laboratories where Cohen and Millman, Kellogg and Zacharias had built their apparatus. The molecular-beam equipment had been dismantled, moved, and discarded: "We didn't come back to anything. We don't have a damn thing from that period. There's no equipment to put into a historical museum."

In 1945–46, however, equipment was the least of Rabi's problems. Money was abundantly available, and he could have bought and/or constructed apparatus. People were another matter altogether. Millman and Kusch were gone. Kellogg and Zacharias were gone ("My whole research team was gone"), and it had become impossible to assemble the kind of team he had had before the war.

Rabi had built his prewar team around postdoctoral fellows and associates. Of course, graduate students were a vital part of the laboratory, but continuity was provided by the senior people. Kellogg and Zacharias were there from 1933 until the war. Millman stayed on long after finishing his dissertation. Kusch came as a postdoctoral fellow in 1937 and was there until the start of the war. Their long tenure with Rabi was a consequence of two facts: first, the work was exciting and they enjoyed it enormously. They sensed the direction the events were taking. (Did they recognize that the work would bring Rabi a Nobel Prize? "It seemed to be inevitable," according to Kusch. "It was a brand new mold of spectroscopy and you can learn all kinds of things about molecules, atoms, and nuclei. We knew this. We didn't underestimate our papers."[6]) The second reason for the long tenure of Rabi's postdoctoral fellows was that in the 1930s there were few jobs and little money. Those young men had few alternatives. They were fortunate to have a job in physics and, even more, to be active participants in first-class physics.

The realities of the 1930s meshed nicely with Rabi's style. He was never interested in the tedious details of experimental physics, and eschewed building, calibrating, and maintaining equipment. The beauty of the 1930s was that he had experienced, gifted people in his laboratory who could carry on this part of the work and, in the process, train graduate students in laboratory skills.

The war changed all this. In 1946 there were jobs for physicists and there was money. The Ramseys and Zachariases of the postwar world could have their own laboratories with their own graduate students spending their own money doing their own research. The time was past for assembling a team such as Rabi wanted—and needed. Indeed, his old groove was gone.

The Nafe-Nelson experiment of 1947 was a natural extension of the long series of hydrogen experiments started back in 1933. The last experiments before the war had employed a beam of *molecular* hydrogen; and, with the new resonance method, the quadrupole moment of the deuteron had been discovered. Nafe and Nelson applied the resonance method to a beam of *atomic* hydrogen.

The earlier beam experiments on atomic hydrogen, carried out by Rabi, Kellogg, and Zacharias in 1934 and 1936, had been nonresonance experiments, and the magnetic moments of the proton and deuteron had been determined by a circuitous route. Two pieces of numerical data were needed: the frequencies ν_H and ν_D of the quantum transitions between the hyperfine states of hydrogen and deuterium. In the 1934 and 1936 nonresonance experiments, these frequencies were not measured directly. Then, the experimental values of ν_H and ν_D—measured indirectly—were put into a theoretical expression, and the magnetic moments of the proton and deuteron were calculated. This was the situation in 1947—not the way that Rabi, who "wanted the answers at the end of the day," liked it.*

The allure of the hydrogens is always the same: their simplicity permits the application of physical theory without any assumptions being made, without any approximations required. Thus, through the resonance method the theoretical expression linking the frequency ν_H with the proton's magnetic moment was exact. The same was true for deuterium. With the experimental values of the magnetic moments measured by Millman and Kusch in 1941, these exact theoretical expressions could be used to calculate the frequencies ν_H and ν_D.

The objective of the Nafe-Nelson experiment was to measure ν_H and

*In 1941, Millman and Kusch measured the magnetic moment of the proton in a way that did not depend on the theory of the hyperfine splitting.

ν_D (which could be done by applying the resonance method to a beam of atomic hydrogen) and to compare the measured values with the values calculated from the exact theory. This was a clever twist: earlier, ν_H and ν_D had been used to determine the magnetic moment; however, with the magnetic moments measured independently by Millman and Kusch, these moments were used by Nafe and Nelson in the calculation to determine ν_H and ν_D.

The results of the experiment were submitted for publication in May 1947. These measured results, along with the calculated values, are:

	Measured	Calculated
ν_H	1420.410 + 0.0006 Mc.	1416.97 + 0.54 Mc.
ν_D	327.384 + 0.003 Mc.	326.53 + 0.12 Mc.
ν_H/ν_D	4.33867 + 0.00004	4.339385 + 0.00003

As can be seen, the values calculated from the theory were smaller than the experimental values by about 0.25 percent—a slight discrepancy. Was this difference real? Rabi, Nafe, and Nelson end their paper with the comment: "Whether the failure of theory and experiment to agree is because of some unknown factor in the theory of the hydrogen atom or simply an error in the estimate of one of the natural constants, only further experiment can decide."[7]

Weeks before the Rabi-Nafe-Nelson results appeared in print, rumors about the experiment were spreading among theoretical physicists: Victor F. Weisskopf, for example, wrote to Hans Bethe in mid-May to ask him what he had heard about the rumored discrepancy. Thus, it is not surprising that this result from Rabi's laboratory, along with the important experimental result from Willis Lamb's laboratory at Columbia University, were both focuses of attention at the Shelter Island Conference on June 2–4, 1947.

The Shelter Island Conference was a landmark in physics.[8] The small number of participants—only twenty-four—constituted the most distinguished group of physicists in the United States. Further, the conference's influence on postwar physics cannot be overestimated. Many of the participants, eager to do physics again after their wartime recess, regard Shelter Island as the most important conference they ever attended.

The excitement at Shelter Island over Rabi's hydrogen results was a tribute both to him and to physics. In the first place, his reputation as a master of precise measurements was established; thus, his data were given due respect. On the other hand, there was every reason to have confidence in the theory. It was a tribute to physics that a discrepancy of only 0.25 percent cried out for explanation.

The first step toward explanation was taken in the form of a question, which served as title to a brief letter that Gregory Breit submitted for publication only three months after the Shelter Island Conference: "Does the Electron Have an Intrinsic Magnetic Moment?"[9] The motivation for this question was the data from the Rabi-Nafe-Nelson experiment. The theoretical expression used to calculate ν_H and ν_D contains a factor for the magnetic moment of the electron which, again from theory, was assumed to be known exactly. If the magnetic moment of the electron was ever so slightly different from the theoretically-assumed value, then the tiny discrepancy between Rabi's data and the theory could be resolved.

"It's something I should have seen right off," said Rabi later, "but I didn't." Within a few months after Breit's question had been asked, Kusch, along with Henry Foley, used the molecular-beam method to measure the magnetic moment of the electron. Instead of having the predicted value of exactly 1.0000 . . . Bohr magneton, its measured value was 1.001146 + 0.000012 Bohr magnetons—a slight difference but, for physics, a significant one. (For this work, Kusch shared the 1955 Nobel Prize in physics; for the theory explaining this very tiny departure from expectations, the physicist Julian Schwinger shared the 1965 Nobel Prize.)

Soon after the Shelter Island Conference, Rabi submitted another paper (with Columbia colleagues W. W. Havens and L. J. Rainwater). The experiment described in this 1947 paper was a departure for Rabi: it was not a molecular-beam experiment. The purpose of the experiment was to investigate the interaction between the electron and the neutron. To accomplish this goal, a beam of neutrons was sent through a piece of lead. In such an experiment, most of the neutrons pass straight through the lead; a few of the neutrons brush against the heavy lead nuclei and are scattered through sizable angles. However, as the neutrons move through the leaden environment, their path can be altered —albeit slightly—by the electrons of the lead atoms. It was this small effect that Rabi and his colleagues were trying to measure.

At the same time Rabi was doing the neutron experiment at Columbia, Fermi was doing the same experiment at the University of Chicago, neither physicist knowing of the other's activity. Both recognized, however, the fundamental importance of the idea behind the experiment.

The final paragraph of the Rabi paper reads: "Experiments of this type can yield exact information which should provide a severe test of the validity of such theories of the structure of elementary nuclear particles."[10] It was a forward-looking conclusion with an implied promise of more experiments to come. As far as Rabi was concerned, however, they never came.

The neutron-scattering experiment could have been the springboard to vault Rabi into experimental particle physics, which became the most active area of inquiry in postwar physical research, and put him in the vanguard of postwar physics just as he had been in physics throughout the 1930s. Although Rabi did continue his molecular-beam research and actually directed more graduate students to their Ph.D.s after the war than he had before, the intensity was gone.

Physics after the war was, for Rabi, only a part-time activity, a part-time duty. The reasons are many. To do physics in the style that had led to his Nobel Prize engaged his attention by day and by night: "Before the war I'd wake up in the middle of the night and design things in my head, think about our experiments. At the Radiation Laboratory, although I was really committed to it, I slept fine." The prewar research that intruded upon his sleep established a standard that could not be equaled unless he focused fully on physics—difficult under the best circumstances. "Unless you are very competitive, you aren't likely to function with the same vigor afterward [after winning the Nobel Prize]. You know, it's like the lady from Boston who said, 'Why should I travel when I'm already here?' "[11]

The acclaim that comes in the wake of the Nobel Prize is general; the response to that acclaim is specific. As the waves of adulation wash over them, many laureates are prompted to ask themselves the unsettling question, "Did I really deserve the prize?" Rabi is a self-confident man and rather enjoys the limelight; therefore, this question did not occupy a prominent place in his thinking. Nonetheless, he was delighted when he learned that Fermi—especially Fermi!—had nominated him for the award. As Emilio Segrè, a Nobel laureate from the University of California, Berkeley, has pointed out:

> Being nominated by Fermi was very impressive. Fermi was completely impervious to favoritism; he had to be just. He may have been somewhat cold, but he was absolutely impartial. He obviously knew physics as well as any living person; thus being nominated by him, considering his knowledge of physics, his character and his type of judgment, made a colossal impression.[12]

Many years later, in 1982, thirty-eight years after winning the prize, Rabi was informed by Abraham Pais, a professor of physics at Rockefeller University, that Einstein had also nominated him for the Nobel Prize. "Are you serious?" asked Rabi. Pais had seen the letter. "Isn't that marvelous?" Rabi said. "Now it's three times. I've had the pleasure three times."[13]

After the war, after his Nobel Prize, Rabi continued his physics, but it could no longer command his entire attention: "The prize opens doors for you, doors which perhaps should not be opened. It attracts you away from your field; it brings many distractions. I'm not a man to open doors and tell people 'Do this, or do that.' If I am invited in, however, then I can go into action. The Nobel Prize *caused* me to be invited, it brought the invitation."

To be sure, Rabi did what he did by choice. He could have thrown himself back into physics, but he did not. He enjoyed, he reveled in, the new "distractions." The open doors brought him onto the public stage in a postwar world profoundly different from the one he had left five years earlier. The gooseflesh from Alamogordo was still with Rabi as he entered this new world. And the invitations came: "If I hadn't won the Nobel Prize, I wouldn't have had the temptation to respond to them . . . nor would I have had the obligation."

Obligation is another tassel on the mantle of a Nobel laureate. He had a department to rebuild and the welfare of East Coast physics to protect. These pursuits alone might have been sufficient to keep him from regaining the focus and intensity that would have been necessary to carry on physics at his prewar level. It was the trips to Washington, D.C., however, trips that came with increasing frequency as the 1940s ended and the 1950s began, that demanded and received Rabi's attention.

CHAPTER

14

The Broader Stage

> Our experience in World War II had a profound
> effect on the scientific community. We saw how
> our command of scientific knowledge and
> method, aided by vast sums of money and sup-
> port, have made it absurdly easy to kill human
> beings. . . . This fateful truth has brought home
> to many scientists the fact that they cannot es-
> cape the social responsibility of their actions.
> No longer can science be just "fun and games."
> —I. I. RABI

WHEN Rabi left his laboratory and his campus in 1940 for Cambridge, he had already been elected to the National Academy of Sciences. With the experimental work for which he won the Nobel Prize behind him, he had already achieved an international standing among physicists. In 1940, he was an academic physicist supreme. It was a simple life.

The academic world that Rabi re-entered in 1945, two months after the dropping of the atomic bombs on Japan, was no simple extension of the one he had left in 1940. Furthermore, the returning Rabi was no simple extension of the man who had left:

I was five years older, and I left Columbia as an ivory-tower professor. I had not had very much experience dealing with indus-try, or technology, or warfare, or politics. I was involved with all of this at the Radiation Laboratory. We had spent several billion dollars and had engaged, more or less, on a world scene. I went to

England in 1942 to show them our 3-centimeter radar equipment, and I saw how things worked in England. We learned from them.

So, dealing at that level, going over to England, being concerned with the actual war plans in order to have the necessary equipment at the right time—all of this was for me a forced growth. In whatever I did, I was always interested in some objective. At the Radiation Laboratory it was winning the war. Basic questions pressed themselves in upon me: Would we invade North Africa? To what degree do we cooperate with the British? What is the value of this for the future of the United States? As a result, I became oriented in a personal way to these more global attitudes. So I was not the same man as when I left.

It was a heady experience to be a physicist in the years immediately following the Second World War. Physicists were celebrities. And Rabi, the most recent American Nobel laureate, was a celebrity among celebrities. He anticipated the halo of fame that would grace the heads of physicists, but underestimated the full extent of the consequences. During the final days of his five-year stay in Cambridge, he looked ahead and expressed his thoughts in an article, "The Physicist Returns from the War":

> Before this paper appears in print, thanks largely to the "atomic" bomb, I hope to be back in my laboratory and, together again with students and colleagues, to resume a life project which was interrupted by "a call to armaments."

While he was undoubtedly sincere in hoping that somehow he could pick up his physical research, bring his students and postdoctoral fellows back together, and pursue the life of a professor once again, he knew that such a hope could not be realized:

> The physicist has become a military asset of such value that only with the assurance of peace will society permit him to pursue in his own quiet way the scientific knowledge which inspires, elevates, and entertains his fellow men.
>
> Thus by the very success of his efforts in this war, the physicist has been placed in an embarrassing position. . . . [He] now is hailed as the messiah who will bring us a new world . . . , new industries, an expanding economy, and jobs for all. . . .

Industry, with considerable success, is trying to lure the physicist from his academic hide-out with glittering pieces of silver and with the promise of unlimited scientific equipment and corps of assistants.[1]

Rabi's anticipations were correct—as far as they went. Postwar physicists found themselves at the hub of potential with opportunity emanating in all directions. There were jobs to choose from within a range of job sectors; there were clubs to address and banquets to attend; there were committees and commissions to be served. Physicists were sages, and their utterances were reckoned with. A writer in *Harper's* described the situation as follows: "Physical scientists are the vogue these days. No dinner party is a success without at least one physicist to explain . . . the nature of the new age in which we live."[2] Samuel K. Allison, a physicist from the University of Chicago who worked on the first nuclear pile with Fermi, caught the spirit of the times when he wrote:

Suddenly physicists were exhibited as lions at Washington tea parties, were invited to conventions of social scientists, where their opinions on society were respectfully listened to by lifelong experts in the field, attended conventions of religious orders and discoursed on theology, were asked to endorse plans for world government, and to give simplified lectures on the nucleus to Congressional committees.[3]

While Rabi had academic job offers to pick from, he rejected them: "I wanted to be at Columbia. I wanted to be in New York. There was no reason for my abandoning Columbia which had been very good to me." His heart belonged to New York and his loyalty was to the university, but he put a condition on his return: he would come back to Columbia only as chairman of the physics department.

There were at least two reasons behind Rabi's demand for the chairmanship. First, the Columbia physics department had to be rebuilt. Universities had been busy recruiting during the final phases of the war, as every major university was eager to add star physicists to its faculty. Fermi and Urey had been lured away from Columbia by Robert Hutchins of the University of Chicago. Other senior professors had left and with them went their students and postdoctoral fellows. "We were really stripped bare," Rabi has said of this situation, "and I started, in 1945, in a very desperate way." With five professorships vacant in the department, he wanted a free hand in the rebuilding program: "You see, my gang had dispersed, and I knew what I wanted. I had grown up, and I was a big shot. I had this reputation, I had connections from Los Alamos and from the Rad Lab, I had the Nobel Prize, and I wanted to build up the physics department. Since I was going to stay in New York, I wanted an environment in which I could live happily."

The second reason behind Rabi's demand for the chairmanship was that he wanted to be free to operate without the burden of having to justify his every move:

> I am an intuitive person, and sometimes it is very clear to me that you must do this or that, but I can't explain it. Or it's just too much: it is more than I can stand to have to *explain* my hunches. My hunches are good, by experience. The only way I could work it so that it would be a good environment for me and for Columbia was to have control—I could no longer go through a chairman and try to persuade him to do this or that.

So Rabi laid down his condition:

> I went to the chairman, Dean Pegram, a very fine person, a brilliant man. He was on most important committees of the university. He also had been chairman of the physics department for some twenty years. I said to him, "I'll come back, but I have to be chairman. I have to work this out, and I have to work this out in my way." Well, he did it. He was my patron, actually, and I asked him to vacate his job. I don't think the department would have elected me necessarily. But Pegram was a *very* powerful man, and he was so universally respected that he just had to suggest it in his way and it was done. I came back as chairman. The department was my responsibility.

Rabi had been a successful recruiter for the Rad Lab and looked optimistically toward continuing that success and building a world-class department of physics—but he was disappointed. With five senior-level positions to be filled, his plan was to bring established physicists to Columbia:

> I had hoped to get Oppenheimer for theoretical physics. And he promised he would come. Then, just before the time came when he was to come, his wife persuaded him not to and he stayed in Cali-

fornia, at Berkeley. That delayed me tremendously because the next one I was going to get would have been Bethe. By that time, however, Bethe had made arrangements with Cornell. I had a whole lot of disappointment. I had five professorships vacant, open, and I couldn't get anybody I really wanted to fill them.

I was chairman along with my other responsibilities, and I had to teach an extra course. I was offering salaries that were five thousand dollars a year more than I was getting to try to attract people . . . and I had the Nobel Prize. I still didn't get them. It was a time to try men's souls. It was so bad that I had to persuade Kramers, who was with the Dutch delegation at the United Nations, to teach a quantum mechanics course at night.* We worked it out and did what we could. The department backed me—at least they weren't in open revolt—even though everyone had to do some extra teaching.

Unable to get the senior people he wanted, Rabi changed his strategy. With no free agents willing to join the Columbia faculty, he looked to the farm system: "I decided that we would have to begin by developing our own young people and bringing in other young people."[4] In the meantime, he was able to attract distinguished physicists to the department as visiting professors. Hans Bethe came, as did Otto Halpern, Gilberto Bernardini, Theodore Von Karman, and Samuel Goudsmit.

There were several promising junior faculty members in the department: J. M. B. Kellogg, Rabi's long-time associate; Willis Lamb, who would soon win the Nobel Prize; and A. Nordsieck, a promising young theorist. If Columbia was to hold these faculty members and to attract equally promising young physicists, Rabi would have to provide the latest facilities so that they could carry out state-of-the-art research. In this regard, Columbia came out of the war at something of a disadvantage.

It irked Rabi that more of the largess of the war had not come to Columbia. The university had been, in fact, the site for critical wartime work. For example, the earliest work on nuclear fission and nuclear reactors had been done at Columbia by Fermi, Szilard, Walter Zinn, and others. All of this work was later consolidated in Chicago by Arthur H. Compton, a University of Chicago physicist. As a consequence of Compton's consolidation, the University of Chicago emerged from the war set

*H. A. Kramers was a distinguished physicist who had been one of the active participants in the development of quantum mechanics.

up to carry on a strong research program in nuclear physics. Moreover, there was, right outside Chicago, the government-supported Argonne Laboratory. The Chicago environment was so attractive that Fermi and Urey left Columbia to accept positions at the University of Chicago after the war.* Again, during the war the University of California at Berkeley had been one of the centers for the isotope separation work that was a necessary precursor to the construction of the atomic bomb. This effort, under the leadership of Ernest Lawrence, brought the Radiation Laboratory to a high state of development, and when the war ended, Berkeley was primed to become a national center for nuclear physics research.

Rabi, no babe in the woods when it came to looking after the interests of the East Coast and Columbia, saw clearly the consequences of Compton's Chicago consolidation and Lawrence's Berkeley buildup. Looking ahead, Rabi was able to transfer some of the MIT Rad Lab work—the 1-centimeter radar development—to Columbia during the war and to form the Columbia Radiation Laboratory. When the war ended, he had the Columbia Rad Lab as a bargaining chip to attract faculty. It was, however, a small chip. After the war, the excitement in physics centered on the nucleus; and, to compete at this research frontier, nuclear reactors and particle accelerators were required. Neither a reactor facility nor an accelerator laboratory was easily accessible to Columbia or, for that matter, to any other university in the Boston-to-Washington northeast corridor.

"Rabi and myself . . . were rather unhappy," Norman Ramsey has said, "and I must confess, slightly jealous due to the fact that . . . the University of Chicago . . . ended up with a very nice reactor. Likewise, the University of California was ending up with a nice high-energy accelerator."[6] As soon as Rabi arrived back at Columbia from the Rad Lab, he and Ramsey carried on discussions about how they could make a nuclear reactor available to Columbia. They discussed the possibility of the department of physics building its own reactor, but recognized that an undertaking of such a magnitude would dominate the activities of a department the size of Columbia's and diminish its vitality.

At the same time that Rabi and Ramsey were trying to find a way to boost Columbia's physics potential, the whole atomic program of the United States was in a state of confusion. When the war ended, many congressmen and policy makers learned for the first time about the

*Actually, Compton began his recruiting activities long before the war was over.[5]

existence of a sprawling complex of governmental laboratories engaged in nuclear research and development. General Groves was still the head of the Manhattan District and, in the absence of established policies, continued to use the funds available to him to support nuclear research. In December 1945, he agreed to provide $170,000 for a new type of accelerator that Edwin McMillan at Berkeley had designed—"a parting gift to Lawrence from General Groves."[7] Likewise, Compton at Chicago was getting money from the Manhattan District.

Into this confusion came Rabi with a proposal. He and Ramsey had been busy. They had discarded the idea of a Columbia reactor; rather, they concluded that the best plan was to get the universities in the greater New York area to join together in a cooperative venture. On January 16, 1946, the New York group (plus Princeton and Yale universities) unanimously agreed to support the establishment of a laboratory for nuclear research. A proposal letter was sent to General Groves three days later.

Zacharias, who was now at MIT, heard about the New York proposal and quickly convened a group of MIT and Harvard physicists who agreed that they, too, needed a laboratory—in Cambridge! Soon General Groves had a second letter. Two letters, two proposed laboratories, two competing groups of physicists.

Groves informed Rabi that he was interested in the proposals, but that he could only consider one of them: the East Coast institutions would have to come together and agree on one proposal. Furthermore, they would have to do it quickly. While the Manhattan District still had some funds, as an entity it was on the way out, merely waiting for Washington policy makers to decide on the form of its successor agency.

The New York and the Cambridge physicists came together on February 16, 1946. It was a difficult session. They agreed on the principle of one laboratory, but argued heatedly over the location—each group wanted the lab in its own vicinity—and over the director. Rabi and Zacharias, long-time teammates, were now in opposition, both tough men accustomed, through one means or another, to getting what they want; neither could be buffaloed. The angry ill-will generated during these discussions required the soothing balm of years to effect a healing.

Rabi and the New Yorkers took a clever, albeit self-serving, step: they added the University of Pennsylvania and the Johns Hopkins University to their group. Johns Hopkins was far to the south, and its addition had the effect of balancing Harvard and MIT to the north. These additions put New York right near the geographic center of all the institutions involved.

On March 23, 1946, representatives from nine universities* assembled at Columbia. They passed a resolution affirming their interest "in promoting and establishing in the northeast of the country a Government research laboratory for nuclear science."[8] They called themselves the Initiatory University Group. Ramsey became the chairman of the subcommittee on site selection. There were a number of criteria agreed upon for the site selection—size, accessibility, availability of services, and so on. When the inevitability of a New York State location was accepted, the group became incorporated, on July 18, 1946, as Associated Universities, Inc., in that state.

Many locations were considered; many sites were visited. During the summer of 1946 it was agreed that a place on Long Island was equally disappointing to everyone, and the site for what was to become the Brookhaven National Laboratory was settled. Within one year after the informal discussions began between the New York and Cambridge physicists, a formal contract was signed—on January 31, 1947—between the Atomic Energy Commission and the Associated Universities, Inc.

Long before the formal agreement was signed, Rabi was looking ahead. Wanting the largest possible accelerator to be built at Brookhaven, he got together with M. Stanley Livingston who, along with Ernest Lawrence, had built the earliest accelerators at Berkeley. Livingston has recalled his instructions:

> Find the highest high-energy machine that can be built. That was specific and that was in '46. I was to report back [to the Associated Universities group] what was the highest energy machine that could be built. I went to Berkeley and talked with them. They had their synchro-cyclotron just under design. They were aiming at 200 million [electron volts] at that time. . . . I came back and reported: "We can build one of that style, 700 volts."[9]

"We ran it with a big barrel of greenbacks," according to Luis Alvarez, who was referring to the Berkeley Radiation Laboratory during the period right after the end of the war.[10] Arthur Roberts wrote another song (sometimes called "The Brookhaven Song") in which he captured the essence of this period. One verse goes as follows:

> It will cost a billion dollars, ten million volts 'twill give,
> It will take five thousand scholars seven years to make it live.

*The universities were Columbia, Cornell, Harvard, Johns Hopkins, MIT, Princeton, Pennsylvania, Rochester, and Yale.

All the generals approve it, all the money's now in hand,
And to help advance our program, teaching students now we've banned.
We have chartered transportation, we'll provide a weekly dance,
Our motto's integration, there is nothing left to chance.
This machine is just a model for the bigger one, of course,
That's the future road for physics, as I hope you'll all endorse.[11]

The verse described the activities that were building toward the establishment of Brookhaven.

As Livingston has continued the story:

Even before I had the design reasonably well-started at Brookhaven for the 700-million volt synchro-cyclotron, Rabi came out and needled Phil Morse [Brookhaven's first director], myself, and others: "Take something that's a bigger challenge," he said, "why don't you take this other idea—the proton synchrotron idea, and make something big up in the billion volts [range]?" And he [Rabi] pushed us into it. I immediately started a second design group. Eventually that took over, and we ended up with the cosmotron as the first multi-BeV [multi-billion-electron volt] machine at Brookhaven.[12]

With Brookhaven, Rabi had his laboratory that would bring the frontier of nuclear physics to Columbia's back door. With an eye to the personnel needs of Brookhaven (his eye was always on the watch for Columbia), he visited Oak Ridge, a Manhattan District laboratory in Tennessee, to give a talk. "Boys," he said, "the war is over. Why should you be stuck here? Why don't you come to an intellectual center?"[13]

Even with the success in establishing Brookhaven, Rabi eventually got his own machine for Columbia: "We did have our own cyclotron. This was a 500- or 600-million-electron volt machine, one of the early ones. At that time, it was the most powerful machine in the world, for a few months. I had decided right from the beginning that to attract people to Columbia, to keep them there, and to give them the opportunity to grow, that we had to have the best equipment we could get." In the postwar years, physicists got what they asked for—especially important physicists like Rabi.

The leaders of the armed services came out of the Second World War with a deep respect for physicists. They were committed to a continuation of the close collaboration between science and the military; they were eager to support basic research because they were confident that it would bring dividends in the form of new and improved weaponry.

Thus, because both sides stood to benefit, a cozy relationship was quick to develop between physics and the military. In 1946, the Office of Naval Research (ONR) was given permanent status by Congress and, by August of the same year, had granted 177 contracts to 81 universities and laboratories. The total of these contracts was $24 million. Of this Rabi has said, "The Navy saved the bacon for American science."[14]

The unimpeded flow of money into the hands of physicists changed physics and changed physicists. Physics became Big. Some physicists viewed these changes with concern and unease. While the verse of Arthur Roberts's Brookhaven song just quoted seems to welcome the influx of money, its title—"Take Away Your Billion Dollars"—as well as its final verse express a nostalgic desire for the physics of bygone days:

> Take away your billion dollars, take away your tainted gold,
> You can keep your damn ten billion volts, my soul will not be sold,
> Take away your army generals; their kiss is death, I'm sure.
> Everything I build is mine, and every volt I make is pure.
> Take away your integration; let us learn and let us teach,
> Oh, beware this epidemic Berkelitis, I beseech.
> Oh, dammit! Engineering isn't physics, is that plain?
> Take, oh take your billion dollars, let's be physicists again.[15]

The characterization of the postwar scientific community as "rudderless in its affluence"[16] is not true. Physicists knew what they wanted: they wanted to do physics. Furthermore, they knew what they had to have in order to do physics: they needed equipment. They found themselves, however, in a social and political environment that could correctly be described as rudderless. Powerful currents caught events in their sweep. But for the crucial role played by science in the war, the conflict could have been (would have been?) lost. Many leaders resolved that the United States could not, and would not, be second in nuclear research.

There was an overwhelming consensus that the government should support basic research. On the other hand, there was widespread disagreement about how that support structure should be organized. Should there be one central agency? Should the control of science funding rest with the President? Should funds be allocated on a geographic basis, or should the allocation of funds be based solely on the significance of proposed research? What yardsticks should be used to measure significance: Society's needs? Defense needs? The needs of science itself?

Strong and effective proponents for differing answers to these questions took positions, and debates ensued. Science was big business, and each congressional voice spoke for its constituency. (The money spent for the wartime projects was focused on very few industries: since 66 percent of all the dollars spent went to only sixty-eight corporations, the didn't-gets and the have-nots were clamoring for their share.) A science-support policy remained an elusive goal.

The issue that separated the policy makers from the scientists was the question of control. From the one side came the cry that if government is supplying the money, then government should decide how it is to be spent. From the scientists came the response that only scientists themselves could make the difficult judgments as to which research programs should be supported. Even with the consequences of Hitler's disastrous control of German science during the war fresh in their minds, still there were those who were seduced by the temptation to bend science toward their own version of Eden. Even Oppenheimer, gifted as he was, had difficulty conveying to Senator J. William Fulbright, astute as he was, the nature of basic research and the dangers of attempting to direct its development.

It is true, as the Second World War clearly demonstrated, that science serves the practical needs of admirals, physicians, businessmen, and so forth; however, it is impossible to predict which innocent basic idea will suddenly spawn a useful product. Only two-and-one-half years before Los Alamos, nuclear physics was so academic, so practically useless, that it served as a smokescreen—via the name Radiation Laboratory—to shield from the enemy the radar work at MIT. As Rabi has written:

If the science of physics lags, the inheritance of technology is soon spent. In the war years, our inheritance of technology was exploited to the point where further substantial progress could come only from a new advance in the science of physics. But the essential unpredictability of the laws of nature beyond our experience, as exemplified in the great discoveries of the past, make scientific research a venture, literally, into the unknown. To set out a detailed program with practical goals for truly scientific research is like trying to make a map of a country no one has ever seen and the very existence of which is in grave doubt. Pure science cannot have any goal other than the appeasement of the human spirit of intellectual adventure.[17]

The hearings went on, and the debates continued. Bills were defeated in the Congress, and bills were vetoed by the president. In the interim, various agencies of government along with the military services were competing in their desires to curry the favor of the physicists. For their part, the physicists reaped a green harvest of dollars. "Isn't physics wonderful?" wrote Rabi to Ernest Lawrence in 1948.[18] It was not until March 1950, almost five years after the war, that the National Science Foundation, the agency charged with supporting the basic research of the nation, was established. During these five years, new patterns of life were thrust upon and adopted by the academic scientist—patterns that remain with us to the present day.

Rabi looks back to these events with pride and with question. He resigned as chairman (executive officer) of the physics department in 1949:

I found that I *did not like* to run people, to be responsible. The actual detail of running the department, the nuts and bolts of it, was not to my taste. I couldn't do it. It was not that I found it beneath me to do it, I just couldn't do it. I appointed a nominating committee of three of the most likely people [to be the new chairman], told them to interview everyone in the department, and to come up with a nomination *not* to exclude one of them. Then I left for Europe so they couldn't consult me at all. They came up with the man I would have appointed anyway; this was Kusch.

Polykarp Kusch, a former postdoctoral fellow with Rabi, was one of the younger men appointed to the faculty during the latter's chairmanship. There were others; in fact, when Rabi resigned as chairman, there were four new professors who would eventually win the Nobel Prize in physics. Columbia was well on its way to regaining its place as one of America's leading centers for physics.

And Brookhaven became a model on which the formation of other laboratories was based. Rabi has described it:

We established it [Brookhaven] as a national laboratory. What Lawrence and McMillan had [in California] was a laboratory, paid for by the government, contracted and run by the University of California. It was a local asset to which others were admitted as guests, very welcome indeed, but as *guests*. I was very much in favor of a national laboratory, a national effort, where people could come as a matter of *right,* providing they had the credentials. People will tell you, and they will be right, that it was not absent from my mind that Columbia was the closest to this [Brookhaven] and that it would be very important to the use of the Columbia physicists. I was manipulating for Columbia. But it wasn't only that. Columbia was *the, the* graduate university, the top place in this region . . . quite a region. Most of the physicists in the country are in the northeastern region. It's true, I had this local patriotism, still have, for New York and for this particular region. My conscience rests very easy with this. I think I did a great deal. I certainly wouldn't have done it for myself. I never worked at Brookhaven and I had no direct benefit myself, individually, from Brookhaven. I got the cyclotron for Columbia, but I never used the cyclotron myself. I had no self-interest in it; I had no intention of working in that field.

It is true that Rabi never used an accelerator in his own research. High-energy physics, accelerator physics, is "big" physics. For Rabi, doing physics is too personal an undertaking for him to be attracted to physics done by groups. His own experimental physics was never influenced by "Berkelitis." On the other hand, he strongly believed that, from a study of the behavior of elementary particles at the high energies made possible by accelerators, a more profound view of matter and antimatter would emerge. Foreseeing entirely new insights coming from big-time physics, he could throw himself behind it. Besides, Columbia University and the New York City region *is* his self-interest.

Much about Rabi and much about those days following immediately after the Second World War is contained in a book, *Elections Away or Tales of a Government Scientist,* by Harold A. Zahl. In this book, Zahl recounts Rabi refusing the largess of government. In late 1945, Lt. Col. James McRae and Zahl met with Rabi to discuss the possibility of converting Columbia's wartime laboratory into long-range unclassified research of military interest. But, Zahl remembers, "Dr. Rabi was afraid of peacetime military control of his laboratory. . . . Dr. Rabi emphasized that, in peacetime, Columbia University was an educational and research organization, and that any contract in which the university would appear must be such as to promote this fundamental objective."[19] Finally they agreed on the conditions of a contract between the Army Signal Corps and Columbia University, and, as Zahl recounts, McRae said:

"Let's talk about money."
"OK, Mac," Dr. Rabi said, "How much do you think?" . . . "Rabi,"

he said, "I would say that about $500,000 a year would keep a good program going. More later, perhaps, after we see how it goes." "Much too much Mac," Dr. Rabi replied, shaking his head very negatively. "Let's get down to something more reasonable."[20]

Rabi, Zahl, and McRae made history that day: they worked to get the amount of money offered *down* to an acceptable level. They finally agreed on a figure of $252,000.[21]

Money *was* available after the war and, for that time, sizable sums indeed. Money was "offered," more money than Rabi was willing to accept—even for Columbia's physics department: "I was chairman at the time, and I didn't want the responsibility of running a laboratory activity big enough to spend $500,000 a year." The money—$250,000 per year—that Rabi *did* accept was put to good use. In the book just cited, Zahl points out that from this support given Columbia, came three Nobel Prize winners, Lamb, Kusch, and Townes.[22]

While Rabi was still executive officer of the physics department, he began to witness the changes that big money was to make upon the conduct of physics. The impact of big money stimulated basic changes in the attitudes of physics faculty members toward the university, changes that eventually spread to other disciplines:

> The whole picture changed as a result of government money. The money was more plentiful so therefore jobs were more plentiful. It became no longer a matter of the department or the university. Each professor who was any good wore a knapsack, he could travel anywhere. It stopped being a collegial affair. I thought it a wonderful thing to give an individual independence; but the costs of it, which were great, I didn't realize until later.

Mobility and specialization has changed the professorate and the university:

> I had the feeling, and I still do, that if you are at a university, you are an educator. And, if you are a gentleman, in addition you do research. I don't like the modern attitude where people treat the university as a research institute. Research institutes exist, Brookhaven and places like it, and such people can go to those places and work. In a university you should live an intellectual life, your interests should go beyond your research speciality.

The money that came after the war changed physicists' approach to their campuses. Collegiality on the campus and within departments was diminished to the point that it was no longer a vital factor in the life of an institution. Money also changed physicists' approach to the discipline of physics: collegiality within physics itself became more restricted. As Rabi has said:

Physicists became narrower. I think that partly came from government money because the competition was along particular lines. There was a sharp drop-off of interest in physics amongst physicists other than for their own particular speciality. They became more and more specialized. That good amateur spirit that existed and was so fascinating to me was disappearing and I think perhaps has now disappeared. I felt the change was deplorable, but it was all done by the scientists themselves.

He is quick to add, however, "But the physics itself was very, very good. The government money was marvelous in the sense that one could afford equipment."

More than the physics being good, the principle was, according to Rabi, correct:

What can you do better with money than to study where you are and what you are? You can't take it with you, so you might as well do this. We don't aim to emulate the Borden Company with its contented cows, so apart from killing one another, which has been a principal activity, we'd better make excuses for *not* giving money to support learning about this world rather than the other way around.

There was another reason the physicists were treated so royally during those early postwar years: the peace was tenuous. The cold war began with V-J Day; and through the late 1940s and early 1950s, its intensity doubled and redoubled. At any time it seemed that the services of the physicists would be needed once again. The specter of Armageddon hung low over the earth. Rabi was spending more and more of his time trying to avert a catastrophe.

CHAPTER

15

"How Well We Meant"

> We cannot put this evil spirit back in a bottle.
> We have to learn to live with it.
>
> I. I. RABI

MANY physicists felt guilty. Rabi did not. The guilt, of course, was a by-product of the Second World War—"the physicists' war."[1]

Nuclear energy is as much a product of human curiosity and ingenuity as the polio vaccine, a Stradivarius violin, or the Declaration of Independence. Knowledge can come in small bits or it can come as a grand overarching synthesis, but once it has come, it is eternal. And it only goes one way. Knowledge can become obsolete; it can be of interest only to historians of our intellectual past; but knowledge cannot be erased. In fact, it flourishes when it is threatened. Almost everyone knows these things; only a few act on them. Rabi acted on them.

Nuclear energy is a reality. It exists. In one form it can exist as a bomb, and there is no way to erase the knowledge required to put a nuclear device together. It is necessary, therefore, to pursue policies and to create structures that promise to keep this potential for destruction from becoming actuality. Within weeks after his return from the Radiation Laboratory, Rabi became engaged in just such pursuits.

The decade following the Second World War was a period of intense emotionalism. From the corridors of Congress to the neighborhood dairy bar, fear, anxiety, uncertainty, and suspicion colored the discourse and established the mood. Behind it all was the ideological conflict between

193

democracy and communism, a cold war conflict that was intensified beyond all precedent by the presence of the atomic bomb. In this psychological cauldron the brew was unsavory: security was pursued with a mania, secrecy was an obsession, and suspicion created communist sympathizers behind every door. Rabi and others had to work in this charged context as they sought rational policies to control this new power.

The times and the issues conspired to bring physicists to the fore in postwar deliberations. Not that any particular group has a monopoly on wisdom. Certainly the physicists did not: as events unfolded, sharp and divisive differences developed within their ranks. But many influential physicists had seen what no other eyes had seen: an unearthly heat had fused the sharp sands of Alamogordo to glasslike smoothness; and, from that searing instant, they returned to bear witness to the realities of the new world.

Physicists had, and have, another advantage. Through training and experience, they can appreciate the significance, both qualitative and quantitative, of "one million": that is, they understand the potential implications of scaling up a quantity—whether the explosive power of a bomb or the weight of a horsefly—by a factor of 1,000,000. Galileo had understood these principles well. Major General James Burns, on the other hand, did not. In testimony urging the quick development of the hydrogen bomb, the general said, "It's a fundamental law of defense that you always have to use the most powerful weapons you can produce"[2]—a frightening remark in that the general made no qualitative distinctions between the best that the legions of Rome could throw against Carthage in the third century B.C. and what the United States could mount against the Soviets twenty-three centuries, and a stockpile of atomic bombs, later. Nuclear energy has changed the rules of war. No one then (or today), from the Joint Chiefs of Staff on down to field commanders, could (or can) look to any military traditions, cite any principles of military strategy, or draw from any battlefield experiences that would apply in a nuclear war. The bomb made novices of everyone. In the babble that followed the Second World War, the physicists spoke with the greatest clarity. They had made the thing and were educated to understand its potential.

Even before the Alamogordo test, questions of controlling atomic energy had been raised. As early as July 1944, for example, Niels Bohr wrote to President Roosevelt pointing out the need to avoid an atomic arms race. By the spring of 1945, expressions of concern were coming from several sources—including Oppenheimer. At a meeting of the Interim Committee on May 31, 1945, a meeting that brought together eminent statesmen, military leaders, and scientists, Oppenheimer projected three stages of nuclear bomb development: Stage I—bombs with an explosive equivalent in the range of 2,000 to 20,000 tons of TNT (the Alamogordo test came in at the upper end of this predicted range); Stage II—bombs in the 50,000-to-100,000-ton range; and, Stage III—bombs equivalent to 10,000,000 to 100,000,000 tons of TNT. After these projections, Oppenheimer suggested the possibility of approaching Russia about the issue of international control. Both the Jeffries Report (November 1944) and the Franck Report (June 1945) elaborated on several topics, including arguments against using the atomic bomb and the need for international controls.*

The discussions and debates concerning the control of atomic energy proceeded simultaneously toward two different goals. First, there were the questions of domestic control. Who would be in charge? In whom would authority be vested to guide the further development of nuclear science? What kind of security restrictions would be applied? The second line of discussion was motivated by the hope of having atomic energy taken out of domestic control altogether and placed under the auspices of an international agency.

The lightning rod that drew the sparks on the subject of domestic control was the May-Johnson bill, introduced in Congress on October 4, 1945. This bill, sponsored by Representative Andrew J. May, of Kentucky, and Senator Edwin C. Johnson, of Colorado, proposed that the absolute authority over all nuclear sources and over all activities associated with nuclear energy—from basic research to bomb design—be placed in a presidentially appointed commission made up of nine members. The bill further provided that the commission would have complete control over the classification of information that came from nuclear research. At the wish of the proposed commission, physical data could be kept a secret.

The May-Johnson bill quickly became identified as an army bill. Young physicists, their passions fired by the vision of an atomic energy commission dominated by the military, converged on Washington. On the last day of October 1945, the Federation of Atomic Scientists (FAS)

---

*Perhaps it was this background that influenced the script writers for the CBS re-enactment of the Alamogordo test, a program hosted by Bill Moyers. During the final countdown of the first nuclear test, Rabi says to Oppenheimer, "It's going to be all right, Robert. And I am sure we'll never be sorry for it."

was formed by a group that was distinguished by its anonymity: there was not a physics star among them. Their principal assets were desire, determination, and credibility through association. As lobbyists they were amateurs, but as atomic scientists they commanded the eager ears of congressmen and the public. They began their assault on the May-Johnson bill and, in the process, educated the public about radioactivity, chain reactions, and atomic bombs. They also brought attention to the public nature of science and the dangers of censorship.

Rabi did not get involved with the federation; and when asked why, his answer was direct: "They didn't need us. They were doing just fine and we older men would have spoiled the show. I was all for them."[3] Also, his thoughts were elsewhere. He was looking ahead—as was Oppenheimer. Rabi was one of those who wanted to internationalize this new power and remove it from every nation's domestic agenda. Oppenheimer was similarly motivated and, for this reason, supported the May-Johnson bill. He was convinced that an agreement would have to be reached on a domestic policy for atomic energy control before the step toward an international version could be taken. As Szilard has said, "Oppenheimer was all in favor of passing a bill fast—any bill as long as it was a bill."[4]

If any scientist needed his or her fear of military control over atomic research reinforced, that reinforcement was supplied by an event that occurred on November 25, 1945. On a directive from General Grove's office, the forces of General Douglas MacArthur ignited their welding torches, cut apart five Japanese cyclotrons, loaded the fragmented parts onto barges, and buried them deep in the Pacific Ocean. Two of these machines, at Tokyo University, were under the direction of Rabi's old friend from the Copenhagen and Hamburg days, Yoshio Nishina. None of the five machines was in working order, but the two under Nishina's direction were being readied for research in biology, medicine, chemistry, and metallurgy. The physicists had a new rallying point and made the most of it: the May-Johnson bill got bottled up in committee and, ultimately, never made it to the floor of the House of Representatives. In the meantime, a new bill, which promised to gain the support of the atomic scientists, was introduced in the Senate shortly before Christmas of 1945.

Christmas week in New York City was bitterly cold that year. The trees across Riverside Drive were small then, and there was nothing to obstruct the view of the Hudson River from Rabi's living-room windows. Rabi and Oppenheimer looked out on the river as they talked. The sun was setting and the ice floes were bathed in pink as they moved with the tide toward the sea. Smoke from two pipes streamed smoothly upward, and twisted into wispy swirls. There was no one else in the room.

The atom and the energy contained within its nucleus had brought Rabi and Oppenheimer together on this cold December day. And humanity, the welfare of the world, the desire for peace, motivated their thoughts. They were both aware that many congressmen were tempted by the fact that the United States alone possessed the bomb to keep the knowledge of the atom within the United States, to build more bombs, to increase our research into the mysterious atom, and to become so powerful that no nation could threaten us. The many congressmen who doubted the ability of the Russians to build an atomic bomb regarded the Russian threat as significant only for the distant future.

Both Rabi and Oppenheimer saw the fallacies in these views and, further, recognized the inevitability of an atomic arms race if the United States came to regard itself as the exclusive custodian of the new atomic knowledge. They were convinced that the atom had to be dissociated from the colors of any particular flag. As they sat together in Rabi's living room, they posed questions to each other and, with deliberate care, shaped their answers. When evening came, a core of stirring and far-reaching ideas for the international control of atomic energy had taken form in their minds.

Less than one month after Oppenheimer left Rabi's Riverside apartment later that evening, the opportunity came for their ideas to move onto a larger stage. On January 23, 1946, Oppenheimer was appointed to a board of consultants whose charge was to develop a proposal that might be presented by the United States to the United Nations Atomic Energy Commission (UNAEC)—a commission formally established a week later, on January 31. The Board of Consultants, appointed by the Dean Acheson Committee, had as its chairman David E. Lilienthal.* Oppenheimer effectively took control of this group and presented the ideas that had come from his and Rabi's Christmas-week discussion. Oppenheimer's proposal to the board members was divided into parts with each member assigned to write up one of them. The work began —writing and rewriting.

As the Lilienthal group was drafting its report, and just as the UNAEC was in the act of getting organized, a controversy was precipitated by

*Other members, in addition to Lilienthal and Oppenheimer, were Chester I. Bernard, Charles Allen Thomas, and Harry A. Winne.

the navy's January announcement that it was going to conduct atomic bomb tests in the Marshall Islands. Confident that the proposed tests and the growing controversy would be detrimental to the hope of achieving an eventual agreement at the United Nations, Rabi and eleven other senior members of Columbia's faculty sent to the *New York Times* (February 16, 1946) a letter calling on President Truman

1. To stop at once the production of bombs;
2. To stop the accumulation of fissionable materials;
3. To regard our stockpile of bombs as a negotiable item in agreements with other governments.

Rabi, who describes himself as a "behind-the-scenes man," was happy for Oppenheimer to be taking the lead in presenting their ideas on international control; however, in his behind-the-scenes fashion he was doing what he could to enhance the likelihood of success.

By mid-March, Lilienthal's Board of Consultants had been working essentially full time for six weeks. Acheson's committee had studied their report, had suggested revisions, and had finally approved it. On March 17, a report went to the secretary of state, James F. Byrnes, entitled "A Report on the International Control of Atomic Energy." This report came to be called the "Acheson-Lilienthal Report." Four days later, it went to President Truman and to Bernard M. Baruch, the newly appointed U.S. Representative to the United Nations Atomic Energy Commission.

The response to the Acheson-Lilienthal Report was polarized: some saw it as the vehicle to carry away all our hard-earned secrets, and some saw it as a testimony to the nobility of humankind. The Federation of Atomic Scientists was delighted with it: it was more than they had dared to hope for. The majority was decidedly enthusiastic with the report—a majority of which, unfortunately, Baruch was not a part.

Baruch was the man who was to present to the UNAEC the United States plan for the international control of atomic energy. The ideas of Rabi and Oppenheimer, beautifully elaborated in the Acheson-Lilienthal Report, was the basis for this plan. Baruch was strongly at odds with parts of the plan: indeed, he was appalled at the very quality of the plan that others regarded as its strength—namely, its flexibility. Baruch wanted more regulations and controls. Above all, however, he wanted built into the plan a system of penalties or sanctions for violators. Moreover, in regard to questions on the subject of atomic energy, Baruch wanted to abolish the veto in the United Nations Security Council so that there would be no escape for violators.

The Baruch Plan, which was in fact the Baruch-modified Acheson-Lilienthal plan, was presented at the opening session of the UNAEC on June 14, 1946. The heart of the program came straight out of Rabi's living room via the pages of the Acheson-Lilienthal Report, and Baruch put it to the dignitaries who had assembled for this historic meeting in the gymnasium of Hunter College. Baruch proposed the creation of an international authority which would have jurisdiction over all aspects of the development and use of atomic energy; furthermore, all production of atomic bombs would cease, and all existing bombs would be dismantled as soon as the questions of control were resolved.

"It was a wonderfully generous thing we did," said Rabi later. "We proposed giving up our nuclear weapons. I think it was our greatest day. That was the peak." To be sure, the proposal of the United States to surrender its atomic energy monopoly to the nations of the world was noble in purpose. After what appeared to be an initial receptiveness, the Soviet delegation, headed by Andrei Gromyko, dug in and resisted. For the next six months, vagueness became the means of intransigence for Gromyko. Working committees attempted to resolve differences and to establish compromise positions, but all to no avail. On December 30, 1946, a Russian vote ended the hope that had taken form one year earlier in the minds of two long-time friends. Lost was that rare and precious opportunity to alter history. By the spring of 1947, the arms race had begun.

While Oppenheimer and the Board of Consultants were drafting what would be the basis for the abortive attempt to place atomic energy under *international* control, scientists were hard at work in support of the McMahon bill, introduced in the Senate on December 20, 1945, whose purpose was to establish the framework for the *domestic* control of atomic energy. In drafting his bill, Representative Brien McMahon, of Connecticut, chose his words carefully to describe the makeup of the commission whose authority would control atomic energy, to define the controls on fissionable material, and to outline the restrictions that would be applied to the dissemination of information. The scientists liked what they read. Through the winter and spring of 1946, the bill was subjected to the scrutiny of many concerned groups. Hearings were held, and scientists, including Rabi, were asked to testify. He favored a completely civilian commission with liaisons providing channels to the military. After the usual House-Senate conferences and compromises, the bill passed the Congress; and on August 1, 1946, President Truman signed it into law, thereby establishing the Atomic Energy Commission.

It took Truman almost three months to find the men he wanted to serve as the charter commissioners. David Lilienthal was named chairman of the AEC on October 28, 1946. Appointed to serve with him were Professor Robert F. Bacher, Cornell physicist; Sumner T. Pike, prominent citizen from Maine; Lewis L. Strauss, Wall Street broker; and William W. Waymack, newspaper editor. The McMahon bill authorized the commission to "establish advisory boards to advise with and make recommendations to the Commission on legislation, policies, administration, and research."[5]

Since, except for Bacher, no one on the commission was conversant with the intricacies of nuclear energy, one of its earliest actions was to staff an advisory committee. The commissioners appointed a group of distinguished men. The first members of the General Advisory Committee of the Atomic Energy Commission (GAC of the AEC) took their places on December 9, 1946: given six-year terms were James B. Conant, president of Harvard University—a chemist; Lee A. DuBridge, president of California Institute of Technology—a physicist; and J. Robert Oppenheimer, director of the Institute for Advanced Study, Princeton—a physicist. Receiving four-year terms were Enrico Fermi, a physicist; Hartley Rowe, an engineer; and Glenn Seaborg, a chemist. Finally, appointed for two-year terms were Cyril S. Smith, a metallurgist; Hood Worthington, of the du Pont Chemical Company; and I. I. Rabi. Oppenheimer became the chairman. Everything was in place when President Truman transferred control of atomic energy from General Groves and the army to the new AEC on December 31, 1946.

A fatal inconsistency has poisoned the atmosphere of all attempts to deal convincingly with nuclear weapons. The flaw that has plagued most discussions on the weapons subject is this: on the one hand, there is the deep and sincere desire to outlaw the bomb; on the other hand, there is the equally felt desire to have the bomb available. As long as the bomb is available, even if outlawed, the arms merchants will flourish. Such is the confidence of man in man. Elements of this dilemma were nowhere more apparent than in the issue that launched the GAC into the limelight. The issue was: "The Super, yes or no?"

The atomic bomb is a fission device that draws its energy from the cleavage of a large nucleus into smaller nuclei. From the earliest days of the Manhattan Project, a few people—notably Edward Teller—had been interested in the idea of building a fusion bomb. In a fusion device, energy is released when small nuclei combine to form a larger nucleus. Whereas the destructive power of the fission bomb, albeit awesome, is inherently limited, both the size of the fusion bomb as well as its destructive potential are, more or less, open ended. The power of this bomb is beyond the reach of our imagination; it can be considered a viable weapon only by the irrational or the suicidal. Throughout the late 1940s and into the early 1950s, the fusion, or hydrogen, bomb was simply called the "Super."

When the Second World War ended, the United States was in sole possession of the atomic bomb, but, looking ahead, various experts were called in to predict how long it would take the Russians to develop their own atomic weapon. Physicists based their predictions on technical considerations, and their predictions were consistently around five years. The predictions of nonscientists were much longer. A few, apparently regarding the Russians as equivalent to Neanderthal people, predicted never. General Groves, for example, predicted twenty years. So the predictions ranged from five years to never.

It took the Russians four years. On September 23, 1949, President Harry S. Truman announced to the nation that an event had occurred in the Soviet Union on August 29—an event that subsequent analysis showed to be the explosion of an atomic bomb. Foreboding and anxiety shook the American people.* The proponents of the Super could not have designed a more effective incident to promote their cause.

Even the prudent can be shocked by the deceptive passage of time: by some quirk, the starting point of a prediction seems to move along with the predictor so that the predicted zero hour is always the predicted time ahead. Thus, even though most physicists had predicted five years as the time required for the Russians to develop an atomic bomb, most physicists were also shocked. Rabi himself was surprised by the Russian accomplishment; and when Ernest Lawrence and Luis Alvarez visited him at Columbia on October 11, 1949, he was happy to see these action-oriented men rocking the boat once again. In fact, when they left his office, they were confident that, along with them, he agreed that the program to build the Super should be started immediately.

Teller's seven years of agitation on behalf of his *idée fixe,* the thermonuclear bomb, together with the stunning shock of Russia's achieve-

---

*I was a paper boy at the time and remember laying the paper, headlined "Russia Explodes A-Bomb," on the counter of a dairy bar. Its owner, one of my customers, said to me, "Johnny, quit your paper route. We'll all be dead in a few days."

ment triggered a knee-jerk reaction on the part of many influential people: "We must build the Super before they do." This was the response of Lewis Strauss, an old friend of Edward Teller and a commissioner of the Atomic Energy Commission. Strauss urged Lilienthal to call the GAC together as soon as possible to consider the U.S. response to Russia's nuclear success. A meeting was scheduled for October 29–30.

A few days before the meeting, Oppenheimer wrote to Conant, anticipating the upcoming GAC meeting and addressing the subject that faced the committee. It was a troubled letter, and for good reason: passion was obfuscating all questions relating to the super. The entire letter follows:

Dear Uncle Jim:

We are exploring the possibilities for our talk with the President on October 30. All members of the Advisory Committee will come to the meeting Saturday, except Seaborg who must be in Sweden, and whose general views we have in written form. Many of us will do some preliminary palavering on the 28th.

There is one bit of background which I would like you to have before we meet. When we last spoke you thought perhaps the reactor program offered the most decisive example of the need for policy clarification. I was inclined to think that the Super might also be relevant. On the technical side, as far as I can tell, the Super is not very different from what it was when we first spoke of it more than 7 years ago: a weapon of unknown design, cost, deliverability and military value. But a great change has taken place in the climate of opinion. On the one hand two experienced promoters have been at work, i.e., Ernest Lawrence and Edward Teller. The project has long been dear to Teller's heart; and Ernest has convinced himself that we must learn from Operation Joe [the Russian explosion] that the Russians will soon do the Super and that we had better beat them to it.

On the technical side, he [Lawrence] proposes to get some neutron producing heavy water reactors built; to this, for a variety of reasons, I think we must say amen [since there are three military applications other than the Super which these reactors would serve]* and many other things will all profit by the availability of neutrons.

*The bracketed portion of the text was so paraphrased for security purposes by Oppenheimer during the 1954 Gray Board Hearings.

But the real development has not been of a technical nature. Ernest spoke to Knowland* and McMahon, and to some at least of the Joint Chiefs. The Joint Congressional Committee, having tried to find something tangible to chew on ever since September 23rd, has at last found its answers. We must have a Super and we must have it fast. A subcommittee is heading west to investigate this problem at Los Alamos and Berkeley. The Joint Chiefs appear informally to have decided to give the development of the Super overriding priority, though no formal request has come through. The climate of opinion among the competent physicists also shows signs of shifting. Bethe, Teller, McCormick and LeBaron are all scheduled to turn up within the next 36 hours. I have agreed that if there is a conference on the Super program at Los Alamos, I will make it my business to attend.

What concerns me is really not the technical problem. I am not sure the miserable thing will work, nor that it can be gotten to a target except by ox cart. It seems likely to me even further to worsen the unbalance of our present war plans. What does worry me is that this appears to have caught the imagination, both of the Congressional and of the military people, as the answer to the problem posed by the Russian advance. It would be folly to oppose the exploration of this weapon. We have always known it had to be done, and it does have to be done, though it appears to be singularly proof against any form of experimental approach. But that we become committed to it as a way to save the country and the peace appears to me full of danger.

We will be faced with all this at our meeting; and anything that we do or do not say to the President will have to take it into consideration. I shall feel far more secure if you have an opportunity to think about it.

I still remember my visit with gratitude and affection.

Robert Oppenheimer[6]

Three vital aspects of the Super issue appear in this letter—two explicitly and one by implication. One aspect is the technical. Even with obsessive devotion driving a mind that his harshest detractors acknowledge as brilliant, Teller had been unable to develop a technically sound proposal for actually building a thermonuclear bomb. Unanswered

*William Knowland was a Republican senator from California.

questions obscured the way ahead. Another troubling aspect of the whole issue was the fact that technical considerations were becoming subservient to passion. The climate of opinion was contrary to rational discourse. Finally, more important than all, was the question of whether humankind would be well served by the addition of this "miserable thing." As Oppenheimer wrote, the commitment to the Super seemed "full of danger."

A few days before the GAC meeting, Oppenheimer was back in Rabi's New York apartment. Since the visit of Lawrence and Alvarez, Rabi's thinking had been evolving. While they left him thinking that he favored the Super, Rabi was still committed to the concept of international control. During Oppenheimer's visit, he suggested that the United States might take a tough stand with the Russians and, for example, say to the Soviet Union: "Now you have an atomic bomb, and we have lots of them. The atomic arms race is over. We'll both give up our weapons to international control. If you don't agree with this plan, we'll force it on you."[7] This approach may have sounded reckless to Oppenheimer because it was not discussed at the GAC meeting.

All the committee members except Seaborg assembled on the morning of October 29, 1949. (Oliver E. Buckley, president of Bell Laboratories, had been named to replace Hood Worthington.) During the two-day meeting, the committee heard from two Los Alamos veterans: Hans Bethe, who was opposed to the hydrogen bomb; and Robert Serber, who was for it. The members also heard from the chairman of the Joint Chiefs of Staff and from George F. Kennan, prominent diplomat and former ambassador to the Soviet Union.

No formal minutes were kept during the two-day meeting. Lilienthal attended the sessions and from his journal we learn: "Conant was flatly against it [the Super]," and Hartley Rowe agreed with him. Further, Oppenheimer leaned toward the Conant view. Buckley did not see it as a moral question; Conant disagreed; "Rabi completely on the other side." On the second day, "they were in full agreement: that they would not be for it." On the third day, October 31, they wrote their report.[8]

The report consists of three parts and two addenda. Part I is, in essence, a call for increased research and development in the areas related to the fission bomb. The implied conclusion was that the security of the United States could be maintained with fission-type weapons. As Rabi had reportedly said to Oppenheimer, "we have lots of them [atom bombs]."

Parts II and III of the report were simply entitled "Super Bombs." A factual account of the Super was the substance of part II. It discussed in a general, somewhat guarded, way the basic design principles of the Super, the technical uncertainties associated with it, and the unlimited destructive potential of such a weapon. Part II gave the estimate of five years as the time required to build such a bomb provided a concerted effort was mounted; however, the report pointed out explicitly that no member of the GAC endorsed such a concerted effort. Part II ended on a doubtful note: Was the Super a weapon that would be militarily useful? Was it cost effective *vis-à-vis* the atom bomb? On both of these questions, the judgment expressed was on the negative side.

The committee members made their recommendations in part III. They were unanimous:

1. in their hope that "the development of these weapons can be avoided";
2. in their reluctance "to see the United States take the initiative in precipitating this development"; and
3. in their agreement "that it would be wrong at the present moment to commit ourselves to an all-out effort toward its development."

They were all committed in their view that the Super should not be built; however, they differed on how far that commitment should be extended. It was this difference that spawned the two addenda.

The first addendum, written by Conant, was signed by all members of the GAC except Fermi and Rabi who supported a minority view. The addendum signed by the majority was an unqualified commitment against the development of the Super, and concluded as follows:

We believe a super bomb should never be produced. Mankind would be far better off not to have a demonstration of the feasibility of such a weapon until the present climate of world opinion changes.

It is by no means certain that the weapon can be developed at all and by no means certain that the Russians will produce one within a decade. To the argument that the Russians may succeed in developing this weapon, we would reply that our undertaking it will not prove a deterrent to them. Should they use the weapon against us, reprisals by our large stock of atomic bombs would be comparably effective to the use of a super.

In determining not to proceed to develop the super bomb, we see a unique opportunity of providing by example some limitations on the totality of war and thus of limiting the fear and arousing the hopes of mankind.

The minority addendum, signed by Fermi and Rabi, was shorter in length but went further. In its entirety, the Rabi-Fermi opinion reads:

An Opinion on the Development of the "Super"

A decision on the proposal that an all-out effort be undertaken for the development of the "Super" cannot in our opinion be separated from considerations of broad national policy. A weapon like the "Super" is only an advantage when its energy release is from 100–1000 times greater than that of ordinary atomic bombs. The area of destruction therefore would run from 150 to approximately 1000 square miles or more.

Necessarily such a weapon goes far beyond any military objective and enters the range of very great natural catastrophes. By its very nature it cannot be confined to a military objective but becomes a weapon which in practical effect is almost one of genocide.

It is clear that the use of such a weapon cannot be justified on any ethical ground which gives a human being a certain individuality and dignity even if he happens to be a resident of an enemy country. It is evident to us that this would be the view of peoples in other countries. Its use would put the United States in a bad moral position relative to the peoples of the world.

Any postwar situation resulting from such a weapon would leave unresolvable enmities for generations. A desirable peace cannot come from such an inhuman application of force. The postwar problems would dwarf the problems which confront us at present.

The application of this weapon with the consequent great release of radioactivity would have results unforeseeable at present, but would certainly render large areas unfit for habitation for long periods of time.

The fact that no limits exist to the destructiveness of this weapon makes its very existence and the knowledge of its construction a danger to humanity as a whole. It is necessarily an evil thing considered in any light.

For these reasons we believe it important for the President of the United States to tell the American public, and the world, that we think it wrong on fundamental ethical principles to initiate a program of development of such a weapon. At the same time it would be appropriate to invite the nations of the world to join us in a solemn pledge not to proceed in the development or construction of weapons of this category. If such a pledge were accepted even without control machinery, it appears highly probable that an advanced stage of development leading to a test by another power could be detected by available physical means. Furthermore, we have in our possession, in our stockpile of atomic bombs, the means for adequate "military" retaliation for the production of use of a "super."

Rabi and Fermi parted company with their fellow committee members, first, in tone and emphasis. The moral revulsion with which these two physicists regarded the Super not only colored their language but also was expressed explicitly. Second, there was the veiled implication that, if other nations did not join in the pledge to eschew the Super, the United States might reconsider its position. (This veiled implication becomes more explicit if the addendum is read in the context of the concluding paragraph of the report.) Many years later, Rabi pointed out that he and Fermi thought a world conference should have been called and an attempt made to reach an agreement to forgo research on thermonuclear weapons: "Fermi and I felt that if the conference should be a failure and we couldn't get agreement to stop this research and had to go ahead, we could do so in good conscience."[9]

Since the destruction wrought by a super bomb could not be confined to a military target or a military objective, both addenda questioned (again implicitly) whether it should be thought of as a military weapon. Also, both addenda carried an explicit affirmation of this nation's ability to respond to a foreign power, even in possession of the Super, with our own stockpile of atomic weapons.

As an advisory committee to the commissioners of the AEC, the GAC report went first to them. Lilienthal, the chairman, was in agreement with the proposals and the conclusions of the GAC; Lewis Strauss was strongly opposed to them.

The commission's report with the GAC report appended to it was taken in person to President Truman by Lilienthal on November 9. Strauss, not content with his influence within the commission, wrote to

Truman on November 25 urging him to make the development of a thermonuclear bomb the subject of highest priority.

There was active and intense lobbying on the question of the Super —all by those who were passionate in their belief that the security of the United States was utterly dependent upon its possession of the hydrogen bomb. As McGeorge Bundy has written, "Quite different choices were available, and no one presented them to the president."[10] The options were not simply a gung-ho "Yes, build it!" versus an absolute "No!" The suggestion made in the Fermi-Rabi minority report "to invite the nations of the world to join us in a solemn pledge not to proceed in the development or construction of weapons in this category" was one such option. Neither this approach nor any other entered into the decision process. If the opponents of the Super had done their lobbying, perhaps some compromise alternatives might have at least entered the discourse. As Rabi has said, "We just wrote our report and then went home, and left the field to the others. That was a mistake. If we hadn't done that, history might have been different."

If any stimulus was required to tip the balance in favor of a crash program to develop the hydrogen bomb (and no additional stimulus was needed), it was provided on January 27, 1950 when Klaus Fuchs, a British physicist, confessed that he was a spy for the Soviet Union.* Fuchs had been at Los Alamos during the war and had participated in some of the early discussions on the Super. Twenty-five years later, when asked, "Who was responsible for overruling such influential advisors as those on the GAC?" Teller answered, "Senator Brien McMahon, Lewis Strauss, and Klaus Fuchs."[11]

On January 10, 1950, President Truman announced his decision. He directed the Atomic Energy Commission "to continue its work on all forms of atomic weapons including the so-called hydrogen or super-bomb." Rabi, Conant, Fermi, Oppenheimer, and the other members of the GAC were distraught and angered over the *form* of Truman's announcement. As Rabi said:

> However it's worded, this will be taken as a statement that we're going ahead and building a hydrogen bomb. The Russians are certainly going to take it that way. Only we're not building a hydrogen bomb, because we don't know how. We're going to try. We don't even know that it can be done. But the Russians will never believe

*Some people believe the Fuchs confession was propitiously timed to smooth the public response to a decision already made.

that an American President could be so stupid as to say we're going to build the most powerful weapon in the world when we don't know how. We've got the worst of both worlds. We haven't got a super, but we've spurred the Russians on to an all-out effort to build one.[12]

Truman's decision to launch a crash program to build the Super was irreversible in its influence on subsequent events—and everlasting in its consequences. "I never forgave Truman for buckling under pressure," said Rabi later. "He simply did not understand what it was about. . . . He didn't have his scientific people to consult and give him an impartial picture."[13]

On November 1, 1952, the United States tested its first "hydrogen" bomb—but this was not the Super considered by the GAC in October 1949. Shortly after Truman's decision to build a thermonuclear bomb, the Super, in the form considered by the GAC in 1949, was shown to be unworkable, a physical impossibility, thus justifying the earlier skepticism (by members of the GAC in 1949) about its technical feasibility. And then, in early 1951, Teller, always creative, and the mathematician Stanislaw Ulam conceived an entirely new method of making a thermonuclear bomb. It was on the basis of the Teller-Ulam idea that thermonuclear weapons were eventually developed.

On August 8, 1953, only nine months after the first U.S. hydrogen bomb, the Russians announced the existence of their own hydrogen bomb and, to prove their words, tested it four days later. Once again, the scale of destructive potential had increased: whereas a conventional bomb can destroy a building, an atomic bomb can destroy a city; whereas an atomic bomb can destroy a city, a hydrogen bomb can destroy a major metropolitan area—from the core of the metropolis out through the quiet lanes of the suburbs. Today, with the stockpiles of thermonuclear weapons crowding the armories of nations, the world can be destroyed. One rash moment could destroy civilization. "I don't mind dying," Rabi has said. "My ancestors did that. What I do mind is the destruction of civilization. Take all my work . . . it is in libraries. . . . Well, all that goes up in smoke. I mean the whole civilization. This is the holy thing which they are violating by pushing in the direction of an annihilating war."[14]

Forty years after the formation of Los Alamos there was a reunion: physicists were brought back to where it all began—back to the sun-baked mesa, to the sprawl of buildings far more permanent looking and prosperous in appearance than the temporary structures that housed the first heroes of the atomic age. "I'm seeing an abomination," said Rabi as his car approached Los Alamos. "We should have put it to rest 30 years ago."[15] Later, he addressed the large gathering of physicists. His talk was entitled, "How Well We Meant." "We meant well," he said, "but what we did was to turn over this power to people who did not understand, people who do not respect the human spirit."[16]

CHAPTER

16

Rabi and Oppenheimer

[Rabi], a man . . . of such rare qualities as
scientist and man.

—J. ROBERT OPPENHEIMER

We were friends. . . . Oppenheimer meant a great
deal to me. I miss him.

—I. I. RABI

ON the surface, there were uncanny parallels between Rabi and Oppenheimer. Both were Jewish; both were New Yorkers; both had an early
interest in science; both were wide-ranging readers; both came to physics from chemistry; both finished their education in Europe; during certain periods, each was drawn to left-wing political movements; both
became focuses in the emergence of American physics; both were intimately involved in the war effort; at the conclusion of the war, they both
worked to find ways to curb the spread of nuclear weapons; they both
held many influential advisory positions in government after the Second
World War.

Along with these parallels in their lives and professional careers run
deep differences. Rabi is, in his way, profoundly Jewish. The Orthodox
Hebrew environment of his boyhood, the devotion he saw demonstrated by his parents for their religious faith, and their respect for the
Jewish cultural heritage allowed him to respond positively to his Jewishness. While the practice and ritual of Judaism was undercut early by the
objective appeal Rabi found in science, his self-identity remained al-

ways secure within the tradition of his people, and he chose, self-consciously, to stay within it.

By contrast, Oppenheimer, also self-consciously, rejected and fled from that tradition. To be sure, in his upbringing there was no rabbinical teaching, no Sukkah celebrating the harvest, no synagogue on the Sabbath. Since little in the lives of Oppenheimer's parents would have acquainted him with the traditions and practices of Judaism, he never had a system of religious beliefs to discard. Yet, from his youth onward, he demonstrated an uneasiness with the fact of his Jewishness.

Rabi and Oppenheimer grew up on opposite sides of Manhattan, the three geographical miles separating their boyhood neighborhoods equivalent to three light-years in socioeconomic terms. The Oppenheimer home on Riverside Drive looked to the west over the Hudson River. There was domestic help—maids and a chauffeur. Paintings by Van Gogh, Cézanne, and Gauguin hung on the walls of their eleventh-floor apartment. The Oppenheimers escaped the heat of a New York summer by retreating to their second home on Long Island, where they relaxed in the cool sea air aboard one of their two sailboats. Robert's boyhood was enriched by trips to Europe as well as by the benefits of private schooling at the Ethical Culture School. He knew nothing about the ghetto on the Lower East Side where Rabi lived.

As for left-wing politics, Rabi's foray into it occurred during his youth; this a brief flirtation, based more on the intellectual content of socialism than on its emotional appeal, was behind him before he finished high school. Oppenheimer's fascination with communism came much later— he was in his thirties—and lasted longer. Unlike the youthful Rabi, for whom the political events of the world were like Roman candles going off, Oppenheimer ignored the affairs of the world. He never voted until the presidential election of 1936—at the age of thirty-two. He was unaware of the Great Depression until he saw its effects in the lives of his own graduate students: though gifted, they could not get jobs. The Depression along with the rise of fascism in Europe awakened in Oppenheimer awareness of "how deeply political and economic events could affect men's lives."[1] When Oppenheimer awakened, he came, in the mid-1930s, into contact with left-wing political groups—a contact that became a crucial part of Oppenheimer's life and brought tragedy twenty years later.

Both Rabi and Oppenheimer had lapses in their formal education. While both started in chemistry, Oppenheimer knew he wanted physics by the time he graduated from Harvard in 1925. Rabi's awakening came four years after graduation from Cornell, after four years of floundering. Oppenheimer, wanting to get "more near the center" of physics, went to Cambridge where Rutherford was the reigning presence in physics.[2] Unfortunately for Oppenheimer, Rutherford was nowhere near the center of physics in 1925; and Oppenheimer spent a trying and frustrating year in Cambridge trying to be an experimental physicist in J. J. Thomson's laboratory.

Similar reasons drew both men to Europe in the 1920s, where they were apprenticed to the creators of the new physics: "I learned the music," said Rabi. "They gave me . . . some taste in physics," said Oppenheimer.[3] In the summer of 1929, they both came home. Rabi, always the New Yorker, began his long career at Columbia University; Oppenheimer, seeking the opportunity to be the instigator of a new center of theoretical physics, went to California where he accepted a joint appointment at the University of California in Berkeley and at the California Institute of Technology in Pasadena.

Rabi and Oppenheimer came back from Europe with a shared determination: they wanted American physics to be world class. Oppenheimer became the center of theoretical physics on the West Coast and, throughout the 1930s, trained and educated a generation of theorists. He became a cult figure with a mystique surrounding him—a mystique he did nothing to dispel. His quick mind and acid tongue, his willingness to praise in a language of learned elegance, and his enthusiasm over the logical structure he saw in physics all came together to produce a legendary whole greater than the sum of the parts. His students respected him, feared him, adored him, idolized him. His students mimicked him: he smoked Chesterton cigarettes, they smoked Chesterton cigarettes; his gestures became their gestures; the intonations and inflections that characterized his conversations were so carefully—and successfully— cultivated by his disciples that, when overheard, some of them could be mistaken for Oppenheimer himself.

By contrast, the respect given to Rabi by his students and postdoctoral fellows was down to earth and unadorned. No myths. They all recognized that none of the great things that happened in Rabi's laboratory would have happened without him. He was the linchpin. However, they saw in Rabi a combination of strengths and weaknesses. He did not have the hands of an experimentalist. Quite the contrary: his students shuddered when he put his hands to the equipment. If there was a mystique about Rabi, it was his eerie ability to be absent from the laboratory when some piece of equipment was misbehaving and his uncanny ability to walk into the laboratory at precisely the time an important result was taking shape.

The desire of Rabi and Oppenheimer to see American physics rise to world prominence was fulfilled by the end of the 1930s. Each of them contributed in vital ways to that rise. Throughout the years between 1930 and 1940, Oppenheimer and his students were contributing to quantum electrodynamics, quantum field theory, and nuclear physics— all subjects at the forefront of the discipline. More than his own physics *per se,* however, Oppenheimer strengthened American physics by helping to put theoretical physics on a footing equal to that of experimental physics.

For his part, Rabi's laboratory at Columbia University became acknowledged as the world's foremost molecular-beam laboratory. His experimental results were seminal for nuclear physics, and the resonance method he developed came to have a pervasive influence on the whole of physics and chemistry. The Rabi Tree is a graphic testimony to the global impact Rabi and his students have had on the subject of physics.

The physics of Oppenheimer and that of Rabi were different—as were their styles of mind. In physics, Rabi regards Oppenheimer as having the best mind of his generation, and is quick to acknowledge, "I was never in the same class with him."[4] These are strong words from a man who has no doubts about his own abilities; and he has said further, "I never ran into anyone who was brighter than he [Oppenheimer] was."[5] Oppenheimer was bright—on this, there is no disagreement. There was a "whiz-kid" brilliance to his mind. "A darting mind," said Harvard professor Wendell Furry, one of Oppenheimer's early postdoctoral fellows.[6] "He knew everything that had been done and could quickly reformulate something in quite a different language," according to MIT professor Philip Morrison, one of Oppenheimer's graduate students.[7] Columbia professor Robert Serber, another Oppenheimer postdoctoral student, recalls his "astonishing quickness of mind."[8] Stephen White, who came to know Oppenheimer well while he was a science writer for the New York *Herald Tribune,* has remarked, "I never knew a man in my life who could understand 95 percent of something faster."[9]

The disparity between Oppenheimer's talent and his lack of scientific accomplishment has puzzled many observers, including the English physicist-turned-novelist C. P. Snow:

> Robert Oppenheimer was one of the most interesting figures in
> world science. Among a mass of very clever men, he was probably

the cleverest. . . . He had genuine scientific talent, and could talk on equal terms with the greatest scientists in the place. Bohr . . . had a very high opinion of Oppenheimer's scientific gift. So had Rabi, the least soft of touches. The curious thing was that Oppenheimer had no great scientific achievement to his name. This is hard to explain. He lived through a period in which men with a tenth of his talent made major discoveries.[10]

Stephen White went on from his previous comment to say, "The other 5 percent he never got to. He could live forever, and he'd never get to it."[11] Abraham Pais, an associate of Oppenheimer at the Institute for Advanced Study, refers to his "talent for almost understanding every-thing."[12] "Probably it's true," Morrison has speculated, "that he knew so much and was so swift in his understanding and insight that he couldn't seize a problem and stick with it."[13] Frank Oppenheimer, Robert's younger brother, put it still another way: "What my brother did, and was terribly interested in, is a kind of teaching and talking with other people, getting them to get their ideas straight. So that part of his scatteredness was reacting to the ideas around him. In that sense my brother had a breadth rather than a depth."[14]

Quick brightness, though an impressive attribute of mind, does not carry with it either the capacity to be original or that special instinct that is needed to focus on a truly important question and, with sustained concentration, stay with it until one has thought it through. Oppen-heimer's mind was the more facile, but Rabi's the more original—as Rabi himself has recognized: "As far as general creativity and novelty is concerned, I think I always had more than Oppenheimer, although he was a better theoretical physicist by far. I think I had a stronger intui-tion." Many physicists would agree with Rabi's comparative assess-ment.

"Rabi was a great experimentalist," Wendell Furry has said, "and he was no slouch as a theorist."[15] Indeed, Rabi will be remembered as a great physicist. Oppenheimer would certainly have wanted to be so remembered, but will not be. He will be remembered for other reasons: as a great teacher of physics; for his command of language, his elo-quence; and, as his brother Frank said, as the "least lazy guy."[16] Most of all he will be remembered as the director of the Manhattan Project (1942–45) and as the central figure of a tragedy—both personal and national—that played itself out in 1954.

The Second World War was a turning point in the lives of Rabi and Oppenheimer. Afterward, each became a man of world affairs: Oppenheimer, a public figure, the acknowledged leader of atomic scientists, a man around whom stories and myths accumulated; Rabi, by contrast, was relatively unknown to the public. His influence, however, was pervasive within the counsels of physics and within the circles of high-placed science advisors. No aura of publicity surrounded Rabi; he was not the subject of myths. "Rabi, you know," Wendell Furry has said, "is just Rabi."[17]

When the war broke out, Oppenheimer admitted the envy he had felt for those men he "had known [who] went off to work on radar and other aspects of military research."[18] And it was not until the spring of 1942 that Arthur Compton asked him to take charge of the scattered studies that were then under way on the nuclear physics related to atomic energy. The technical challenge of creating a military weapon to exploit the energy concentrated in the atomic nucleus excited Oppenheimer, who recognized that, if he were successful, the project, and he along with it, would be a part of history.[19]

Oppenheimer did not eschew notoriety. Perhaps by 1942 he was aware that his accomplishments in physics were falling short of his aspirations and would not bring him immortality. In any event, he was avid to be a principal part of the atomic-bomb project and, to achieve this desire, was willing to adjust his life accordingly. In a taped telephone conversation with Arthur Compton, Oppenheimer said, "I'm cutting off every Communist connection. For if I don't the government will find it difficult to use me. I don't want to let anything interfere with my usefulness to the nation."[20] His eagerness to be suitable extended to his willingness to become an army colonel and to have the entire atomic-bomb project militarized. Only the blunt counsel of Rabi and Robert Bacher convinced him that the success of the project depended upon the talents of physicists who could not and would not work within a military chain of command.

When the decision was made to centralize most of the research activities related to the bomb project (a decision influenced by Rabi), when Los Alamos was selected as the location (a decision influenced by Oppenheimer), and when Oppenheimer—early in 1943—was named to direct the project, he brought his persuasive powers to bear on Rabi to become associate director of the Manhattan Project—an offer that, for reasons discussed earlier, Rabi refused.

Though never a citizen of Los Alamos, Rabi was, from the beginning, Oppenheimer's most valued consultant. As mentioned earlier (chapter 11), on February 26, 1943, Oppenheimer sought Rabi's help through a letter, which reads, in part, as follows:

Dear Rabi:

I made in Washington a strong and extremely painful attempt to have our project transferred to O.S.R.D. [Office of Scientific Research and Development] under a special committee established for that purpose. I did not get to first base. . . . I do not know whether the arrangements as now outlined will work, for that will take in the first instance the good will and cooperation of quite a few good physicists; but I did not draw out from my position, and I am willing to make a faithful effort to get things going. I think if I believed with you that this project was "the culmination of three centuries of physics," I should take a different stand. To me it is primarily the development in time of war of a military weapon of some consequence. I do not think the Nazis allow us the option of [not] carrying out that development.

I know that you have good personal reasons for not wanting to join the project, and I am not asking you to do so. Like Toscanini's violinist, you do not like music. I am asking two things of you, within the limits set by your conscience.

(1) I hope that we can have a conference on the physics ahead of us in April, perhaps from the 10th to the 30th, at Los Alamos. The theoretical people I should like to have there at that time, and some of the experimental ones will be there too, though they may be busy with installation. I should like to have you come to that to talk over the physics, and to give us the benefit of your advice at a critical time. This is not a method of tricking you into the project, and it is not for the purpose of talking politics. It is just for the physics, and such relatively simple arrangements as we have to make at that time to see that the physics gets done.

(2) There are two men whom I should be more than reluctant not to have on the project: Bethe and Bacher. I think that you know the reasons in each case and agree with them. You have a great deal of influence with these two men, and they in turn on many others who are involved with the project. I am asking that you use that influence to persuade them to come rather than to stay away.[21]

On issues of policy, physics, and personnel, Rabi was, according to Hans Bethe, "the fatherly advisor to Oppie."[22]

While Rabi's talents and Rad Lab experience were reasons enough for Oppenheimer to want him on the mesa, there was an even more compelling reason: their personal relationship. A person with great influence often has difficulty getting straight and honest responses from those of lesser standing. There is a story about Niels Bohr and his son Aage who, during one of their visits to the United States, met Richard Feynman. Bohr was well aware that his vast reputation tempered people's response to his ideas. In a talk with Feynman, the senior Bohr realized that the young man was attending to the substance of the ideas they were discussing, and was not influenced by his (Bohr's) reputation. After the discussion ended, Bohr is said to have told his son that they should remember this man Feynman because they could get an honest appraisal from him.

Oppenheimer's charismatic personality, his rapid brilliance, and his talent for lucid expression exerted a powerful influence on all people. Many—even those famous in their own right—were intimidated by him, in awe of him, and entranced by him. Such people stepped lightly in his presence, tended toward flattery, and they expressed themselves with studied care, not wanting Oppenheimer to catch them out. Oppenheimer knew all this and, on balance, rather enjoyed it.

His relationship with Rabi was different, as the latter has recalled:

> I first met him [Oppenheimer] in Leipzig in the late fall—or was it the winter?—of 1928. He had just gotten his degree a year or so before, and there were a lot of stories about him—*as* a personality: his good wit, his sarcasm, and so on. But I only met him. Then when I went to Zurich, about February or so, 1929, I got to know him quite well because our intellectual interests about various things—science, philosophy, religion, painting—were similar and different from the interests of most young physicists at that time. We saw a good deal of one another, as purely personal friendship. Then he left, I left, and he went west [to California]. . . . We'd meet occasionally, every few years, but we felt a certain kinship. In other words, I thought he was a friend of mine and he felt I was a friend of his. . . . It's the kind of friendship which we had, both fairly young, that sort of lasts. You start off just where you left off. I was not, as it were, put off by his manner. For one thing, though, I never flattered him, I was always honest with him. Then came the war.

Everyone who knew both men recognized the special quality of their relationship. "They understood each other," says Philip Morrison.[23] This understanding was on many levels and was, in part, a by-product of Rabi's direct honesty with Oppenheimer. As Felix Bloch has said, "Rabi appreciated Robert and when you appreciate the man you tell him, at

of judgment had always been in Oppenheimer's favor. But it was not evidence that did him in.

Furthermore, Oppenheimer was not done in by other men. It is true that there were many people who did not share Rabi's positive feelings toward Oppenheimer; indeed, many did not like him; some hated him. Oppenheimer's detractors saw him as an intellectual snob with a large dose of phoniness. Although Rabi recognized that with Oppenheimer, "you carried on a charade. . . . He lived a charade,"[27] Rabi went along with it and even enjoyed the Oppenheimer mystique: "It was fine—matching wits and so on. Oppenheimer was great fun, and I took him for what he was."[28] Many others could never determine *what* Oppenheimer was, and were unwilling to engage in the charade.

Famous after the war, Oppenheimer wore his fame as an outer garment—it was on display. A friend of both Oppenheimer and Rabi admits that "Oppenheimer had Oppenheimer on his mind all the time. Oppenheimer was sensitive to the way he appeared at all times—I don't think Rabi ever was."[29] Some who had been close to Oppenheimer before and during the war cooled toward him afterward. They saw the Washington environment and his influence within it as having an intoxicating effect on him so that "he began to consider himself God Almighty, able to put the whole world to rights."[30] While Oppenheimer's self-importance troubled many of his friends, to his enemies it was insufferable.

Furthermore, Oppenheimer's eloquent tongue bruised many an ego. "He could cut you cold and humiliate you right down to the ground," said Seth Neddermeyer, a Los Alamos colleague of Oppenheimer.[31] One man had been humiliated on June 13, 1949, in public, under the bright lights of a congressional hearing: that man was Lewis Strauss, a commissioner on the Atomic Energy Commission. At this hearing, the question was whether radioactive isotopes should be allowed to leave the United States—a measure Strauss strongly and publicly opposed. Oppenheimer, as chairman of the General Advisory Committee, was asked to comment on Strauss's concerns, and did so forthrightly:

No one can force me to say that you cannot use these isotopes for atomic energy. You can use a shovel for atomic energy; in fact, you do. You can use a bottle of beer for atomic energy. In fact, you do. But to get some perspective, the fact is that during the war and after the war these materials have played no significant part, and to my knowledge, no part at all.[32]

People in the audience snickered, and those watching Lewis Strauss saw his eyes narrow, the muscles in his jaws begin to work, and the color rise in his face. Five years later, Lewis Strauss, then chairman of the AEC, brought the charges against Oppenheimer that resulted in the formal hearing and the judgment against him.

The hearing on the matter of J. Robert Oppenheimer began in Washington, D.C., on April 12, 1954, in Building T-3 of the Atomic Energy Commission. The scene was Room 2022—a "long dark room," as Rabi recalls it.[33] Into that gloomy room came a succession of witnesses who included some of America's greatest scientists. Robert Bacher, Hans Bethe, Vannevar Bush, James Conant, Lee DuBridge, Norman Ramsey, John von Neumann, and Rabi came in support of Oppenheimer; the prosecutor, Roger Robb, brought Luis Alvarez, Kenneth Pitzer, and Edward Teller to testify against him.

At issue in the hearing was whether Oppenheimer was a threat to the security of the United States. To settle the issue, the adversaries of Oppenheimer scrutinized his veracity, his conduct, and his loyalty. A prime exhibit was Oppenheimer's conversation with his close friend Haakon Chevalier during the winter of 1942 to 1943. Chevalier had informed Oppenheimer that a way was available to transmit atomic secrets to the Russians. While refusing to have anything to do with Chevalier's proposal, Oppenheimer did not report the incident to the appropriate security officers until much later and, when he did, he refused to identify Chevalier. Further, he lied about specific details of the Chevalier incident.

Of all the witnesses, Rabi's testimony focused the most sharply and cogently on the issues and was far and away the most dramatic. Roger Robb, who represented the Atomic Energy Commission against Oppenheimer, was an experienced trial lawyer with an impressive record of convictions to his credit. Robb made a fool of Oppenheimer, who never seemed to realize what was happening. The hearing was *de facto* a half-trial. As prosecutor, Robb used all the tricks in the courts of law to implement what was, in essence, a vendetta against Oppenheimer. Traps were skillfully set, and into them fell Oppenheimer and some of the witnesses. Bullying tactics unsettled and confused many witnesses. By contrast, Oppenheimer's counsel, Lloyd K. Garrison, approached the hearing as a hearing and was not prepared to match Robb's ruthlessness. (At the conclusion of the first week of the hearing, the general counsel of the AEC, Joseph Volpe, urged Oppenheimer and Garrison to "pick up their papers and leave the hearing"[34] if the tactics of the first week were continued—advice that Oppenheimer ignored.) Besides the differences in the tactics employed, the rules of the hearing were set up so as to put Oppenheimer and his lawyers in a distinctly defensive and strictly reactionary position. Strauss's hand-picked lawyer Robb held all the trump cards. Oppenheimer, unable to see what was happening, did not mount an appropriate response. Rabi, on the other hand, had a clear perception of what was happening and was more than a match for the attorney Robb and for the occasion itself.

On the morning of April 21, the second week of the hearing, Rabi sat down in the witness chair. Robb's direct examination focused on three issues. First, one of the more important issues in the hearing, the thermonuclear bomb program. The prosecution attempted to establish that Oppenheimer's suspicious political ties had motivated him to delay and even to subvert America's development of the fusion bomb.

Second, the defense of the United States. This issue was related to what writers of a *Fortune* magazine article had seen as ominous: namely, the activities of the so-called ZORC group during the summer of 1952. The ZORC group was comprised of *Z*acharias (Jerrold), *O*ppenheimer, *R*abi, and *C*harles Lauritsen. According to the anonymous writer in *Fortune,* the ZORC group wanted to make redundant offensive nuclear weapons by means of an air-defense system.[35] At the time, the actions of the ZORC group were interpreted as an attempt to foil the development of the hydrogen bomb.

Finally, there was Rabi's personal appraisal of Oppenheimer.

It had been Oppenheimer's committee, the GAC, that recommended against the development of the fusion bomb. The members carried out their deliberations, during the fall of 1949, in an atmosphere of national fear and tension. The Russians had just exploded their first atomic bomb. How would the United States respond? The witness Rabi recounted the issues:

> Following the announcement of the Russian explosion of the A-bomb, I felt that somehow or other some answer must be made . . . to regain the lead which we had. There were two directions in which one could look: either the realization of the super [the fusion bomb] or an intensification of the effort on fission weapons to make large ones, small ones, . . . to get a large variety and very great military flexibility. . . . There was a real question there where the weight of the effort should lie.[36]

The question of "where the weight . . . should lie" really entailed a whole nexus of issues. "There was the question of the military value of this weapon [the fusion bomb]," as Rabi said in his testimony. "What sort of target it was good for. . . . We felt—and I am talking chiefly about myself—that this was not a good weapon. But by its very nature, if you attacked a target, it took in very much more. . . . We discussed [in the 1949 GAC meetings] a great deal what you were buying if you got this thing."[37] Rabi's testimony touched on many of the practical questions that faced the 1949 GAC as they formulated their recommendations about the fusion-bomb program for the AEC. For example, the effect a crash program to develop the Super would have on the availability of nuclear material for fission bombs; the deliverability of a fusion weapon; the economics of the program. Underlying all these practical considerations was the fact that no one knew how to make the super bomb. "We didn't even know whether this thing contradicted the laws of physics," Rabi testified.[38] He made it clear that, in terms of the knowledge that existed in October 1949, there were no creditable ideas for initiating the fusion-bomb project: "There has been all this newspaper stuff about delay. The subject which we discussed in the 1949 meeting, that particular thing [the then-proposed Super] has never been made . . . and we still don't know to this day whether something like that will function."[39]

There were many technical and quasi-technical reasons for Oppenheimer and the GAC members to recommend against a crash program to develop a fusion weapon. The committee, however, went beyond the technical. "We felt," testified Rabi, "that the whole discussion raised an opportunity for the President of the United States to make some political gesture which would be such that it would strengthen our moral position."[40] Rabi was asked what made him think it appropriate to speak on nontechnical aspects of the issue. "That is a good question," he responded. ". . . Somehow or other we didn't feel it was inappropriate."[41] Oppenheimer's detractors, of course, had their own answer to that question.

Just before the luncheon recess, Rabi testified that, in his judgment, Oppenheimer was a "man of upstanding character, . . . a loyal individual," and said that he did not believe that "Dr. Oppenheimer [was] a security risk."[42]

After the noon recess, Rabi's cross-examination began.

The "Chevalier incident" had proved to be the most damning to Oppenheimer's cause, and his own testimony in this regard only exacerbated the issue. Rabi tried to set the incident in perspective by distinguishing between the context of the event (1943) and the context of the hearing (1954). In 1943, Russia was our ally in war; in 1954, the Soviet Union was our enemy in a cold war. Rabi underscored the difficulty of judging a man's behavior in 1943 by claiming that he himself "[couldn't] say what [he] would have done at that time."[43] Whereas, "If a man in 1954 came with such a proposal, my God,—it would be horrifying."[44]

The prosecutor, Robb, attempted to weaken Rabi's testimony by using a ploy that had succeeded with an earlier witness.

ROBB: Dr. Rabi, getting back to the hypothetical questions that have been put to you . . . about the Chevalier incident, if you had been put in that hypothetical position and had reported the matter to an intelligence officer, you of course would have been [*sic*] told the whole truth about it, wouldn't you?

RABI: I am naturally a truthful person.

ROBB: You would not have lied about it? [Oppenheimer had admitted lying.]

RABI: I am telling you what I think now. The Lord alone knows what I would have done at that time. This is what I think now.

ROBB: Of course, Doctor, as you say, only God knows what is in a man's mind and heart, but give us your best judgment of what you would do.

RABI: This is what I think now; I hope this is what I would have done then. . . .

ROBB: Of course, Doctor, you don't know what Dr. Oppenheimer's testimony before this board about that incident may have been, do you?

RABI: No.

ROBB: So perhaps in respect to passing judgment on the incident, the board may be in a better position to judge than you?

Robb had used this approach earlier in the hearing with the witness James Conant who, in agreeing with the prosecutor that "the board may be in a better position to judge," had, in effect, given the board *carte blanche.* Rabi would not allow Robb to get off so easily. The testimony continues:

RABI: I have the highest respect for the board. I am not going to make any comment about the board. They are working very hard, as I have seen.

Unable to permit the matter to rest here, Robb pressed further:

> ROBB: Of course, I realize you have complete confidence in the board. But my point is that perhaps the board may be in possession of information which is not now available to you about the incident.
> RABI: It may be. On the other hand, I am in possession of a long experience with this man, going back to 1929, which is 25 years, and there is a kind of seat of the pants feeling in which I myself lay great weight. In other words, I might even venture to differ from the judgment of the board without impugning their integrity at all.
> ROBB: I am confining my question to that one incident, Doctor. I think we have agreed that the board may be in possession from Dr. Oppenheimer's own lips about the incident which is not now available to you, is that correct?
> RABI: Is this a statement?
> ROBB: Yes.
> RABI: I accept your statement.
> ROBB: And therefore it may be that the board is now in a better position than you, so far as that incident is concerned, to evaluate it?
> RABI: An incident of that sort they may be. I can't say they are not. But on the other hand, I think that any incident, . . . you have to take it in sum.
> ROBB: Of course.
> RABI: You have to take the whole story.
> ROBB: Of course.
> RABI: That is what novels are about. There is a dramatic moment and the history of the man, what made him act, what he did, and what sort of person he was. This is what you are really doing here. You are writing a man's life.[45]

Adamant in his testimony that no single incident could be divorced from the whole life of a man, Rabi thus defused the questions on the "Chevalier incident." He would not allow Robb to escape behind the shroud of secrecy, to invoke information known only to the board, and thereby, to cast doubt on his own testimony. Rabi had to acknowledge, as Oppenheimer had before him, that a "tissue of lies" surrounded the incident, but concluded, "that it is part and parcel of the kind of foolish behavior that occurred in the early part of the record. . . . It was a foolish action, but I would not put a sinister implication to it. The record is full of actions before Oppenheimer became the sort of statesman he now is."[46]

At one point during his testimony, Rabi was asked whether he had ever spoken to Chairman Strauss on Oppenheimer's behalf. Rabi's answer was no, but he continued, "I never hid my opinion from Mr. Strauss that I thought that this whole proceeding was a most unfortunate one." And here Rabi dramatically put the Oppenheimer hearing into perspective:

> The suspension of the clearance of Dr. Oppenheimer was a very unfortunate thing and should not have been done. In other words, there he was; he is a consultant, and if you don't want to consult the guy, you don't consult him, period. Why you have to then proceed to suspend clearance and go through all this sort of thing, he is only there when called, and that is all there is to it. [At the time of the hearing, Oppenheimer's role in government was that of high-level consultant. He was not a member of any vital committee of government.] So it didn't seem to me the sort of thing that called for this kind of proceeding . . . against a man who has accomplished what Dr. Oppenheimer has accomplished. There is a real positive record. . . . We have the A-bomb and a whole series of [them] . . . what more do you want, mermaids? This is just a tremendous achievement. If the end of that road is this kind of hearing, which can't help but be humiliating, I [think it is] a pretty bad show.[47]

And a bad show it was. In spite of Oppenheimer's outstanding record of service, in spite of the fact that there was no evidence of disloyalty, his accusers got their satisfaction. The board, by a 2-to-1 vote, decided against him.

It is not adequate to conclude that the Oppenheimer affair was simply a product of the times. Galileo's trial before the Inquisition could also be so dismissed; however, that historical tragedy is still with us today, 350 years later. Galileo's trial and Oppenheimer's hearing serve as indictments against systems—whether they be an ecclesiastical system or a security system—that can be used as a shield for angry men as they go about destroying a man.

While it is true that the cards were stacked against him, Oppenheimer's disgrace and humiliation were brought on, to a large extent, by his own conduct during the hearing. *Time* magazine concluded that, "in the list of witnesses against J. Robert Oppenheimer, the most effective was J. Robert Oppenheimer himself."[48] Roger Robb, the attorney personally selected by Lewis Strauss to represent the security board, said to his wife one evening during the hearing that he "had seen a man destroy himself on the witness stand."[49] Oppenheimer himself acknowledged later that during the hearing, "I had very little sense of self."[50] Oppenheimer's sense of self, however, was not temporarily misplaced in the adversarial, tension-wracked hearing. Felix Bloch remembered an exchange he had with Rabi: "I once said, 'You know, I wonder of all the Oppenheimers I have seen, which is the real one?' " And Rabi's response was: "I'll bet you Robert doesn't know himself."[51] "Identity," as Rabi has said, was "his problem."[52]

It is this "sense of self" or "identity" that so profoundly distinguishes the two men, Rabi and Oppenheimer. Both men were Jewish, but as Bloch has remarked, "he [Oppenheimer] tried to act as if he were not a Jew and succeeded well because he was a good actor."[53] From his youth, Oppenheimer eschewed his Jewishness. In 1922, when he accompanied his English teacher Herbert Smith (from the Ethical Culture School) on a trip to the Southwest, Oppenheimer, then eighteen years old, asked to travel as Smith's brother so he could be Robert "Smith."[54] By contrast, Rabi's youthful response to anti-Semitism was also to change his name, but in the other direction: from Isidor Rabi to Isidor Isaac Rabi. In Germany, during his postdoctoral years, not only would he identify himself as Jewish, but did so with the declarative statement, *"Ich bin ein Aus-Jude"* ("I am an Austrian Jew"). Austrian Jews were the most disliked. "I was never sailing under false colors," Rabi has said. "This is it. Whatever dealings we have will be on that basis— I know who you are and you'll know who I am."

Rabi has discussed Oppenheimer and the question of religion at length:

> Oppenheimer was Jewish but he wished he weren't and tried to pretend he wasn't. I have said of him that he would have been a much better physicist if he had studied the Talmud rather than Sanskrit. . . . It would have given him a greater sense of himself. The Jewish tradition, even if you don't know it in detail, is so strong that you renounce it at your own peril. Doesn't mean you have to be orthodox, or even practice it, but if you turn your back on it, having been born into it, you're in trouble. So that poor Robert, an expert in Sanskrit and French literature . . .

Rabi's voice trailed off.

"Oppenheimer," said Rabi, "was a man who was passionately religious in the sense that he had the capacity for being that." One of the prerequisites for a nontrivial religious sense is a profound sense of self. Rabi knows who he is. Rabi is deeply religious. Eschewing religious practices, and an anthropomorphic concept of God, Rabi has what Einstein referred to as a "cosmic religious feeling"[55]—a religious sense that transcends dogma and institutions:

> Nothing in the world can *move* me as deeply as some of these orthodox Jewish practices. People go to Israel, to Williamsburg in Brooklyn, or to those places where Orthodox Jews go . . . and they pray and shake back and forth. Some people are appalled by it, but to me it is great. These are my people. I could join them, shake back and forth, and feel all right about it. The thing that saves me from *any* of those feelings is that I'm a scientist which I firmly believe transcends, doesn't oppose, but transcends these particular things. I am of this and there is no question, but I'm not *in* it, couldn't be in it. I love it and I respect it, but as a scientist I am at a more universal level . . . and this comes back to God.

For Rabi, the circle is complete.

For Oppenheimer, the circle never closed. According to Rabi:

> He never got to be an integrated personality. It happens sometimes, with many people, but more frequently, perhaps, because of their situation, with brilliant Jewish people. With enormous capacities in every direction, it is hard to choose. He wanted everything. He reminded me very much of a boyhood friend of mine, who's a lawyer, about whom someone said, "He'd like to be president of the Knights of Columbus and B'nai B'rith." God knows I'm not the simplest person, but compared to Oppenheimer, I'm very, very simple.

The complex Oppenheimer was a man of many roles, but one he took to naturally after the war was that of a Washington insider, as Philip Morrison has commented:

> [By 1949,] Robert became a victim of his own view, that he could be the determiner of history. He worked under the illusion that his

powerful abilities and his remarkable public reputation of 1945 would make him a major figure in the United States administration. And it did for a while . . . as long as he didn't buck anything. But he was committed to feeling that there should be some solution to the problem of the cold war. . . . He was caught by his own earnest, incredible passion to get something good done for the sake of the future. The flaw, that he had done so well as a committee man and laboratory leader and insider, was that the inside way was the only way. In order to be an insider he then cut away more and more of his independence. In the end, they destroyed him.[56]

In the aftermath, Oppenheimer became a martyr. His martyrdom, however, was viewed suspiciously by some. One of Oppenheimer's famous students said, "I'm afraid he has only assumed a new role in his big repertoire. Just now he happens to be, of necessity, saint and martyr, but if ever the wind changes, he'll be busy again in Washington with the rest of them."[57]

Oppenheimer's chief antagonists, Strauss and Teller, were, on the other hand, ostracized. Eventually, the Senate refused to confirm the nomination of Strauss as secretary of commerce and he faded from public life. A few weeks after the verdict against Oppenheimer, Rabi and Teller were in Los Alamos attending a conference, in whose festive atmosphere many old friends were gathered. At lunch on the opening day, Teller breezed up to Rabi and Robert Christy, a physicist from the California Institute of Technology—but his outstretched hand was deliberately ignored. Coldly, Rabi "congratulated" Teller on the "brilliance" of his testimony at the Oppenheimer hearing, a testimony whose oblique phrases cast direct doubt on Oppenheimer's loyalty. Teller was so shaken by Rabi's treatment that he excused himself from the luncheon and spent the remainder of the day in his room. He did not return to Los Alamos for nine years.

Today, as Rabi reflects on the Oppenheimer hearing, he feels a sense of both guilt and anger. He recognizes the special influence he had with Oppenheimer:

I was one of the few living who could sit down and say [to Oppenheimer], "Now don't be a fool. If you want to cause trouble for yourself, if you want to write a Rousseau autobiography, do it after the show is over." If I'd been in on it [the hearing], maybe I could have gotten him to manage the case in the way I thought. I would simply have advised him to stand up and say, "This is what I accomplished for the United States. There is a record. I see no reason for a retrial. If you find it in your hearts to do this, there it is. I hope you have a long life and live to regret it. I will have no part of it." Period. And walk out. Instead he stood up there and spilled his guts.

While feeling he should have made a more overt attempt to influence Oppenheimer's conduct in the hearing, Rabi recognizes that Oppenheimer, being Oppenheimer, probably would not have followed his advice: "I'm also a bit angry that Robert . . . let it happen."

In a real sense, Robert Oppenheimer did let it happen. One would think that with his quickness of mind, with his amazing ability to synthesize ideas, he should have seen the direction the hearing was taking, he should have seen the extent to which the hearing had been "set up" to get him, and, seeing this, he should have altered his own conduct at the hearing. But he did not. As Frank Oppenheimer acknowledged, he played right into their hands. "I don't know why he did it," said Frank Oppenheimer.[58]

"Oppenheimer was a man who was put together of many bright shining splinters," says Rabi. Rabi's statement is not intended to be denigrating; rather, it is for Rabi a statement of fact about a man he liked deeply. If Rabi is correct, then the suggestion that Oppenheimer "lost his sense of self" is misleading. It might be more correct to suggest that in the hostile hearing room, there was no sense of self in which Oppenheimer could take refuge. There were many facets to J. Robert Oppenheimer, but there was no facet for functioning effectively within the adversarial setting created by Lewis Strauss.

Rabi and Oppenheimer: many parallels, basic differences. Both men deeply concerned with the events of their day; both men eager to do good for the sake of the future. Rabi, the wiser; Oppenheimer, the more brilliant. Rabi the effective operator behind the scenes; Oppenheimer, the eloquent spokesman.

Of all their similarities and of all their differences, it is perhaps the sense of identity, to themselves and to others, that separates the two men most decisively. If Rabi and Oppenheimer, like Humpty-Dumpty, each fell from a wall and shattered into many pieces, the King's men would never be able to restore the splintered brilliance of the original Oppenheimer. For Rabi, the King's men would have it easy: the pieces fit together in only one way.

C H A P T E R

17

Statesman of Science

Science [is] a great intellectual force which liberates the mind from outworn prejudice and
provides understanding and illumination.
—I. I. Rabi

"REAL peace means more than the absence of violent war. To fulfill
human expectations, peace must be a condition which permits the release of the latent creative energies of all people to the end of enhancing
and elevating the quality of human life on this globe."[1] Rabi spoke these
words when delivering the opening address, in 1971, to the Fourth International Conference on the Peaceful Uses of Atomic Energy.

The sad proposition can be persuasively argued that, since the Second World War, the foreign and, to an extent, the domestic policies of
the United States have been influenced more by what the nation stands
against than by what it stands for. Pre-eminent among those things we
stand against is communism.

The enervating arms race that has dominated the affairs of state ever
since the nucleus was tapped as an energy source is a prime example
of how this stand against communism has dominated national policies.
Consider, for example, the report "The Impact of Science and Technology" printed in *A Task Force Report by the Republican Committee on
Program and Progress.* This task force report was issued in the fall of
1959, when Rabi's power and influence were at their peak. In the section
entitled "The Maintenance of Peace," reference to the evil and powerful

232

Communists provides the springboard for this statement: "We have no choice but to maintain superior military strength, and military strength means a rapidly advancing science and technology." This logic—communism is strong and evil; *ergo,* the most advanced weapon systems must be developed and deployed; *ergo,* science and technology must be supported and utilized—was the dominant influence on decision makers in the late 1940s. (The statement I have just quoted could, unfortunately, have been written yesterday.)

Rabi thinks by a different logic. He is not a pacifist and has never advocated that the United States should disarm unilaterally. However, since the end of the Second World War, he has promoted policies that, in his judgment, would enhance the security of the United States:

> Our country developed on the basis of complete security: the Atlantic Ocean to the east, the Pacific Ocean to the west, and no threat from either the north or the south. So we could have our own peculiar institutions which we developed. If we want to remain the United States of America, we have to try to keep that security. Every time a superior weapon is developed it turns us into a continental state. And there is no example in history of a continental state remaining a democracy. Germany, France, and Italy were never democracies in our sense at all. They aren't now, not in the American sense. So our policy should have been all along to get every arms reduction. Combat all arms as far as we could; this was our natural advantage. But after the Second World War we just became intoxicated, we lost sight of American interests. I have *never* seen a negotiation in which I took part where American interests were important; rather, of importance was American *pride.*

For Rabi, reduction of arms enhances the security and vitality of the institutions and the democracy that are so peculiarly American. But there is more. Military strength has its material foundations—armaments—more important, military strength derives from principles shared by a people. The blind concentration on the material side of military strength can destroy the political, intellectual, and ethical principles on which that strength ultimately rests. "It is a lack of these other qualities that finally destroyed both Hitler and the Kaiser in spite of their great military capacity and devilish skill. Hitler's hopes of world domination were consumed in the furnaces of Auschwitz as much as under the hammerings of the 8th Air Force."[2] Through science itself, Rabi sought to promote and to strengthen those principles that would lessen the perceived need for armaments on the parts of all nations.

The material side of science is there for all to see and to experience. Developments such as those in transportation, communication, sanitation, medical treatment, and energy production have determined to a large extent the very texture of society. The technological exploitation of new scientific understanding dramatically influences the gross national product of a nation. On the personal level, new technologies create new jobs while they render others obsolete. A job, in turn, allows the individual to purchase the material amenities that are themselves the products of the material side of science.

So overwhelming is the material side of science that another side of science is often lost from view. Science is a tradition of original thinking that brings new insights into the nature of humanity, new understanding of our universe, and new conceptions of how the two fit together. The fundamental ideas of science have inevitably led to new modes of thought. The world, seen in the light of science, is a world beyond oneself. By learning to appreciate the human spirit that can discover fundamentally new ideas, we discover something above daily life, above nationality, and beyond a religious affiliation. We understand the basic unity in the spirit of all mankind and exalt mankind as the mind and developing consciousness of the universe.

A universal yearning of the human species is self-understanding, self-realization. Both religion and science are responses to this yearning; however, whereas religion tends to erect barriers between people, science tends to tear those barriers down. The practices of religion are defended locally; the practices of science are shared globally. The culture of religion is sectarian; the culture of science, universal. "Science," Rabi has said, "[is] a great intellectual force which liberates the mind from outworn prejudice and provides understanding and illumination."[3]

The culture of science is shared universally and is respected universally. In this universality Rabi saw a powerful means of bringing people together in a spirit of cooperation. Science could effectively pull aside the Iron Curtain and permit the light of shared understanding to illuminate dark suspicion. Through science the President of the United States could confront divergent advice and formulate sound policies. For Rabi, the survival of humanity hinges on the hope that people will not only recognize that their most noble goal is to understand themselves and their place within the universe but that this goal will override the petty and parochial aims that disturb the peace.

In January 1983, a new fundamental particle was discovered in Geneva, Switzerland, at the laboratory called by its acronym CERN (Center for European Nuclear Research). This particle, called the "W particle," was the subject of speculation long before a theory was created that allowed details of its existence to be predicted. The laboratory at CERN was at that time the site of the world's largest particle accelerator —the only accelerator that could achieve the energy range in which the W particle could be observed. The discovery was a triple triumph: for the theoreticians who predicted it, for the experimentalists whose ingenuity translated prediction into actuality, and for the laboratory itself. It was also a triumph for the diplomacy of I. I. Rabi.

Soon after the end of the Second World War, a vision had grown in Rabi's mind. Ginestra Amaldi, wife of the eminent Italian physicist Eduardo Amaldi, has recalled hearing Rabi talk about his vision:

> It couldn't have been very long after the end of the war. We had been out to dinner with Rabi in Trastevere, and the street car back to the center of town would not come, as usual. Our visitor from the States casually asked my husband: "Why don't the Europeans get together and do physics jointly? At home in the States, nine universities have just pooled their resources and finances to build a large accelerator. You ought to try it too."[4]

Rabi was referring, of course, to the Brookhaven National Laboratory which was, at that very time, taking form outside New York City on Long Island (see chapter 14). He had seen that, despite sharp differences between nine cooperating universities about questions of detail—location, organizational structure, and so on—the desire to establish a laboratory where frontier research in physics could be carried out was so powerful as to enable differences to be resolved.

Rabi envisioned science as being the same unifying influence in Europe. The European nations had borne the brunt of the war and also shared the costly prospect of rebuilding their cities and economies. A European laboratory was something positive, to inspire, to raise war-weary spirits: "Europe was down and out, and I was interested in European unity. Of course, it's one thing to dream of European unity, but here was something where they could actually act together. It had this great political value. At that time, they had nothing else. They wanted to stay important in science and this was it."

A European laboratory could be a model for other forms of cooperation:

Why was I interested in Europeans getting together? It's not that my interest is in Europe as such. I like to go there, but the real point I felt—and still feel—was that Europe was a hostage, it is up for grabs. I wanted to do whatever I could to strengthen Europe to stand on its own feet industrially, psychologically, and in other ways. I saw *no* reason for us to battle with the Russians, I still don't, *except for Europe.* If Europe were independent and had a sense of unity, we could be friendly with the Russians and regard them as curious people trying to live under this funny form of government. We could sympathize with them for their lack of freedom. But with Europe there, that was a problem.

Clearly, Rabi was seeking to stabilize the precarious relationship between the United States and the Soviet Union; and, in his judgment, a strong, unified Europe would be stabilizing. Science was his means to that end.

Rabi's opportunity came when he was named a United States delegate to the Fifth General Assembly of UNESCO (United Nations Educational, Scientific, and Cultural Organization) held in Florence, Italy, in June 1950:

I've always known that sometimes it's best to be silent if you want to get something done in politics. During the crossing to Europe I promised the other delegates that I would hold my tongue when they presented motions for financial aid, from UNESCO, to cultural institutions in the German Federal Republic. I personally did not approve of these motions; I considered them premature. In return, the other delegates agreed to support my motion for the "Establishment and Organization of Regional Research Centers and Laboratories."[5]

Although the members of the U.S. delegation were leery of European scientists, they agreed to Rabi's proposal.

At the assembly meeting, Rabi worked behind the scenes—particularly with his friend Amaldi and with Pierre Auger, the head of natural sciences in UNESCO.

In Florence [Rabi has reported], I talked as little as possible. I got several European friends to speak to the delegates of other countries about the plan for the laboratory, and to campaign for their votes. By going about it that way, there was less suspicion that my proposal was simply to further American interests. Ultimately, I avoided talking about nuclear research altogether. My motion stated only in very general terms that the international cooperation of scientists, in search for new knowledge, should be intensified in those fields . . . where the efforts of a single country of the region would not be enough for the particular problem.[6]

Rabi's strategy was effective. He made his motion in the Green Room of the Palazzo Vecchio on June 7, 1950:

We scientists in the United States want to preserve the international fellowship of science, to keep the light of science burning brightly in Western Europe. Moreover, we want very much to help remove a sense of frustration which is growing among scientists of countries which do not have the material means which we have in the United States of America.[7]

He went on to urge that UNESCO should be "the catalyst for science of the world." He stressed that the role of UNESCO should be limited to the planning of the laboratory; that is, the research laboratory itself should be independent of UNESCO.

The United States resolution, motivated by Rabi, was approved by the Florence General Assembly. In December 1951, delegates from participating nations met to lay the groundwork for an international laboratory. They selected Geneva as its site. On February 15, 1952, representatives from eleven nations signed the document establishing CERN *(Conseil Européen pour la Recherche Nucleaire):* the Federal Republic of Germany, Denmark, France, Greece, Italy, the Netherlands, Sweden, Switzerland, Yugoslavia, Belgium, and Norway. Later that same day, Rabi received a letter that read: "We have just signed the Agreement which constitutes the official birth of the project you fathered at Florence. Mother and Child are doing well, and the Doctors send you their greetings." The letter was signed by Niels Bohr, Werner Heisenberg, Eduardo Amaldi, Hannes Alfvén, Pierre Auger, and eighteen other physicists. Rabi had this letter framed and hung it on the wall of his home office.

On July 6, 1950, one month after Rabi presented his proposal for a European research center to the Florence General Assembly, Dwight David Eisenhower wrote the following words in his diary:

Our people assume that the world knows something about us, our system of government, our international policies, our economic system, etc. Actually we know very little about others, but they know far less about us, and it is essential in the world struggle that the world know something about our good intentions, latent strength, respect for the rights of others. Since our opponent has to depend on lies, and we can tell the truth, the advantage would seem to be with us. But the truth must be nailed, bannerlike to a staff, and we must do that by convincing the whole world that our announced intentions of peace are the truth.[8]

When Eisenhower wrote these words, he was the president of Columbia University, the Korean War was eleven days old, and the world was gingerly making its way into the nuclear era.

The Rabi-Eisenhower acquaintanceship began on the campus of Columbia University and it did so in dramatic fashion. Hans Bethe recalls their meeting:

Rabi got the Nobel Prize and Eisenhower [then president of Columbia University] asked Rabi to come and talk with him. And Eisenhower said, "Professor Rabi, I congratulate you on the Nobel Prize, and besides, I am always very happy to see one of the employees of the University." So Rabi drew himself up to his full height of five feet five inches and said, "Mr. President, the faculty are not the employees of the university. They *are* the university!" Eisenhower was so impressed by that that they were friends ever since.[9]

"I have enormous respect for [Eisenhower]," Rabi said to Edwin Newman in an interview on December 29, 1972. "His besetting sin, to my mind, was his modesty. . . . He was a live body with humor and everything . . . enormous common sense. . . . wonderful judgment and interests. . . . He understood peace."[10]

Eisenhower's regard for Rabi is conveyed by his response to an offer made to the physicist by the Institute of Advanced Study at Princeton:

As President of Columbia, I had to protect the University against the disastrous effect of faculty morale and academic standards should Dr. Rabi leave. We were in no position to match Princeton's offer financially. Could I have, it would have been futile, for Dr. Rabi praised intellectual challenge above money. I could only present to him the probabilities of what might happen to Columbia should he leave, in the hope that his concern for the institution and its function would save him for us. I stressed that to the academic world, he symbolized pure science on Morningside Heights. His departure, I continued, would deprive the University of its chief drawing card—to use layman's language—to bring in brilliant graduate students for whom his presence on our campus meant excellence in science, . . . My arguments were simple, our conversation was man to man. I was only sorry that I could not find the splendid phrases such an appeal and such a figure deserved. Then Dr. Rabi delighted me and assured Columbia against sudden deterioration in science by agreeing to stay on.[11]

Eisenhower need not have worried: many offers came to Rabi; but for him no place could compete with Manhattan and no institution with Columbia.

Eisenhower's diary thoughts of 1950 took public form in 1953 when, on December 8, he stepped to the lectern in the great Hall of Assembly in the United Nations Building in New York. A hush focused the attention of thirty-five hundred people from sixty nations on the president of the United States. At the heart of Eisenhower's speech, which addressed the sober realities of an atomic world, was a specific proposal: for governments to reduce their stockpile of fissionable materials by donating them to an International Atomic Energy Agency, set up under the aegis of the United Nations. The principal purpose of this Atomic Energy Agency would be, in Eisenhower's words, "to devise methods whereby this fissionable material would be allocated to serve the peaceful pursuits of mankind."[12] Such a plan, he continued, would "open up a new channel for peaceful discussions, and initiate at least a new approach to the many difficult problems that must be solved . . . if the world is to shake off the inertia imposed by fear, and is to make positive progress towards peace."[13]

Eisenhower's proposal suited Rabi to a tee. With the nuclear atom as a means of bringing people together, Rabi's imagination took flight. He saw the opportunity for lifting the cover of secrecy—at least partially! —that blanketed atomic research at that time. If we pulled back our cover just a bit, perhaps the Russians would do the same. To the extent that ideas could be shared—ideas about nuclear reactors, about nuclear fission and fission products, about the effects of radiation on materials, about a whole range of topics—to the extent that informed judgments could take the place of paranoid uncertainty, then policies could be based on knowledge rather than on assumption.

Somewhat surprisingly, Eisenhower's proposal also struck a responsive chord in the mind of Lewis L. Strauss, chairman of the Atomic Energy Commission. Strauss, who was in the Assembly Hall when Eisenhower delivered what many regard as one of the great speeches of the century, has described the reaction: "The speech was received, at first, with an impressive aspiration, a sound of indrawn breaths, followed by a gigantic, collective sigh—then wave after wave of applause. Even the Soviet delegation was caught up with the general enthusiasm."[14] It was an emotionally charged moment, and the fervor may have moved Strauss. Here, on the one hand, was Eisenhower proposing "world-wide investigation into the most effective peacetime uses of fissionable material"; and here, on the other hand, was Lewis Strauss who was one of the most "apprehensive about letting atomic information stray beyond the borders of the United States."[15] In fact, just five days before Eisenhower's speech, Strauss had taken the first step to remove the security clearance of J. Robert Oppenheimer (see chapter 16). Yet Strauss was responding positively to the President's proposal while at the very same time he was setting the stage to do in the man whose similar proposals were regarded as inspired by the Communists.

At this time, not only was Strauss the chairman of the Atomic Energy Commission, but Rabi was chairman of the General Advisory Committee to the AEC. At a meeting of the GAC early in 1954—a few weeks after Eisenhower's speech—Strauss asked for ideas on how Eisenhower's proposal could be translated into some form of action. Rabi responded by suggesting an international conference on the peaceful uses of atomic energy. He was made the chairman of a committee to plan such a conference.

During the early months of 1954, Rabi was in a delicate position. On the one hand, he needed the cooperation of Strauss if the international conference was ever to be a reality. On the other hand, Strauss was out to get Rabi's friend Oppenheimer and was preparing for Oppenheimer's hearing. Rabi managed: he pulled no punches on behalf of his friend at the hearing and, at the same time, maintained Strauss's support for the conference.

The early response to Rabi's idea was guarded and cool, a large part of the skepticism being due to the maniacal regard for security that pervaded all things atomic. In August, Rabi traveled to London and went directly to Cambridge where, over lunch at St. John's College, he presented his idea to Lord Adrian, Sir James Chadwick, Sir John Cock-croft, Sir Nevill Mott, Robert Spence, and A. K. Longair. Again, the reaction to Rabi's idea was reserved, as he said later:

> To my surprise, the initial reception of this idea by scientists in this country and in Europe, which I visited twice in the summer of 1954, was even less than lukewarm. There was a hopeless feeling that the Conference could not succeed, that it would be regarded as a propaganda stunt, that the Soviets would not join, that the papers presented at the Conference would be of inferior quality because of atomic secrecy, and that in general more harm than good would come of it.[16]

Like the other English scientists, the reaction of Sir John Cockcroft, director of the United Kingdom Atomic Energy Establishment at Harwell, was tepid. But as Rabi presented a range of topics that could form an agenda of a conference, Cockcroft warmed to the subject. Rabi left England with the latter's support, and others followed. Rabi has said that, "by persistence and persuasion and by presenting an attractive list of topics, the British, the Canadians, and the French were won over to the general idea."[17]

One person who required no persuasion was President Eisenhower. On December 10, 1953, two days after his "Atoms for Peace" speech had been delivered to the United Nations, Eisenhower expressed in his diary the hope that motivated his speech: "to make a clear effort to get the Soviet Union working with us in some phase of this whole atomic field that would have only peace and the good of mankind as a goal. If we were successful in getting even the tiniest starts, it . . . might expand into something broader."[18] He clearly recognized that the apolitical character of science was a potent means of getting that tiny opening. Eventually, in his message to the conference which was read at the opening session, he pointed out that the conference was limited to scientific and technical matters:

> It is expressly non-political. You meet, therefore, as free men of science, interested only in enriching man's store of knowledge about this wonderful discovery. Science speaks in many tongues. The advance of the nuclear arts has been the work of men of many nations. That is so because the atom itself is non-political: it wears

no nationality, and it recognizes no frontiers. It is neither moral nor immoral. Only man's choice can make it good or evil.[19]

As Rabi was using his influence among scientists to promote the conference idea, Eisenhower used the power of his office. He directed the secretary of state, John Foster Dulles, to propose an agenda item for the United Nations. Speaking before the General Assembly of the United Nations on September 23, 1954, Dulles called for, first, the creation of an international atomic energy agency that would include all nations of the world; and, second, the convening of an international scientific conference as early as possible in 1955, under the auspices of the United Nations.

As such things go, these plans developed quickly. On December 4, 1954, resolution 810 (IX) was adopted unanimously by the General Assembly. In part, the resolution read: "that an international technical conference of Governments should be held, under the auspices of the United Nations, to explore means of developing the peaceful uses of atomic energy through international co-operation." Details about the location and time for the conference were delegated to the secretary general of the United Nations.

The then secretary general Dag Hammarskjöld brought to the planning activities not only the prestige of his position but also his wisdom. An advisory committee was formed to work with Hammarskjöld; and, at his insistence, the members of the committee were eminent scientists. Rabi was the United States representative on Hammarskjöld's committee.*

The first meeting of the advisory committee was held in New York from January 17 to 28, 1955. According to Rabi,

> The committee met to decide what sort of conference it should be. The great danger was that it might lead to something terrible. ... We had to have a conference that was run by countries, but with a kind of agreement that nothing political would enter the rules of procedure. That was a terrific thing to arrange. It took a full week for twenty-two simple rules of procedure to be agreed on. The Russians opposed us at every turn, and when the final vote came it was counted: "One, two, three, four, five, six"—and then Ham-

*Other members of the committee were: Sir John Cockcroft (Great Britain); D. V. Skobeltzin (Soviet Union); Homi Bhabba (India); W. B. Lewis (Canada); Bertrand Goldschmidt (France); and J. Costa Ribeiro (Brazil).

marskjöld turned to the Russian delegation and said, "You see, the vote is against you," and the chief Soviet delegate said, "But I haven't voted." Hammarskjöld apologized profusely, and the Russians voted with the rest of the countries. To this day, I don't know whether the Russians' objections to the rules of procedure were an attempt to be able to insinuate politics into the conference or were a test of the sincerity of the West to hold the conference. But, believe me, the effort was tremendous.[20]

The rules of procedure were adopted. Also at the first, long meeting of the advisory committee, a topical agenda was drafted. It was decided that the conference would be held in Geneva, Switzerland, at the Palais des Nations, from August 8 to 20, 1955.

There was early disagreement among the members of the advisory committee over who should fill the position of president of the conference. Rabi conferred with Strauss. Looking directly into his eyes, Rabi said, "I guess we've killed cock robin." Did Strauss catch the allusion? According to Rabi, he did:

> He knew . . . that bastard. The obvious president would have been Robert Oppenheimer. A great international reputation, he could have played the role beautifully. What a terrible thing to have done to a man like Oppenheimer. He was a tremendous national asset. In Europe he'd be followed around wherever he was. In this country, I'd be sitting in some airport with him and people would come up for autographs; they recognized him. He was that kind of an attractive charismatic figure. He was a scientist, but he was also a humanist and was against the atomic bomb in every way. It was a great loss to the United States not to have him to back as president.

Rabi supported Homi Bhabba for president; and, on February 1, Hammarskjöld announced that the distinguished nuclear physicist from India would be appointed president of the conference.

Through the course of the planning for the conference, Rabi and Hammarskjöld became friends. The secretary general looked forward to the meetings with the advisory committee and enjoyed his association with the scientists who were members of it. He, too, came to recognize that the exchange of scientific information could be an effective means of improving the political atmosphere and reducing mistrust and suspicion

—a recognition reinforced by the success of the conference itself. Later, in his 1957–58 annual report, Hammarskjöld wrote:

> It may be worth considering whether those elements of the problem [disarmament] lending themselves to objective study by experts in science and technology . . . might not be singled out for separate treatment . . . in a manner similar to that recently tried in Geneva. Certainly, such an approach . . . might help to improve the atmosphere and clarify many of the problems.[21]

Sometime in early 1955, the apathy on the part of scientists turned to enthusiasm. When American scientists were invited to submit papers to the U.S. government for presentation at the conference, over 1,000 papers were submitted in a very short time. That first International Conference on the Peaceful Uses of Atomic Energy "made a very great difference in the whole idea of atomic secrets," Rabi has said. "We and the Russians were forced to declassify a whole field of nuclear physics and technology in order to take a position at the conference. Declassifying the papers one-by-one would have taken forever. We simply opened up the field."[22] Altogether, 1,132 papers were presented in Geneva at the ICPUAE; there were more than 3,600 participants from 73 different countries. According to Rabi, "[this conference] introduced a human as well as a scientific connection. . . . The scientists met, they got to know one another, and in this way they were able to influence their own governments. I think it changed the whole direction of things."[23] Hammarskjöld considered the conference to be "one of the most important events in the postwar world."[24]

The Russians were also impressed by the conference. After the conference, Professor Vladimir Veksler, a prominent Russian scientist and co-inventor of the synchrocyclotron, made a speech carried by Moscow Radio and beamed to Eastern European countries. In the speech, Veksler said:

> The international scientific conference called in Geneva to deliberate on the peaceful uses of atomic energy, was not only the first truly great international conference in the field of physics . . . it was a conference of scientists unique in history. . . . The circle of topics discussed was very wide. . . . The debates were not confined to sessions of the special groups. In my opinion very fruitful conversations were held in the lobbies and in private within the narrow

circle of experts from various countries. . . . The debates were friendly in tone. . . . It is to be noted with satisfaction that the scientists of the world easily found a common language. . . . The participants of the conference paid constant and great attention to contributions by Soviet delegates. . . . I by no means wish to claim that the contributions of scientists of other countries . . . were less significant than ours. On the contrary, many were most successful. The value of the conference lay precisely in that it fostered an enrichment of knowledge on both sides. . . . Our scientists and engineers were unanimous in their praise for the report of the U.S. scientist, Dr. [Walter H.] Zinn. . . . Most noteworthy were the exhibitions staged by the Western countries, and the U.S. exhibition in particular. Altogether, I consider the Geneva Conference a tremendous success. It has opened up splendid perspectives toward the peaceful utilization of atomic energy.[25]

"If [Veksler's] speech, delivered as propaganda, was representative of the impressions of the Russian scientists, as I know it was ours," said Rabi in December 1955, "I am satisfied with the results of the Conference in helping to re-establish the worldwide community and communion of scientists."[26] Rabi's satisfaction was widely shared; in fact, the 1955 ICPUAE was deemed such a success that the United Nations has sponsored three such conferences since then (1958, 1964, and 1971). Recently asked to look back over his many activities and to identify those in which he takes particular pride, Rabi answered "Number one is the Baruch proposal (see pages 198–99). Another thing of which I am *very* proud and that is the Conference on the Peaceful Uses of Atomic Energy in Geneva."

Rabi was not the first scientist to serve government. There is, indeed, a long history to the relationship between science and government: before Rabi served the United States, Archimedes served Syracuse; and before James Killian served Eisenhower, the Danish astronomer Tycho de Brahe served the Bohemian king Rudolph II. This long history notwithstanding, the current role played by science in the affairs of state is both qualitatively and quantitatively different from that of earlier eras. During the Second World War, the proximity fuse, microwave radar, and the atomic bomb were developed. The bomb ended the war abruptly; however, without radar, the conflict might have come to an end—in favor of the Axis powers—before the bomb was developed. The question is, Would any of these developments have taken place if England's Sir Henry Tizard and the United States's Vannevar Bush had not had access to men of power?

In the years immediately following the war, physicist and poet were united in their concern about questions of policy. The issues of government were issues of science, and the issues of science were issues of passion. During the H-bomb discussions, Truman received the advice of the General Advisory Committee of the Atomic Energy Commission. This committee, comprised of eminent scientists, was charged with advising governmental leaders on matters concerned with atomic energy. Their report conveyed the hope, expressed in compelling language, that an unqualified commitment could be made *against* the development of the thermonuclear bomb. In their minority report, Fermi and Rabi provided the opportunity for Truman to be a statesman. They called for the President "to invite the nations of the world to join . . . in a solemn pledge not to proceed in the development or construction of weapons in [the thermonuclear] category."[27] With the backing of the GAC, Truman could have adopted such a course of action. From the other direction came the urgent call for a crash program, a commitment to build the Super comparable in scope "to that which produced the first atomic weapons"—a course of action for which Lewis Strauss, then a commissioner of the Atomic Energy Commission, was the spokesman. This position was supported by physicists Teller, Lawrence, and Alvarez as well as by some members of Congress who hinted that they would not accept anything other than a full-fledged crash program. Between these two extremes was the Joint Chiefs of Staff, who advocated a development program for the Super but saw no reason for a crash program.

Truman's decision for an all-out effort to build the H-bomb can be praised or damned in accordance with one's convictions. As for Rabi:

> I never forgave Truman for buckling under the pressure. He simply did not understand what it was about. As a matter of fact, after he stopped being President he still didn't believe that the Russians had a bomb in 1949. He said so. So for him to have alerted the world that we were going to make a hydrogen bomb at a time when we didn't even know how to make one was one of the worst things he could have done. It shows the dangers of this sort of thing.[28]

Other observers agree with Rabi's claim that Truman did not understand. For example, McGeorge Bundy has written, "As for President

Harry Truman, I conclude that his way of deciding large matters was badly designed for this [H-bomb] case. . . . The President's duty in nuclear matters is not simply to decide; it is to understand for himself."[29]

"He didn't have his own scientific people to consult and give him an impartial picture," concludes Rabi. Would Truman have made the decision differently if he had had his own Vannevar Bush? The only answer that can be given is "Possibly." At least a trusted advisor could have brought dispassionate enlightenment to the alternatives. Certainly, an advisor could have helped Truman understand the nature of the weapon itself, and then, the grave implications of building it versus not building it could have been weighed objectively.

In September 1949, the Russians sent tremors through the world when they exploded their first atomic bomb. On October 4, 1957, they did it again—this time with the 184-pound satellite called "Sputnik." Sputnik was in orbit, and many Americans were alarmed. Eisenhower later wrote, "This feat precipitated a wave of apprehension throughout the Free World."[30]

At that time, Rabi was the chairman of the Science Advisory Committee of the Office of Defense Mobilization (SAC of the ODM). This committee was created in the wake of the hydrogen-bomb decision, on April 20, 1951, under the chairmanship of Dr. Oliver Buckley, retiring president of Bell Laboratories. President Truman stated that this new committee would be "in a direct position to participate in the mobilization program as it affects scientific research and development."[31] While this committee could do what it wanted to do and examine what it wanted to examine, it had little influence. There were two reasons for this situation. First, Buckley's policy was to wait until advice was specifically sought before he would activate the committee. Second, the committee did not have direct access to the President but, rather, reported to the director of ODM who, as a member of the National Security Council, could relay information to the President. "Something one learns quite early in the advisory business," Rabi has said, "you can sit there in the best offices, but people won't come for advice. You have to be in the position that things come across your desk." Two examples serve to illustrate the ineffectiveness of the SAC of the ODM. The first was the Oppenheimer affair. "I share the feeling," Killian has written, "that Eisenhower was badly advised and made a grievous mistake in his handling of the case. . . . He [Eisenhower] did come to realize that some of the early scientific advice he had received had been one-sided, coming as it did principally from the scientists of whom Edward Teller became the symbol and for whom Admiral Strauss had been the channel."[32] What if the SAC of the ODM had had direct access to Eisenhower in 1953–54 and could have represented a more balanced view of the scientific community and of the facts themselves? It is possible that the Oppenheimer drama would have ended on a somewhat happier note.

Another example where the ODM might have had greater influence was that of earth satellites. During this time, the United States planned to orbit a small satellite as part of the International Geophysical Year. Rabi sent a letter to Arthur Flemming, director of ODM, expressing the opinion of the committee that the Vanguard satellite destined for orbit was too small. Calling both for larger satellites and for a program of space exploration, the committee members based their recommendations on the view that the United States would be facing competition in these areas. Rabi, in his letter, requested that Flemming convey these ideas to President Eisenhower. If Flemming took up the matter with Eisenhower, he did so in a manner that produced no results. Eisenhower did nothing—then. If the SAC of the ODM had direct access to Eisenhower, it is possible that much of the psychological trauma as well as the political fallout associated with Sputnik could have been averted.

> There were two problems created by the Soviet *Sputnik* [wrote Eisenhower]. The first, a short-term one, was to find ways of affording perspective to our people and so relieve the current wave of near-hysteria; the second, to take all feasible measures to accelerate missile and satellite programs. To discuss these matters I asked the members of the Scientific Advisory Committee of the Office of Defense Mobilization, a group of distinguished scientists, to meet with me.[33]

The meeting between Eisenhower and the SAC took place on October 15, 1957, eleven days after Sputnik had been launched. On the previous day, October 14, Rabi had called the SAC into session. "We bandied about what should be changed," said Hans Bethe. "Much of this was on defense, some of it was on science in general."[34] When the President opened the meeting, Rabi and the members of the SAC were ready. Eisenhower has recalled the meeting: "I said that I had invited them in order to learn what ideas and proposals they might like to advance. The question before us was plain: How could all the many governmental and government-connected scientific activities be best supported so as to achieve the best kind of progress? Dr. Isidor Rabi, of Columbia University, was the first to reply."[35]

David Z. Beckler, whose life was to be directly influenced by the events of the day, was there with the President, Rabi, and the other members of the SAC. He took these notes:

Rabi ... remarked spontaneously that from the committee's point of view, most matters of policy coming before the President have a very strong scientific component. Not only a technical but a scientific point of view plays a role. He did not see around the President any person who would help keep the President aware of the scientific considerations, as in the economic field. He did not see the scientific point of view put forward in a way to give daily opportunities to influence attitudes. He [Rabi] observed that science was, in a sense, being called in after the fact.

The President said that he agreed with this, and that more than once he had felt this need. But the lines of organization were frozen. The Office of the President was crammed and inadequate. Congress has traditionally been jealous with respect to this Office. However, something could probably be worked out.[36]

Hans Bethe was one of the SAC members at that memorable October meeting at the White House:

One hour will always be in my mind, and that is the hour when we presented to President Eisenhower the need to have a stronger committee, and that's when we got the "P" in PSAC. It was a memorable hour. Rabi was on very good terms with Eisenhower, partly because Eisenhower had been president at Columbia. Rabi was our spokesman. Rabi presented our [the SAC] case to the President so concisely and so convincingly, six major points in one hour, and Eisenhower immediately understood. This was an unforgettable hour, completely changed my opinion of President Eisenhower. I found that he was extremely quick, understanding almost immediately what we were after, and acted on it. He immediately said to his adjutant, "You see that this is done."[37]

Among the recommendations made by Rabi and the SAC were that the President should have a science advisor: "a personal, unbiased advisor," as Rabi later expressed it, "who can find all the available evidence, analyze it, and lay it before the President in a form which he can digest and apply, in formulating his decision."[38] Rabi stressed that this advisor should be a person the President could live with easily, and further recommended that the science advisor should have a group of scientists to whom he could go for counsel and advice:

> [This] group of scientists, a President's Science Advisory Committee (PSAC), which [the advisor] may or may not chair but which consists of informed people and people of judgment who, although not directly connected with the President on a day-to-day fashion, understand his problems . . . and understand that they're there as advisors and not as experts on particular narrow fields. If those people are of that caliber and also have the reputations I've described, then the President has something to fall back on and is protected in following a course of action which he would not have the time, or sometimes maybe even the capacity, to comprehend fully, to comprehend the ramifications of this course of action in interrelationship with others.[39]

In a television address on November 7, 1957, Eisenhower announced the creation of the Office of Special Assistant to the President for Science and Technology. James R. Killian, Jr., then president of MIT, was named to fill the new position. Two weeks later, Eisenhower reconstituted the SAC of the ODM as PSAC, the President's Science Advisory Committee, and placed it directly under the White House as part of the President's official family. Rabi resigned his chairmanship of the SAC so that Killian could become chairman of the new PSAC. New members were added, bringing the membership of PSAC to eighteen. George Kistiakowsky, the second scientist to hold the position of Special Assistant to the President for Science and Technology, described PSAC as a "coherent thinking machine."[40]

Did Eisenhower ask Rabi to be his science advisor? "No," responded Rabi. "I would have found it very hard to take. I think it is probably beyond my capacity. I am not of that temperament. I know my own weakness. I wouldn't have taken it if he'd offered it to me. He didn't offer it to me."

Through the Eisenhower administration, the PSAC flourished. They quickly laid the groundwork for the nuclear test ban treaty (which came to fruition during the Kennedy administration); they created NASA; they supported the creation of federal programs to strengthen science education throughout the country; they assessed a whole range of military programs that were proposed by the different services.

PSAC owed its immediate success to a combination of factors. It was created at a time when a variety of nuclear, military, and space-related problems made the advice of scientists an important element in policy decisions. Also, scientists still enjoyed the "fair-haired" status they had achieved as a function of their wartime accomplishments. Finally, Eisenhower liked scientists and was accessible to them almost to the end of his life. In 1968, for example, there were hints circulating that nuclear weapons might be used in Vietnam. George Kistiakowsky called James Killian and Rabi to express his concern and to suggest that the three of them urge Eisenhower to use his influence against such military policies that would permit the use of nuclear weapons. Killian, Kistiakowsky, and Rabi sent a telegram to Eisenhower, who acted immediately: a few days later, each man received a telephone call from the secretary of defense, Robert McNamara, who had been requested by President Lyndon Johnson to assure them that the use of nuclear weapons was not under consideration. Killian saw Eisenhower a few months before his death. The former President asked about "my scientists" and said, "You know, Jim, this bunch of scientists was one of the few groups that I encountered in Washington who seemed to be there to help the country and not themselves."[41] Eisenhower, a Republican, worked smoothly with the scientists who were largely Democratic, and neither their political persuasion nor their erudition posed a threat to him.

While PSAC, under Jerome Weisner, functioned well in the early part of the Kennedy administration, it was less influential toward the end. Then, as the Vietnam War intensified during the Johnson and Nixon administrations, the scientists came to be identified by Johnson and particularly by Richard Nixon as part of an intellectual community critical of the war policies. By 1973, when Nixon eliminated the White House science advisory structure, he regarded scientists as adversaries. President Gerald Ford re-established the Office of Science and Technology Policy, Executive Office of the President, on May 11, 1976. During the Carter administration, science advisors were active, on a modest scale, once again.

While the White House science advisory machinery remains intact in the administration of Ronald Reagan, its influence is meager. It is hard to imagine a program where objective, analytical advice would be more valuable than it would be in the President's proposed Strategic Defense

Initiative, or "Star Wars," program. Yet this program provides a prime example of the differences between PSAC during the late 1950s and early 1960s and the White House Science Council of the Reagan years. President Reagan presented his proposal for an "impenetrable shield" on March 23, 1983. The council, not having been informed about the proposal, had no opportunity to discuss it. This fact was a contributing factor to the resignation of John Bardeen, two-time winner of the Nobel Prize in physics, from the White House Science Council.[42] The White House Science Council does not seem to function as a "thinking machine" in the Reagan administration.

Many reasons can be cited for the diminution of influence of scientists within the executive branch of government. One reason is the low caliber of the scientists recent administrations have employed. ("A degree in chemistry or physics doesn't make you a scientist.") Eisenhower's PSAC was constituted of men with global reputations (see appendix B, page 266). There was Edwin Land, president and founder of the Polaroid Corporation, an "authentic genius";[43] there was Hans Bethe, Nobel laureate, "a man of tremendous intellect, an idealist with a whiplash of a mind."[44] Bethe, a calculator without peer, could reduce many a vague idea to hard numbers. There was Edward Purcell, Nobel laureate, a man who "did not speak often, but when he did, there would be enormous silence in the room because everybody knew that whatever he said was going to be worth listening to with careful attention."[45] Every man on the committee, from Robert Bacher to Jerrold Zacharias, was an accomplished intellect.

Rabi provides another reason for the decline in the effectiveness of the PSAC concept:

[As the years passed], we were confronted with problems that had strong economic and social overtones and they [PSAC members] said, "We ought to have help on this, we ought to have some social scientists." It was a dreadful mistake. I knew if I fought against it, I would have lost. It doesn't matter whom they selected, even somebody as good as James Tobin who just won the Nobel Prize in economics, any congressman or senator can argue with them. The economist or the social scientist doesn't know anything the senator doesn't know, or at least, anything that they don't feel confident about. No senator is going to argue with me about physics, but they will argue with any social scientist. So we lost that aura, we lost that mystique. It was the beginning of the end. It eroded our self-confidence because what the social scientists have to contribute to social questions wasn't fresh.

Rabi continued as an active member of PSAC through 1961. Since that time, he has been a consultant-at-large for the committee. While he is proud of the accomplishments of the first PSAC and of its influence, the influence of science itself did not penetrate into the policy-making apparatus as deeply as he would have wished. As always, he sees the universal culture as a means for promoting international understanding. In an article, "The President and His Scientific Advisors," Rabi expressed his fundamental belief:

A great deal of the international prestige of the United States has come about because of the high level of scientific achievement in the United States in the World War II and postwar years. This prestige is something that is very important to preserve in foreign relations. It is a very important asset to trade on—it's very attractive, one of the most attractive portions of the whole American image abroad. We have on the one side this tremendous military power, and this is not the sort of thing we would like to use very much; but implicit in it is the prestige of the scientific achievement which is universally respected and desired on all sides. This is one branch of American power which is not readily understood by the political mind. The Department of State, for example, considering the personnel which goes in there, service officers, and even the political appointees, have not adequately understood the scientific community, the domestic scientific community—have not understood how to use it. This is a very important element in American policy which has been used very successfully sometimes and has been very much neglected at other times. But, as a source of influence and power, it is equivalent to a great deal of military hardware; and it's also something to trade.

Thus there is this very important other element of presenting the United States not just as a great and powerful giant but as this very highly cultivated country, in fields of culture which are universally respected and which all nations desire. So the Science Advisor has to have close connection with the President and the State Department to aid them in utilizing this fundamental strength, not just in horse-trading or haggling but in an actual important element of respect for our country, so that where the United States sits is the head of the table, not only because of power, military or commercial, but also because of this highly prized intellectual capacity and achievement.[46]

To Rabi's sorrow, the science advisors and the advisory apparatus have not been successful in promoting the use of our culture as a fundamental strength:

> We need to have people around the President who love the United States more than they hate the Russians. I had an experience when I was the U.S. Representative on the Science Committee of the United Nations. We were getting ready for the International Conference on the Peaceful Uses of Atomic Energy. I went to see [Henry Cabot] Lodge, who was the Ambassador to the United Nations. He gave me a lecture, how to be tough: don't shake hands with them, don't be friendly, that sort of thing. I thanked him very much. The difference between us was that I wanted [the conference] to succeed. What he wanted was to show that he was a real honest-to-goodness anti-Communist who hated Russia.
>
> We consider ourselves superior to the Russians in every way, morally, culturally, scientifically; therefore, it's our job to understand them; not to imitate them and not to imitate them in their worst features. It's what I have against Israel: they had the West Bank for ten years, in control, and they didn't succeed to understand the inhabitants or to make the inhabitants understand Israel. We—and the Israelis—feel we're a superior culture. All right, show it! Not just that you're stronger.

In Rabi's judgment, the policies of the United States have, since the Second World War, been determined as much by what we, as a nation, stand against as by what we stand for. The principles we stand for are powerful. They have encouraged inquiry to be pursued freely and have allowed science to prosper. If we believe in our own culture and if we have the strength of our convictions, it is time to demonstrate this belief in terms other than through armaments. When asked how this is to be done, Rabi talks about the universal culture of science.

CHAPTER

18

Wisdom: Toughness with a Smile

> Wisdom is inseparable from knowledge; it is
> knowledge plus a quality which is within a
> human being. Without it knowledge is dry, al-
> most unfit for human consumption, and dan-
> gerous in application. The absence of wisdom is
> clearly noticeable; the learned fool and the edu-
> cated bore have been with us since the begin-
> nings of recorded history. Wisdom adds flavor,
> order, and measure to knowledge. Wisdom
> makes itself most manifest in the application of
> knowledge to human needs.
>
> —I. I. RABI

TODAY Rabi is an elder statesman, the dean of American physics. But
Rabi was an elder statesman forty years ago, a gray eminence even
then.

He was a relatively young man (in his forties) when Rabi made his
trips to Los Alamos and consulted with Oppenheimer. On one of these
visits he told Richard Feynman to contemplate the neutron. Feynman
answered, in essence, "If Rabi says to contemplate on the neutron, I'll
contemplate on the neutron," and added, "He already was sort of an
elder statesman."[1]

RABI: Scientist and Citizen

The primary attribute of an elder statesman is wisdom. Throughout his adult life, Rabi built a reputation by virtue of his infectiously buoyant, albeit tough-minded, wisdom.

In 1955, Rabi was given an honorary degree by Harvard University and, later that year, was the Morris Loeb Lecturer on Physics at Harvard. Rabi's Loeb Lecture, on October 21, 1955, was entitled "Science and the Humanities." This address speaks as powerfully to us today as it did then:

> How can we hope to obtain wisdom, the wisdom which is meaningful in our own time? . . . Not the wisdom of the Monday morning quarterback, but the wisdom of the man of balanced judgment based on knowledge, the wisdom of the man with the well-stored mind and feeling heart as expressed in word and action. . . . We certainly cannot attain it [such wisdom] as long as the two great branches of human knowledge, the sciences and the humanities, remain separate and even warring disciplines. . . . Only by the fusion of science and the humanities can we hope to reach the wisdom appropriate to our day and generation.[2]

In his address, Rabi acknowledges the contemporary argument that science is inherently simple while the study of man is inherently complicated. But, he points out:

> Wise laws for government and personal conduct were known in remotest antiquity. The literature of antiquity shows a profound understanding of human natures and emotions. Not man but the external world was bewildering. The world of nature instead of seeming simple was infinitely complex and possessed of spirits and demons. . . . To revere and trust the rational faculty of the mind, to allow no taboo to interfere in its operation, to have nothing immune from its examination is a new value which has been introduced into the world. The progress of science has been the chief agent in demonstrating its importance and riveting it into the consciousness of mankind. . . .
>
> To my mind, the value content of science or literary scholarship lies not in the subject matter alone, or even in greater part. It lies chiefly in the spirit and living tradition in which these disciplines are pursued. The spirit is almost always conditioned by the subject.

Science and the humanities are not the same thing; the subject matter is different and the spirit and tradition are different. Our problem in our search for wisdom in a contemporary world is to blend these two traditions in the minds of individual men and women. . . .

The greatest difficulty which stands in the way of a meeting of the minds of the scientist and the nonscientist is the difficulty of communication. . . . The mature scientist, if he has any taste in these directions, can listen with pleasure to the philosopher, the historian, the literary man, or even the art critic. There is little difficulty from that side because the scientist has been educated in our general culture and living in it on a day-to-day basis. He reads newspapers, magazines, books, listens to music, debates politics and participates in the general activities of an educated citizen. Unfortunately, this channel of communication is often a one way street. The nonscientist cannot listen to the scientist with pleasure and understanding. Despite its universal outlook and its unifying principle, its splendid tradition, science seems to be no longer communicable to the great majority of educated laymen.

Rabi concluded his 1955 Loeb Lecture with the following words:

Only by the fusion of science and the humanities can we hope to reach the wisdom appropriate to our day and generation. The scientists must learn to teach science in the spirit of wisdom, and in the light of the history of human thought and human effort, rather than as the geography of a universe uninhabited by mankind. Our colleagues in the nonscientific faculties must understand that if their teachings ignore the great scientific tradition and its accomplishments, however eloquent and elegant in their words, they will lose meaning for this generation and be barren of fruit. Only with a unified effort of science and the humanities can we hope to succeed in discovering a community of thought, which can lead us out of the darkness, and the confusion, which oppress all mankind.

Rabi's concern about the deep division between science and the humanities was discussed with Charles P. Snow in 1957 while Rabi was in a London hospital recovering from a heart attack. Two years later,

257

Snow further developed these ideas in his Rede Lectures and introduced the phrase that made him famous: "The Two Cultures."*

The schism between science and the humanities is particularly disturbing to anyone who seeks unity; and Rabi, his thinking so influenced by physics, sees a unified world.

The theoretical systems of physics such as Newtonian dynamics, thermodynamics, or quantum mechanics are, among other things, powerful organizational schemes. They bring together a diverse range of phenomena, they correlate factual information. Karl Popper, philosopher of science, refers to the theories of physics as nets to catch the world. The great physicists like Hans Bethe or Richard Feynman understand the few basic principles of physics so thoroughly that any question asked of them is immediately grasped and their response springs directly from their ability to use these principles as a bridge between the question and the appropriate answer.

In a similar, though in a much more general, sense, a few powerful principles seem to be the foundation of Rabi's thinking. These principles give a connectedness to his thoughts, his opinions, and his judgments. He can be asked a question that he has never been asked before, and his response will have shape and context. His thoughts are of a piece, anchored by these deep principles.

Principles of thought provide a framework that must retain its integrity as one confronts new knowledge, new information, new situations. When Rabi was a child, religion provided an all-embracing framework for thought. God, the creator of the world; God, the administrator of the world; God, the father of Abraham, Isaac, and Jacob—all of these, but more: this same God was a presence in the home: "God was present all the time. In conversation, not a paragraph—hardly a sentence—would go by without reference to God."[3]

For Rabi, this pervasive religious environment did two things. First, it instilled the awareness that there is a reality both greater than and external to himself. The universal God became the standard by which things could be judged and, in the process, the God concept itself became the standard by which he judged other standards. Second, the God concept developed in the child Rabi the *capacity* for rapturous awe, the *capacity* to be inspired, the *capacity* for aspiration.

When the young Rabi discovered Copernicus, he saw the majestic

*Many years later, Sir Charles and his son were visiting the Rabis in New York City. Helen heard Snow tell his son, "That man [Rabi], sitting on the sofa there, is the man who gave me the idea for the two cultures."

regularity of the planets in their orbital trajectories around the sun and the vision of Copernicus became a new source of inspiration. The rational need to embrace the planetary motions with understanding became a new source of aspiration. The stages of religion and science have similar underpinnings, so it is not difficult to recast the former into the latter. "They spring from the same thing," says Rabi, "from human aspiration, from the depths of the soul, from deep thinking and feeling."[4]

For Rabi, the recasting took place in his teenage years. When the recasting was complete, a new system of thought had taken its place but the aura of religion was still very much in evidence:

> The idea of God helps you to have a greater feeling for the mystery of modern physics. . . . I never thought of physics as a profession. . . . I never thought of doing it as a living. . . . But science was something I would follow and admire. And enjoy. I think that most of the people I knew who studied physics in my time, who were more or less my age, didn't have this attitude, quite. They were doing it as something that they liked to do. Some said, "It's fun." I always hated the idea that it was "fun." I knew other ways to have fun. Physics has a much deeper emotional quality for me than that.[5]

Science can be regarded as a growing body of knowledge that brings understanding to the phenomena of nature and that, from time to time, pays off with a practical bonus such as a laser, a fiber, or a vaccine. Science can also be regarded as a creative human activity that has as its principal objective the appeasement of the human spirit that comes with intellectual adventure. Taken in these senses, science is a large stage from which to observe the affairs of the world and the affairs of men; it is a living framework that can bring perspective, clarity, and even wisdom to the manifold issues that interest and excite, that plague and trouble peoples of the world. As Rabi has written:

> Every generation of mankind has to remake its culture, its values, its goals. Wisdom does not come in formulas, proverbs, or wise laws, but out of a living actuality. The past is important for understanding the present, but it is not the present. . . .[6]

Man is made of dust and to dust returneth, he lives in a universe of which he is also a part. He is free only in a symbolic sense; his nature is conditioned by the dust out of which he is made. To learn to understand himself he must learn to understand the universe in which he lives and of which he himself is a part.[7]

Mankind is puny and feeble under the heavens as long as it is ignorant. It is ignorant in so far as it is self-limited by dogma, custom, and most of all by fear, fear of the unknown. To science the unknown is a problem full of interest and promise; in fact, science derives its sustenance from the unknown; all the good things have come from that inexhaustible realm. Science is the greatest uncentralized, undirected cooperative effort of all time, not only among people of the same culture but also among people of the most diverse origins and cultures. Furthermore, the traditions of science provide us with a set of values and an ethic which are rational and therefore accessible to all men. The universal respect in which science is held by people who differ extremely in other matters indicates that the scientific tradition can become a means to bring nations of the world together for peace and cooperation.[8]

Science, the humanities, and the cultures of the world—Rabi's interest in these topics is no less intense in the middle 1980s than it was in 1955. At banquets, on television, and in print, Rabi has a platform. On successive days in December 1985, his ideas were featured in columns by Jimmy Breslin in the *New York Daily News* and by Anthony Lewis in the *New York Times*—different writers, with markedly different political convictions. However, these columnists both were inspired by their conversations with Rabi, thus exemplifying his vision of a world where the rational principles of science counteract the passions of culture, religion, and politics that tend to separate members of the human species.

Today Rabi enjoys the attention and the veneration that comes to the survivor of an age of heroes. Rabi was a contemporary of physicists who created the intellectual revolutions of twentieth-century physics, and his own contributions to the discipline are part of history, part of the unfolding future. An American physicist when American physics was ordinary, Rabi helped make American physics extraordinary. The many honors coming to him today recognize Rabi the physicist, Rabi of the MIT Radiation Laboratory, Rabi the statesman, and Rabi the wise counselor. In 1984, Bill Moyers featured Rabi on a television program aptly called "Rabi: Man of the Twentieth Century."

In September 1971, Rabi addressed the Fourth International Conference on the Peaceful Uses of Atomic Energy, held in Geneva, Switzerland. Not only did he look back to the first such conference that he had been instrumental in creating, but he also looked ahead to goals commanding dedication and commitment. His address ended with these words:

The exploration of modern science connects mankind most directly with the universe as a whole. From the basic laws of physics one can begin to understand the special properties of the various atomic species which make possible life itself, and the same basic laws extend universally from the most distant parts of space to the innermost fastnesses of matter of the infinitesimally small. The special properties of matter which make life possible turn out to be no accident, but rather a direct result of the most basic general laws of physics as manifested in quantum mechanics and relativity. From these studies we learn that man is unique and yet a part of totality, subject to universal laws. It is part of the glory of the race that these laws were discovered by mankind.

It has been stated that the proper study of mankind is man, but we now see that this cannot be approached narrowly but only through the whole, which is science. Mankind is the mind and the developing consciousness of the universe.

We can hope that if indeed we survive into the future, that men will realize deeply that their most noble goal is to understand themselves within the universe and that this goal will override all the petty and parochial aims that so disturb the peace and endanger mankind's future existence.[9]

I. I. Rabi, man of the twentieth century, still stands by these words.

Epilogue

BY I. I. RABI

THIS book closes an account of eighty-eight years of this brilliant twentieth century. No idea which existed eighty-eight years ago is untouched. All the basic ideas of science have been re-examined, enlarged, and brought out in new and more powerful forms. Relativity, quantum mechanics, and genetics have been transformed from inspiring revelations and now form a part of the everyday tools of the working scientist. These sciences have become more like technology. This intellectual equipment plus the powerful instrumentalities which have been devised for further exploration could give us the means for a pause—a pause for assimilation. Perhaps some might think that this is a time for reflection, a time for assimilation of scientific ideas and achievements into the general stream of Western culture.

To my way of thinking, the time for reflection is never the now at the end of a period of great accomplishment. People of the present get to be so impressed with the past, with the unbelievable achievements of their ancestors, that the ideas of the past become hardened into dogma. That is when application drives out innovation.

Physics is now a very mature science and may be losing its attraction to young Americans of eager minds. Of this we must beware in our teaching. Understanding the eighteenth- and nineteenth-century physics can be a tremendous intellectual experience. In the twentieth century, physics begins to lose its hard, fructifying contact with the real world and human experience. The wonderful phenomena and discoveries have been made hard to reach except through an esoteric mathematical language. I feel my generation and the current generation have not devoted the time and profound effort to make the extraordinary phenomena of relativity and quantum mechanics accessible to the intelligent, educated person. I am sure it can be done because that's the way

I understand it. This failure to make the subject accessible to the general educated person has, to my mind, resulted in driving science, particularly physics, out of the secondary schools. Unless a great effort, a really great effort, is expended in this direction, the outlook for the future is bleak.

There is a ray of hope. Just as we learned a great deal from the Russian success of Sputnik, which awoke us to many deficiencies, the industrial success of the Asian world—Japan, Korea, Singapore—may spur us on to recover our depleted native intellectual élan. We can rely on nobody but ourselves to get us out of this intellectual slump. We must start with our schools, the training of our teachers, and the restoration of our ideals of learning for its own sake.

APPENDIX A

As in past years the committee found it difficult to choose from almost equally meritorious contributions in scientific fields so different that comparison and contrast were impossible.

Notwithstanding this difficulty, the committee reached a unanimous decision in favor of Dr. Rabi's research as outlined in his paper, "Radio Frequency Spectra of Atoms and Molecules" because it extends the range of scientific knowledge regarding atoms in a very significant way.

Dr. Rabi has not only discovered radiations, emitted by atoms, that are pitched lower than any hitherto observed but also devised a method of measuring them. Although they lie within the range of radio, they are too feeble by far for detection by even the most sensitive devices now known in radio.

Dr. Rabi's work has opened a way of measuring such subtle properties of atoms and molecules as the magnetism of their component parts a hundred times more accurately than was possible by any instrument available up to the present time. Of special significance is his conclusion that "there are no forces between the nucleus and the electrons because of their spins, other than those arising from the fact that the nucleus, as well as the electron, is a magnet."

APPENDIX B

*The President's Science Advisory Committee and its consultants,
as of December 1, 1957*

Dr. Robert F. Bacher, Professor of Physics, California Institute of Technology; and member of the National Academy of Sciences.

Dr. William O. Baker, chemist, Vice President for Research, Bell Telephone Laboratories; and member of the National Academy of Sciences.

Dr. Lloyd V. Berkner, physicist, President, Associated Universities, Inc.; and member of the National Academy of Sciences.

Dr. Hans A. Bethe, Professor of Physics, Cornell University; member of the National Academy of Sciences; and recipient of the Nobel Prize in Physics, 1967.

Dr. Detlev W. Bronk, physiologist, President, Rockefeller Institute for Medical Research; President, National Academy of Sciences; Chairman of the Board, National Science Foundation; and President, Rockefeller University.

Gen. James H. Doolittle, aeronautical engineer, Vice President, Shell Oil Company.

Dr. Hugh L. Dryden, physicist, Director, National Advisory Committee for Aeronautics; and member of the National Academy of Sciences.

Dr. James B. Fisk, physicist, Executive Vice President, Bell Telephone Laboratories; and member of the National Academy of Sciences.

Dr. Caryl P. Haskins, physiologist, President, Carnegie Institution of Washington; and member of the National Academy of Sciences.

Dr. Albert G. Hill, Professor of Physics, Massachusetts Institute of Technology; and Director of Research, Weapons Systems Evaluation Group.

Dr. James R. Killian, Jr., President, Massachusetts Institute of Technology; and member of the National Academy of Engineering.

Dr. George B. Kistiakowsky, Professor of Chemistry, Harvard University; and member of the National Academy of Sciences.

Dr. Edwin H. Land, physicist, President, Polaroid Corporation; and member of the National Academy of Sciences and the National Academy of Engineering.

Dr. Emanuel R. Piore, physicist, Director of Research, International Business Machines Corporation; and member of the National Academy of Sciences and the National Academy of Engineering.

Dr. Edward M. Purcell, Professor of Physics, Harvard University; member of the National Academy of Sciences; and recipient of the Nobel Prize in Physics, 1952.

Dr. Isidor I. Rabi, Professor of Physics, Columbia University; member of the National Academy of Sciences; and recipient of the Nobel Prize in Physics, 1944.

Dr. H. P. Robertson, Professor of Physics, California Institute of Technology; and member of the National Academy of Sciences.

Dr. Herbert Scoville, Jr., physical chemist, Assistant Director, Central Intelligence Agency.

Dr. Alan T. Waterman, physicist, Director, National Science Foundation.

Dr. Jerome B. Wiesner, engineer, Director, Research Laboratory of Electronics, Massachusetts Institute of Technology; and member of the National Academy of Sciences and the National Academy of Engineering.

Dr. Herbert F. York, physicist, Director, Livermore Laboratory, University of California.

Dr. Jerrold R. Zacharias, Professor of Physics, Massachusetts Institute of Technology; and member of the National Academy of Sciences.

NOTES

Any quotes in the text made by I. I. Rabi that are not noted come from interviews and conversations with the author that took place from September 1981 to August 1986.

Introduction. American Physics Becomes Pre-eminent

1. Spencer R. Weart, "The Physics Business in America, 1919–1940: A Statistical Reconnaissance," in *The Sciences in the American Context: New Perspectives,* ed. Nathan Reingold (Washington, D.C.: Smithsonian Institute Press, 1979), 295–358.
2. Daniel J. Kevles, *The Physicists* (New York: Vintage Books, 1979), 163.
3. J. Robert Oppenheimer, quoted in Stanley Coben, "The Scientific Establishment and the Transmission of Quantum Mechanics to the United States, 1919–32," *American Historical Review* 76 (1971): 455.
4. Robert Wayne Seidel, "Physics Research in California: The Rise of a Leading Sector in American Physics" (Ph.D. diss., University of California, Berkeley, 1978), 508.
5. Felix Bloch, interview by Charles Weiner, Stanford University, Stanford, Calif., 15 August 1968, transcript, Center for History and Philosophy of Physics, American Institute of Physics, New York, 14–15.
6. Werner Heisenberg, *Physics and Beyond* (New York: Harper & Row, 1971), 94.
7. See Kevles, *The Physicists,* chap. 15.
8. Ibid., 282.
9. Jeremy Bernstein, *Hans Bethe, Prophet of Energy* (New York: Basic Books, 1979), 43–44.
10. Lee A. DuBridge, in *A Tribute to I. I. Rabi: A Collection of Papers and Addresses Delivered at the Symposium in Pupin Laboratories on May 23, 1967* (New York: Department of Physics, Columbia University, 1970), 15.

Chapter 1. Copernicus Comes to Brooklyn

1. I. I. Rabi, interview by Edwin Newman, December 1972, transcript, William E. Wiener Oral History Library, New York, 4–5.
2. Israel Rubin, *Satmar: An Island in the City* (Chicago: Quadrangle Books, 1972), 92.
3. Jeremy Bernstein, "Profiles: Physicist," *New Yorker,* 13 October 1975, 48.
4. Ibid., 49.
5. Irving Howe, *World of Our Fathers* (New York: Harcourt Brace Jovanovich, 1976), 256.
6. Bernstein, "Profiles: Physicist," 48.
7. Gertrude Rabi, interview with author, New York, 14 February 1983.
8. Bernstein, "Profiles: Physicist," 49.
9. Ibid., 50.
10. For population data, see Alter F. Landesman, *Brownsville,* 2d ed. (New York: Bloch Publishing, 1971), 46.
11. G. Rabi, interview with author.
12. Bernstein, "Profiles: Physicist," 49.

13. I. I. Rabi, interview by Barbara Land, 12 November 1962, transcript, Columbia Oral History, Columbia University, New York, 4.

14. Bernstein, "Profiles: Physicist," 49–50.

15. Arthur Koestler, *The Sleepwalkers* (New York: Grosset & Dunlap, 1959), 254.

16. I. I. Rabi, interview by Stephen White, 11 February 1980, transcript, Rabi private collection, 20.

17. I. I. Rabi, interview by Newman, 16.

18. Hutchins Hapgood, *The Spirit of the Ghetto* (Cambridge, Mass.: Belknap Press/Harvard University Press, 1967), 18.

19. Landesman, *Brownsville,* 6–7.

20. I. I. Rabi, interview by Land, 8.

21. I. I. Rabi, interview by White, 31.

22. I. I. Rabi, interview by Newman, 24.

23. G. Rabi, interview with author.

24. I. I. Rabi, interview by Newman, 20.

25. I. I. Rabi, interview by Land, 6–7.

26. I. I. Rabi, interview by White, 24–25.

27. Ibid., 25.

28. Bernstein, "Profiles: Physicist," 53–54.

29. I. I. Rabi, interview by Land, 8.

30. I. I. Rabi, interview by Newman, 19.

31. I. I. Rabi, interview by White, 33.

Chapter 2. The Physicist Emerges from the Wilderness

1. Jeremy Bernstein, "Profiles: Physicist," *New Yorker,* 13 October 1975, 54.

2. Gertrude Rabi, interview with author, New York, 14 February 1983.

3. I. I. Rabi, interview by Edwin Newman, December 1972, transcript, William E. Wiener Oral History Library, New York, 27.

4. Ibid.

5. I. I. Rabi, interview by Barbara Land, 12 November 1962, transcript, Columbia Oral History, Columbia University, New York, 9.

6. Ibid., 10, 12.

7. Ibid., 11.

8. I. I. Rabi, interview by Newman, 26.

9. G. Rabi, interview with author.

10. I. I. Rabi, interview by Thomas S. Kuhn, 8 December 1963, transcript, American Institute of Physics, New York, 5.

11. I. I. Rabi, interview by Land, 16.

12. Ibid.

13. I. I. Rabi, interview by Kuhn, 6.

14. Henry Rowland, "The Highest Aim of the Physicist," in *The Physical Papers of Henry Augustus Rowland* (Baltimore: Johns Hopkins University Press, 1902), 669.

15. Henry Rowland, "A Plea for Pure Science," in *The Physical Papers of Henry Augustus Rowland* (Baltimore: Johns Hopkins University Press, 1902), 594.

16. I. I. Rabi, interview by Kuhn, 6.

17. I. I. Rabi, interview by Land, 18.

18. Ibid.

19. Bernstein, "Profiles: Physicist," 50.

20. I. I. Rabi, interview by Land, 18.

21. I. I. Rabi, interview by Kuhn, 7.

22. A. W. Browne, letter to Professor F. Bedell, 14 March 1923, Department of Physics, Cornell University, Ithaca, N.Y.

23. G. Rabi, interview with author.

24. Helen Rabi, interview with author, 15 February 1983.

25. G. Rabi, interview with author.

26. H. Rabi, interview with author.
27. I. I. Rabi, interview by Kuhn, 8.
28. I. I. Rabi, interview by Land, 19.
29. Ernest Merritt, letter to Professor William Fox, 18 June 1924, Department of Physics, Cornell University, Ithaca, N.Y.
30. I. I. Rabi, interview by Kuhn, 9.
31. Bernstein, "Profiles: Physicist," 58.
32. Ibid.
33. I. I. Rabi, interview by Land, 21.
34. I. I. Rabi, interview by Kuhn, 13.
35. Ibid., 16.
36. Bernstein, "Profiles: Physicist," 60.
37. I. I. Rabi, interview by Kuhn, 12.
38. Ibid., 12–13.
39. I. I. Rabi, interview by Land, 22.
40. I. I. Rabi, "On the Principal Magnetic Susceptibilities of Crystals," *Physical Review* 29 (1927): 174–85.
41. J. H. Van Vleck, an American physicist, became the authority on electric and magnetic susceptibilities. K. S. Krishnan is an Indian physicist whose career largely consisted of applying Rabi's dissertation method to the measurement of susceptibilities.
42. I. I. Rabi, interview by Kuhn, 12.

Chapter 3. Learning the Melody

1. James Franck and Gustav Hertz, "Über Zusammenstösse zwischen Elektronen und den Molekülen des Quecksilberdampfes und die Ionisierungs-spannung desselben," *Verhandlungen der Deutschen Physikalischen Gesellschaft Berlin* 16 (1941): 457–67.
2. Arnold Sommerfeld, "Zur Theorie des Zeeman-Effekts der Wasserstofflinien, mit einen Anhang über den Stark-Effekt," *Physikalische Zeitschrift* 17 (1916): 491–507.
3. Peter Debye, "Quantenhypothese und Zeeman-Effekt," *Physikalische Zeitschrift* 17 (1916): 507–12.
4. Louis Victor deBroglie, "Ondes et quanta," *Comptes Rendus* 177 (1923): 507–10.
5. Wolfgang Pauli, "Über den Zusammenhang des Abschlusses der Elektronengruppen im Atom mit der Komplex-struktur der Spektren," *Zeitschrift für Physik* 31 (1925): 765–85.
6. G. E. Uhlenbeck and S. A. Goudsmit, "Ersetzung der Hypothese vom unmechanischen Zwang durch eine Forderung bezüglich des innuen Verhaltens jedes einzelnen Elektrons," *Die Naturwissenshaften* 13 (1925): 953–54.
7. Werner Heisenberg, "Über quantentheoretische Umdeutung kinematischer und mechanischer Benziehungen," *Zeitschrift für Physik* 33 (1925): 879–93.
8. Erwin Schrödinger, "Quantisierung als Eigenwertproblem," *Annalen der Physik* 79 (1926): 361–76, 79 (1926): 489–527; 80 (1926): 437–90; 81 (1926): 109–39.
9. Ralph Kronig, quoted by I. I. Rabi, interview with author.
10. Fritz Reiche and Hans Rademacher, "Die Quantelung des symmetrischen Kreisels nach Schrödingers Undulationmechanik," *Zeitschrift für Physik* 39 (1926): 444–64; Hans Rademacher and Fritz Reiche, "Die Quantelung des symmetrischen Kreisels nach Schrödingers Undulationmechanik, II. Intensitätsfragen," *Zeitschrift für Physik* 41 (1926): 453–92.
11. Wolfgang Pauli, quoted in Max Jammer, *The Conceptual Development of Quantum Mechanics* (New York: McGraw-Hill, 1966), 326.
12. Werner Heisenberg, "Über den anschaulichen Inhalt der quantem theoretischen Kinematik und Mechanik," *Zeitschrift für Physik* 43 (1927): 172–98.
13. I. I. Rabi, interview by Thomas S. Kuhn, 8 December 1963, transcript, American Institute of Physics, New York, 20.
14. Rudolf Peierls, a German-born American physicist, most recently worked at Oxford University. Hans Bethe, also a German-born American physicist, was a student of Sommerfeld at Munich and came to Cornell University in 1935. He won the Nobel Prize for Physics in 1967.

15. Hans Bethe, interview with author, Harvard University, Cambridge, Mass., 23 November 1982.

16. I. I. Rabi, interview by Barbara Land, 12 November 1962, transcript, Columbia Oral History, Columbia University, New York, 25.

17. Daniel J. Kevles, *The Physicists* (New York: Vintage Books, 1979), 201.

18. There are many versions of this story. One version is in Hendrik B. G. Casimir, *Haphazard Reality: Half a Century of Science* (New York: Harper & Row, 1983), 85.

19. Jeremy Bernstein, "Profiles: Physicist," *New Yorker,* 13 October 1975, 73.

20. Ibid., 83.

21. I. I. Rabi, interview by Kuhn, 22.

22. I. I. Rabi, "Refraction of Beams of Molecules," *Nature* 123 (1929): 163–64; I. I. Rabi, "Zur Methode der Ablenkung von Molekularstrahlen," *Zeitschrift für Physik* 54 (1929): 190–97.

23. I. I. Rabi, interview by Kuhn, 22.

24. Ibid.

25. Bernstein, "Profiles: Physicist," 88.

26. I. I. Rabi, interview by Kuhn, 29–30.

27. Bernstein, "Profiles: Physicist," 88.

28. Ibid.

29. Helen Rabi, interview with author, 15 February 1983.

30. Paul Dirac, "The Quantum Theory of the Electron," *Proceedings of the Royal Society of London (A)* 117 (1928), 610–24; 118 (1928), 351–36.

31. Rockefeller Foundation, letter to I. I. Rabi, 16 January 1929, Rabi private collection.

32. Rockefeller Foundation, letter to I. I. Rabi, 29 January 1929, Rabi private collection.

33. Walter Heitler, a German-born physicist, was a professor at the University of Zürich; Fritz London, also a German-born physicist, went to Duke University, N.C., in 1929; Wheeler Loomis was a long-time chairman of the physics department at the University of Illinois, Champaign-Urbana; John Slater was a professor of physics at Massachusetts Institute of Technology in Cambridge; Leo Szilard, a Hungarian-born physicist, was professor of bio-physics at the University of Chicago; Eugene Wigner, a Hungarian-born physicist, was a professor of physics at Princeton University, N.J.; and John von Neumann, a Hungarian-born mathematician, was a professor of mathematics at the Institute for Advanced Studies, Princeton University.

34. Shirley Quimby, interview with author, Columbia University, New York, 23 July 1982.

Chapter 4. Classroom Lecturer

1. Edwin C. Kemble, The General Principles of Quantum Mechanics. Part I, *Reviews of Modern Physics* 1 (1929): 157–215; E. C. Kemble and E. L. Hill, The General Principles of Quantum Mechanics. Part II, Rev. Mod. Phys. 2 (1930): 1–58.

2. I. I. Rabi, interview by Morris Krieger, 28 March 1963, transcript, Columbia Oral History, Columbia University, New York, 110.

3. Jeremy Bernstein, "Profiles: Physicist," *New Yorker* 13 October 1975, 96.

4. I. I. Rabi, interview by Krieger, 110–11.

5. Shirley Quimby, interview with author, Columbia University, New York, 23 July 1982.

6. Sidney Millman, "Recollections of a Rabi Student of the Early Years in the Molecular Beam Laboratory," in *A Festschrift for I. I. Rabi,* vol. 38 of *Transactions of the New York Academy of Science,* ed. Lloyd Motz (New York: New York Academy of Sciences, 1977), 87.

7. Quimby, interview with author.

8. Frank Press, in *Celebration of the Fiftieth Anniversary of the Pupin Laboratories* (New York: Columbia University, n.d.), 49.

9. Leon Lederman, in *Celebration of the Fiftieth Anniversary of the Pupin Laboratories* (New York: Columbia University, n.d.), 123.

10. Irving Kaplan, conversation with author, Fall 1982.

11. Norman Ramsey, interview by Joan Safford, Harvard University, Cambridge, Mass., July 1960, transcript, Columbia Oral History, Columbia University, New York.

Notes

12. William Nierenberg, interview with author, La Jolla, Calif., 8 January 1982.
13. Quimby, interview with author.
14. Helen Rabi, interview with author, 15 February 1983.
15. John S. Rigden, "1981 Oersted Medal Citation—I. I. Rabi," *American Journal of Physics* 50 (1982): 971.

Chapter 5. Nearer to God

1. George Pegram, letter to I. I. Rabi, 14 May 1929, Rabi private collection.
2. J. M. B. Kellogg, letter to I. I. Rabi, November 1947, Rabi private collection.
3. F. W. Loomis and R. W. Wood, "The Rotational Structure of the Blue-Green Bands of Na₂," *Physical Review* 32 (1928): 223–36.
4. Harold Urey, "The Alternating Intensities of Na₂ Bands," *Physical Review* 38 (1931): 1074–75.
5. G. Breit and I. I. Rabi, "The Measurement of Nuclear Spin," *Physical Review* 38 (1931): 2082–83.
6. I. I. Rabi, "The Nuclear Spin of Caesium by the Method of Molecular Beams," *Physical Review* 39 (1932): 864.
7. I. I. Rabi and V. W. Cohen, "The Nuclear Spin of Sodium," *Physical Review* 43 (1933): 582–83.
8. I. I. Rabi, interview by Thomas S. Kuhn, 8 December 1963, transcript, American Institute of Physics, New York, 26.
9. V. W. Cohen, conversation with author, 1964.

Chapter 6. The Resonance Method

1. P. Kusch, "The Magnetic Dipole Moment of the Electron" (unpublished lecture), Kusch private collection.
2. Sidney Millman, "Recollections of a Rabi Student of the Early Years in the Molecular Beam Laboratory," in *A Festschrift for I. I. Rabi, Transactions of the New York Academy of Science,* ed. Lloyd Motz (New York: New York Academy of Science, 1977), 88.
3. Jeremy Bernstein, "Profiles: Physicist," *New Yorker,* 13 October 1975, 96.
4. I. I. Rabi, "On the Process of Space Quantization," *Physical Review* 49 (1936): 324–28.
5. I. I. Rabi, "Space Quantization in a Gyrating Magnetic Field," *Physical Review* 51 (1937): 652–54.
6. Jerrold Zacharias, interview with author, New York, 19 March 1982.
7. Polykarp Kusch, interview with author, University of Texas, Dallas, 12 November 1981.

Chapter 7. The Hydrogens: 1933–40

1. A version of this story is in Immanuel Estermann, "History of Molecular Beam Research: Personal Reminiscences of the Important Evolutionary Period 1919–1933," *American Journal of Physics* 43 (1975): 670.
2. Otto Frisch, interview by Thomas S. Kuhn, Cavendish Laboratory, Cambridge, England, 8 May 1962, transcript, Archive for the History of Quantum Physics Project, American Institute of Physics, New York.
3. R. Frisch and O. Stern, "Über die magnetische Ablenkung von Wasserstoffmolekulen und das magnetische Moment des Protons I.," *Zeitschrift für Physik* 84 (1933): 4–16; I. Estermann and O. Stern, "Über die magnetische Ablenkung von Wasserstoffmolekulen und das magnetische Moment des Protons II.," *Zeitschrift für Physik* 85 (1933): 17–24.
4. I. Estermann and O. Stern, "Über die magnetische Ablenkung von Wasserstoffmolekulen und das magnetische Moment des 'Deutons,' " *Zeitschrift für Physik* 86 (1933): 132–34.

5. Ibid., 132.

6. Estermann, "History of Molecular Beam Research," 661–71.

7. Jerrold Zacharias, interview with author, New York, 19 March 1982.

8. Ibid.

9. Ibid.

10. Ibid.

11. Shirley Quimby, interview with author, Columbia University, New York, 23 July 1982.

12. I. I. Rabi, J. M. B. Kellogg, and J. R. Zacharias, "The Magnetic Moment of the Proton," *Physical Review* 46 (1934): 157–63; I. I. Rabi, J. M. B. Kellogg, and J. R. Zacharias, "The Magnetic Moment of the Deuton," *Physical Review* 46 (1934): 163–65.

13. I. Estermann and O. Stern, "Magnetic Moment of the Deuton," *Nature* 133 (1934): 911.

14. Rabi, Kellogg, and Zacharias, "Magnetic Moment of the Proton," 163.

15. I. I. Rabi, interview by Thomas S. Kuhn, New York, 8 December 1963, transcript, American Institute of Physics, New York, 27.

16. J. M. B. Kellogg, I. I. Rabi, and J. R. Zacharias, "The Gyromagnetic Properties of the Hydrogens," *Physical Review* 50 (1936): 472–81.

17. I. Estermann, O. C. Simpson, and O. Stern, "The Magnetic Moment of the Proton," *Physical Review* 52 (1937): 535–45.

18. Jeremy Bernstein, "Profiles: Physicist," *New Yorker,* 13 October, 1975, 97.

19. J. M. B. Kellogg et al., "An Electrical Quadrupole Moment of the Deuteron," *Physical Review* 55 (1939): 318–19.

20. J. Schwinger, "On the Neutron-Proton Interaction," *Physical Review* 55 (1939): 235.

21. J. M. B. Kellogg et al., "The Magnetic Moments of the Proton and the Deuteron: The Radiofrequency Spectrum of H_2 in Various Magnetic Fields," *Physical Review* 56 (1939): 728–43.

22. J. M. B. Kellogg et al., "An Electrical Quadrupole Moment of the Deuteron: The Radiofrequency Spectra of HD and D_2 Molecules in a Magnetic Field," *Physical Review* 57 (1940): 677–95.

23. Hans Bethe, interview by Charles Weiner and Jagdish Mehra, 27–28 October 1966, transcript, Center for the History and Philosophy of Physics, American Institute of Physics, New York.

24. I. I. Rabi, "The Moments of the Light Nuclei," in Enrico Fermi et al., *Nuclear Physics* (Philadelphia: University of Pennsylvania Press, 1941), 23.

Chapter 8. The Human Side of Physics: The Birth of Radiofrequency Spectroscopy

1. Vivian Gornick, *Women in Science: Portraits from a World in Transition* (New York: Simon & Schuster, 1983), 36.

2. Polykarp Kusch, interview with author, University of Texas, Dallas, TX, November 12, 1981.

3. Polykarp Kusch, interview with author, November 12, 1981.

4. Jerrold Zacharias, interview with author, New York, NY, March 19, 1982.

5. Ibid.

6. Norman Ramsey, interview by Joan Safford, Harvard University, Cambridge, Mass., July 1960, transcript, Oral History Research Office of Columbia University, New York.

7. Jeremy Bernstein, "Profiles: Physicist," *New Yorker* 13 October 1975, 50.

8. Norman Ramsey, interview with author, Harvard University, Cambridge, Mass., 18 March 1982.

9. J. M. B. Kellogg, et al., "The Magnetic Moments of the Proton and the Deuteron: The Radiofrequency Spectrum of H_2 in Various Magnetic Fields," *Physical Review* 56 (1939): 728–43.

10. Ibid.

11. P. Kusch, S. Millman, and I. I. Rabi, "The Radiofrequency Spectra of Atoms: Hyperfine Structure and Zeeman Effect in the Ground State of Li^6, Li^7, K^{39} and K^{41}," *Physical Review* 57 (1940): 765–80.

Notes

Chapter 9. Rabi Goes to War

1. Hans Bethe, letter to I. I. Rabi, 30 September 1937, Rabi private collection.
2. P. P. Ewald, letter to I. I. Rabi, August 1938, Rabi private collection.
3. Edward Condon, letter to Herbert Stuart, 3 April 1940, Rabi private collection.
4. Jerrold Zacharias, interview with author, New York, 19 March 1982.
5. *Five Years at the Radiation Laboratory* (Cambridge, Mass.: MIT Press, 1947), 12.
6. James Phinney Baxter, III, *Scientists Against Time* (Boston: Little, Brown, 1946), 142.
7. Lee A. DuBridge, interview with author, Laguna Hills, Calif., 9 January 1982.

Chapter 10. The MIT Rad Lab

1. Ernest C. Pollard, *Radiation: One Story of the M.I.T. Radiation Laboratory* (Durham, N.C.: Woodburn Press, 1982), 39.
2. Jeremy Bernstein, "Profiles: Physicist," *New Yorker* 20 October 1975, 48.
3. Lee A. Dubridge, "Organization of the Radiation Laboratory," in *Index,* ed. Keith Henney, Rad Lab Series, vol. 28 (New York: McGraw-Hill, 1953), xvii.
4. Lee A. DuBridge, interview with author, Laguna Hills, Calif., 9 January 1982.
5. Daniel J. Kevles, *The Physicists* (New York: Vintage Books, 1979), 304.
6. Lee A. DuBridge, interview with author, 9 January 1982.
7. *Five Years at the Radiation Laboratory* (Cambridge, Mass.: MIT Press, 1947), 19.
8. Henry Guerlac (unpublished history of the Radiation Laboratory), no. CI-3, Massachusetts Institute of Technology Archives, Cambridge, Mass.

Chapter 11. Los Alamos Advisor

1. Spencer R. Weart and Gertrude Weiss Szilard, eds., *Leo Szilard: His Version of the Facts* (Cambridge, Mass., MIT Press, 1978), 54.
2. Vannevar Bush, *Piece of the Action* (New York: William Morrow, 1970), 59.
3. Hans Bethe, interview with author, Harvard University, Cambridge, Mass., 23 November 1982.
4. Robert A. Bacher, interview with author, California Institute of Technology, Pasadena, 11 January 1982.
5. J. Robert Oppenheimer, letter to James Conant, 1 February 1943, reprinted in Alice Kimball Smith and Charles Weiner, *Robert Oppenheimer: Letters and Recollections* (Cambridge, Mass.: Harvard University Press, 1980), 247.
6. J. Robert Oppenheimer, letter to James Conant, November 30, 1942, reprinted in Smith and Weiner, *Robert Oppenheimer,* 240.
7. J. Robert Oppenheimer, letter to I. I. Rabi, 26 February 1943, reprinted in Smith and Weiner, *Robert Oppenheimer,* 250.
8. Helen Rabi, interview with author, New York, 15 February 1983.
9. Felix Bloch, interview with author, Stanford University, Stanford, Calif., 9 November 1982.
10. Robert A. Bacher, interview with author.
11. J. Robert Oppenheimer, letter to I. I. Rabi, 26 February 1943, reprinted in Smith and Weiner, *Robert Oppenheimer,* 250.
12. Robert A. Bacher, interview with author.
13. Hans Bethe, interview with author.
14. Jeremy Bernstein, "Profiles: Physicist," *New Yorker* 20 October 1975, 53.
15. I. I. Rabi, "Approaches to the Atomic Age" (Address to the Boston Institute for Religious and Social Studies, Boston, 3 January 1946), reprinted as Chapter 12 in I. I. Rabi, *Science: The Center of Culture* (New York: World Publishing, 1970), 142.
16. Rabi, *Science: The Center of Culture* 138–39.

Chapter 12. Radar and the Bomb in War and in Peace

1. Ernest C. Pollard, *Radiation: One Story of the M.I.T. Radiation Laboratory* (Durham, N.C.: Woodbarn Press, 1982), 156.

2. Pollard, *Radiation,* 153–55.

3. Karl T. Compton, "Establishment of the Radiation Laboratory," in *Index,* ed. Keith Henney, Rad Lab Series, vol. 28 (New York: McGraw-Hill, 1953), viii–xv.

4. Edward M. Purcell, interview by Katherine Sopka, Harvard University, Cambridge, Mass., 8 June 1977, transcript, American Institute of Physics, New York, 25–26.

5. General Admiral Karl Doenitz, quoted in James Phinney Baxter, III, *Scientists Against Time* (Boston: Little, Brown, 1946), 35.

6. Henry Guerlac (unpublished history of the Radiation Laboratory), no. E1, Massachusetts Institute of Technology Archives, Cambridge, Mass.

7. Baxter, *Scientists Against Time,* 46.

8. Ibid., 46.

9. Guerlac, unpublished history, no. E-VII, 8.

10. Lee A. DuBridge, interview with author, Laguna Hills, Calif., 9 January 1982.

11. Ibid.

12. Ibid.

13. Purcell, interview by Katherine Sopka, 31.

14. The song, "It Ain't the Money," quoted by permission of the author and copyright owner, Arthur Roberts.

Chapter 13. The Part-Time Physicist

1. Jeremy Bernstein, "Profiles: Physicist," *New Yorker* 20 October 1975, 54.

2. Lee A. DuBridge, interview with author, Laguna Hills, Calif., 9 January 1982.

3. Bernstein, "Profiles: Physicist," 54.

4. I. I. Rabi, "Radiofrequency Spectroscopy" (Richtmyer Lecture, delivered at the joint meeting of the American Physical Society and the American Association of Physics Teachers, New York, 19 January 1945), Rabi private collection.

5. I. I. Rabi, "Oersted Response," *American Journal of Physics* 50 (November 1982): 972.

6. Polykarp Kusch, interview with author, University of Texas, Dallas, 12 November 1981.

7. J. E. Nafe, E. B. Nelson, and I. I. Rabi, "The Hyperfine Structure of Atomic Hydrogen and Deuterium," *Physical Review* 71 (1947): 914–15.

8. Silvan S. Schweber, "Shelter Island, Pocono, and Oldstone: The Emergence of American Quantum Electrodynamics after World War II," *Osiris* 2 (1986): 265–302.

9. Gregory Breit, "Does the Electron Have an Intrinsic Magnetic Moment?," *Physical Review* 72 (1947): 984.

10. W. W. Havens, Jr., I. I. Rabi, and L. J. Rainwater, "Interaction of Neutrons with Electrons in Lead," *Physics Review* 72 (1947): 636.

11. Bernstein, "Profiles: Physicist," 54.

12. Emilio Segrè, interview with author, Berkeley, Calif., 8 November 1982.

13. Stephen White, interview with author, New York, 5 October 1982.

Chapter 14. The Broader Stage

1. I. I. Rabi, "The Physicist Returns from the War," *The Atlantic,* October 1945, 107.

2. Daniel J. Kevles, *The Physicists* (New York: Vintage Books, 1979), 375.

3. Daniel S. Greenberg, *The Politics of Pure Science* (New York: New American Library, 1967), 65.

4. Jeremy Bernstein, "Profiles: Physicist," *New Yorker,* 20 October 1975, 62.

5. Greenberg, *Politics of Pure Science,* 100.

6. Norman F. Ramsey, interview by Joan Safford, Harvard University, Cambridge,

Notes

Mass., July 1960, transcript, Oral History Research Office of Columbia University, New York.

7. Kevles, *The Physicists,* 368.

8. Norman F. Ramsey, "Early History of Associated Universities and Brookhaven National Laboratory," Brookhaven Lecture Series, no. 55, 30 March 1966.

9. Charles Weiner, ed., *Exploring the History of Nuclear Physics,* American Institute of Physics Conference Proceedings, no. 7 (New York: American Institute of Physics, 1972), 76–77.

10. Greenberg, *Politics of Pure Science,* 132.

11. The song, "Take Away Your Billion Dollars," quoted by permission of the author and copyright holder, Arthur Roberts.

12. Weiner, *Exploring the History of Nuclear Physics,* 77–78.

13. Greenberg, *Politics of Pure Science,* 133.

14. Ibid., 134.

15. The song, "Take Away Your Billion Dollars," quoted by permission of the author and copyright holder, Arthur Roberts.

16. Greenberg, *Politics of Pure Science,* 122.

17. I. I. Rabi, *Science: The Center of Culture* (New York: World Publishing, 1970), 5.

18. Kevles, *The Physicists,* 369.

19. Harold A. Zahl, *Electrons Away: Tales of a Government Scientist* (New York: Vantage Press, 1968), 97.

20. Ibid., p. 97.

21. Ibid., p. 97.

22. Ibid, p. 98.

Chapter 15. "How Well We Meant"

1. Daniel J. Kevles, *The Physicists* (New York: Vintage Books, 1979), 302.

2. James R. Shepley and Clay Blair, *The Hydrogen Bomb* (New York: David McKay, 1954), 81.

3. Alice Kimball Smith, *A Peril and a Hope: The Scientists' Movement in America: 1945–47* (Chicago: University of Chicago Press, 1965), 251.

4. Spencer R. Weart and Gertrude Weiss Szilard, eds., *Leo Szilard: His Version of the Facts* (Cambridge, Mass.: MIT Press, 1978), 226.

5. Richard G. Hewlett and Oscar E. Anderson, Jr., *The New World: 1939–1946,* vol. 1 (University Park: Pennsylvania State University Press, 1962), 720.

6. J. Robert Oppenheimer, letter to James Conant, 21 October 1949, reprinted in Stanley A. Blumberg and Gwinn Owens, *Energy and Conflict: The Life and Times of Edward Teller* (New York: Putnam, 1976), 206–7. See also United States Atomic Energy Commission, *In the Matter of J. Robert Oppenheimer* (Cambridge, Mass.: MIT Press, 1970), 242–43.

7. Norman Moss, *Men Who Play God: The Story of the Hydrogen Bomb* (London: Victor Gollancz, 1968), 17.

8. David E. Lilienthal, *The Atomic Energy Years 1945–1950,* vol. 2 of *The Journals of David E. Lilienthal* (New York: Harper & Row, 1964), 581–82.

9. Jeremy Bernstein, "Profiles: Physicist," New Yorker, 20 October 1975, 77.

10. McGeorge Bundy, "The Missed Chance to Stop the Hydrogen Bomb," *New York Review of Books* 13 May 1982, 13–22.

11. Blumberg and Owen, *Energy and Conflict,* 213.

12. I. I. Rabi, quoted in Norman Moss, *Men Who Play God: The Story of the Hydrogen Bomb* (London: Victor Gollancz, 1968), 40.

13. Bernstein, "Profiles: Physicist," 78.

14. I. I. Rabi, quoted on "Our Times with Bill Moyer," Columbia Broadcasting System, 27 June 1983.

15. Ibid.

16. I. I. Rabi, quoted in Charles E. Claffey, "A Father of the A-Bomb Looks Back in Torment," *Boston Globe,* 15 April 1983, p. 1.

Chapter 16. Rabi and Oppenheimer

1. Philip M. Stern, *The Oppenheimer Case: Security on Trial* (New York: Harper & Row, 1969), 14.

2. Alice Kimball Smith and Charles Weiner, *Robert Oppenheimer: Letters and Recollections* (Cambridge, Mass.: Harvard University Press, 1980), 75.

3. J. Robert Oppenheimer, quoted in Stanley Coben, "The Scientific Establishment and the Transmission of Quantum Mechanics to the United States, 1919–32," *American Historical Review* 76 (1971): 455.

4. Nuel Pharr Davis, *Lawrence and Oppenheimer* (New York: Simon & Schuster, 1968), 23.

5. Jeremy Bernstein, "Profiles: Physicist," *New Yorker,* 13 October 1975, 84.

6. Wendell Furry, interview with author, Harvard University, Cambridge, Mass., 20 July 1983.

7. Philip Morrison, interview with author, Massachusetts Institute of Technology, Cambridge, 26 July 1983.

8. Smith and Weiner, *Robert Oppenheimer,* 150.

9. Stephen White, interview with author, New York, 5 October 1982.

10. C. P. Snow, *The Physicists* (Boston: Little, Brown, 1981), 107.

11. White, interview with author.

12. Abraham Pais, *Subtle Is the Lord* (New York: Oxford University Press, 1982), 11.

13. Morrison, interview with author.

14. Frank Oppenheimer, interview with author, San Antonio, Tex., 30 January 1984.

15. Wendell Furry, interview with author, 20 July 1983.

16. Oppenheimer, interview with author.

17. Furry, interview with author.

18. United States Atomic Energy Commission, *In the Matter of J. Robert Oppenheimer* (Cambridge: MIT Press, 1971), 11.

19. U.S. Atomic Energy Commission, *In the Matter of J. Robert Oppenheimer,* 13.

20. Arthur Holly Compton, *Atomic Quest: A Personal Narrative* (New York: Oxford University Press, 1956), 126.

21. J. Robert Oppenheimer, letter to I. I. Rabi, 26 February 1943, reprinted in Smith and Weiner, *Robert Oppenheimer,* 250–51.

22. Hans Bethe, interview with author, Harvard University, Cambridge, Mass., 23 November 1982.

23. Morrison, interview with author.

24. Felix Bloch, interview with author, Stanford University, Stanford, Calif., 9 November 1982.

25. Bethe, interview with author.

26. J. Robert Oppenheimer, letter to Charles Lauritsen, ca. 27 August 1945, reprinted in Smith and Weiner, *Robert Oppenheimer,* 299.

27. Bernstein, "Profiles: Physicist," 84.

28. Ibid.

29. White, interview with author.

30. Robert Jungk, *Brighter Than a Thousand Suns* (New York: Harcourt Brace & World, 1956), 241.

31. Davis, *Lawrence and Oppenheimer,* 220.

32. Stern, *Oppenheimer Case,* 129.

33. Barton Bernstein, "In the Matter of J. Robert Oppenheimer," *Historical Studies in the Physical Sciences,* vol. 12, no. 2 (Los Angeles and Berkeley: University of California Press, 1982), 222.

34. Stern, *Oppenheimer Case,* 300.

35. "The Hidden Struggle for the H-Bomb," *Fortune,* May 1953, 110.

36. U.S. Atomic Energy Commission, *In the Matter of J. Robert Oppenheimer,* 452.

37. Ibid., 453.

38. Ibid., 454.

39. Ibid., 456.

Notes

40. Ibid., 455.
41. Ibid.
42. Ibid., 459.
43. Ibid., 468.
44. Ibid., 465.
45. Ibid., 469–70.
46. Ibid., 472.
47. Ibid., 468.
48. *Time,* 28 June 1954, quoted in Stern, *Oppenheimer Case,* 359.
49. Barton Bernstein, "In the Matter of J. Robert Oppenheimer," 227.
50. *Life,* 13 December 1963, quoted in Barton Bernstein, "In the Matter of J. Robert Oppenheimer," 228.
51. Bloch, interview with author.
52. Bernstein, "Profiles: Physicist," 84.
53. Bloch, interview with author.
54. Smith and Weiner, *Robert Oppenheimer,* 9.
55. Albert Einstein, *Ideas and Opinions* (New York: Bonanza Books, 1954), 38.
56. Morrison, interview with author.
57. Jungk, *Brighter Than a Thousand Suns,* 333.
58. F. Oppenheimer, interview with author.

Chapter 17. Statesman of Science

1. I. I. Rabi, *Peaceful Uses of Atomic Energy,* vol. 1 (New York: United Nations, 1972), 79.
2. I. I. Rabi, *My Life and Times as a Physicist* (Claremont, Calif.: Claremont College, 1960), 11.
3. Ibid.
4. Robert Jungk, *The Big Machine* (New York: Charles Scribner, 1968), 29.
5. Ibid., 19.
6. Ibid., 39.
7. Walter H. C. Laws and Charles A. Thomson, *UNESCO—Purpose, Progress, Prospects* (Bloomington: Indiana University Press, 1957), 194.
8. Robert H. Ferrell, ed., *The Eisenhower Diaries* (New York: W. W. Norton, 1981), 176.
9. Hans Bethe, interview with author, Harvard University, Cambridge, Mass., 23 November 1982.
10. I. I. Rabi, interview by Edwin Newman, December 1972, transcript, William E. Wiener Oral History Library, New York, 155.
11. Dwight D. Eisenhower, *At Ease: Stories I Tell My Friends* (New York: Doubleday, 1967), 347–48.
12. Dwight D. Eisenhower, *Peace with Justice* (1961; reprint, New York: Columbia University Press, 1967), 63.
13. Ibid., 64.
14. Lewis L. Strauss, *Men and Decisions* (New York: Doubleday, 1962), 361.
15. Philip M. Stern, *The Oppenheimer Case: Security on Trial* (New York: Harper & Row, 1969), 114.
16. I. I. Rabi, "International Cooperation in Science," *Columbia Alumni News* 47 (December 1955): 9.
17. Rabi, "International Cooperation in Science," 9.
18. Ferrell, *Eisenhower Diaries,* 261.
19. *Proceedings of the International Conference on the Peaceful Uses of Atomic Energy,* vol. 16 (New York: United Nations, 1956), ix.
20. Jeremy Bernstein, "Profiles: Physicist," *New Yorker,* 20 October 1975, 92.
21. Brian Urquhart, *Hammarskjöld* (New York: Alfred A. Knopf, 1972), 321–22.
22. Bernstein, "Profiles: Physicist," 91.
23. Ibid., 91–92.

24. Joseph P. Lash, *Dag Hammarskjöld* (New York: Doubleday, 1961), 152.
25. Vladimir Veksler, quoted in Rabi, *My Life and Times*, 19.
26. Rabi, "International Cooperation in Science," 12.
27. Herbert F. York, *The Advisors: Oppenheimer, Teller, and the Super* (San Francisco: W. H. Freeman, 1976), 54.
28. Bernstein, "Profiles: Physicist," 78.
29. McGeorge Bundy, "The Missed Chance to Stop the Hydrogen Bomb," *New York Review of Books*, 13 May 1982, 20.
30. Dwight D. Eisenhower, *Waging Peace* (New York: Doubleday, 1965), 205.
31. David Z. Beckler, "The Precarious Life of Science in the White House," *Daedalus* 103 (1974): 117.
32. James R. Killian, Jr., *Sputnik: Scientists and Eisenhower* (Cambridge, Mass., MIT Press, 1977), 233.
33. Eisenhower, *Waging Peace*, 211.
34. Bethe, interview with author.
35. Eisenhower, *Waging Peace*, 211.
36. Beckler, "Precarious Life of Science," 118.
37. Bethe, interview by author.
38. Rabi, *My Life and Times*, 26.
39. I. I. Rabi, "The President and His Scientific Advisors," *Technology in Society* 2 (1980): 16.
40. Killian, *Sputnik*, 111.
41. Ibid., 241.
42. John Bardeen, letter, *Science*, 17 January 1986, 203.
43. Killian, *Sputnik*, 87.
44. Ibid., 154.
45. Ibid., 123.
46. Rabi, "The President and His Scientific Advisors," 17.

Chapter 18. Wisdom: Toughness with a Smile

1. Richard P. Feynman, interview by Charles Weiner, Altadena, Calif., 4 March 1966, transcript, American Institute of Physics, New York.
2. I. I. Rabi, "Science and the Humanities" (Loeb Lecture, Harvard University, Cambridge, Mass., 21 October 1955).
3. Jeremy Bernstein, "Profiles: Physicist," *New Yorker*, 13 October 1975, 48.
4. I. I. Rabi, "Approaches to the Atomic Age" (Address delivered at the Boston Institute for Religious and Social Studies, Boston, 3 January 1946), reprinted in I. I. Rabi, *Science: The Center of Culture* (New York: World Publishing, 1970), 138–47.
5. Bernstein, "Profiles: Physicist," 50, 53.
6. Rabi, *Science*, 30.
7. Ibid., 33.
8. I. I. Rabi, "Science as a Way of Life" (Speech delivered at Columbia University, New York, 26 September 1950), Rabi private collection; I. I. Rabi, "Man's Right to Knowledge" (Speech delivered at California Institute of Technology, 11 June 1954), Rabi private collection.
9. I. I. Rabi, "Opening Remarks" (Speech delivered at the Fourth International Conference on the Peaceful Uses of Atomic Energy, Geneva, Switzerland, 6 September 1971), Rabi private collection.

ACKNOWLEDGMENTS

The author would like to thank the following people for permission to quote from interviews conducted with them: Robert A. Bacher, Hans Bethe, Felix Bloch, Lee A. DuBridge, Wendell Furry, Polykarp Kusch, Phillip Morrison, William Nierenberg, Frank Oppenheimer, Shirley Quimby, Gertrude Rabi, Helen Rabi, I. I. Rabi, Norman Ramsey, Emilio Segre, Stephen White, and Jerrold Zacharias. I would also like to thank Irving Kaplan and V. W. Cohen for their contributions through conversations I had with them. Complete information for all interviews and conversations can be found in the notes.

Special thanks to I. I. Rabi for permission to use the photographs which appear in the book, to quote from his memoir which is reposited at the William E. Wiener Oral History Library in New York City, and to quote from the following material in the Rabi Private Collection: "Science and the Humanities" (Loeb Lecture, Harvard University, 21 October 1955); "Radiofrequency Spectroscopy" (Richtmyer Lecture, delivered at the joint meeting of the American Physical Society and the American Association of Physics Teachers, New York, 19 January 1945); and "Opening Remarks" (Speech delivered at the Fourth International Conference on the Peaceful Uses of Atomic Energy, Geneva, Switzerland, 6 September 1971).

Grateful acknowledgment is made to the following sources for their permission to reprint:

Song lyrics on pages 167, 185–86, and 187 are from "It Ain't the Money" and "Take Away Your Billion Dollars" by Arthur Roberts. Quoted by permission of the author and copyright owner, Arthur Roberts.

Quoted statements made by I. I. Rabi in Chapter 15 from an on-screen interview, "Our Times with Bill Moyers," 27 June 1983. © CBS Inc. 1983. All rights reserved. Originally broadcast over the CBS Television Network as part of the "Our Times with Bill Moyers" program series.

Interview of Felix Bloch by Charles Weiner, Stanford University, Stanford, California, 15 August 1968. Transcript, Center for History and Philosophy of Physics, Niels Bohr Library, American Institute of Physics, New York City.

Interview of I. I. Rabi by Thomas S. Kuhn, 8 December 1963. Transcript, Niels Bohr Library, American Institute of Physics, New York City.

Interview of Otto Frisch by Thomas S. Kuhn, Cavandish Laboratory, Cambridge, England, 8 May 1962. Transcript, Archive for History of Quantum Physics, copies at American Institute of Physics, New York City.

Interview of Hans Bethe by Charles Weiner and Jagdish Mehra, 27–28 October 1966. Transcript, Center for History and Philosophy of Physics, Niels Bohr Library, American Institute of Physics, New York City.

Interview of Edward M. Purcell by Katherine Sopka, Harvard University, Cambridge,

Massachusetts, 8 June 1977. Transcript, Niels Bohr Library, American Institute of Physics, New York City. Reprinted by permission of Edward M. Purcell and the American Institute of Physics.

Interview of Richard P. Feynman by Charles Weiner, 4 March 1986, Altadina, California. Transcript, Niels Bohr Library, American Institute of Physics, New York City.

Quoted statements made by Frank Press and Leon Lederman in chapter 4 from the *Celebration of the Fiftieth Anniversary of the Pupin Laboratories,* Columbia University. Reprinted by permission of Frank Press and Leon Lederman.

Robert Wayne Seidel, "Physics Research in California: The Rise of a Leading Sector in American Physics" (Ph.D. Dissertation, University of California, Berkeley, 1978).

Polykarp Kusch, "The Magnetic Dipole Movement of the Electron" (unpublished lecture), Kusch Private Collection.

Henry Geurlac (unpublished history of the Radiation Laboratory), M.I.T. Archives.

In addition, grateful acknowledgment is made to I. I. Rabi and the following institutions for their joint permission to reprint material:

William E. Weiner Oral History Library, New York for an interview of I. I. Rabi by Edwin Newman, December 1972.

Oral History Research Office, Columbia University for: Interview of I. I. Rabi by Barbara Land, 12 November 1962. Interview of I. I. Rabi by Morris Krieger, 28 March 1963. Interview of Norman Ramsey by Joan Safford, Harvard University, July 1960.

Finally, I would like to thank the following for permission to quote from their personal letters:

A. W. Browne, letter to Prof. F. Bedell, 14 March 1923, and Ernest Merritt, letter to Prof. William Fox, 18 June 1924. Reprinted by permission of the Department of Physics, Cornell University.

Rockefeller Foundation Officers, letters to I. I. Rabi, 16 January 1969 and 29 January 1969. Reprinted by permission of the Rockefeller Foundation.

George Pegram, letter to I. I. Rabi, 14 May 1929. Rabi Private Collection.

J. M. B. Kellog, letter to I. I. Rabi, November 1947. Rabi Private Collection. Permission granted by Martin Kellog.

Hans Bethe, Letter to I. I. Rabi, 30 September 1937. Rabi Private Collection.

E. P. Ewald, letter to I. I. Rabi, August 1938. Rabi Private Collection.

Edward Condon, letter to Herbert Stuart, 3 April 1940. Rabi Private Collection.

INDEX

NOTE: I. I. Rabi is referred to throughout the index as IIR.

Index

Baruch *(continued)*
sented Acheson-Lilienthal Report to United Nations Atomic Energy Commission, 199

Baruch Plan, *see* Acheson-Lilienthal Report

Battle of Britain, 129

Battle of Coral Sea, 163

Battle of Midway, 163

Battle of the Philippine Sea, 163

Beckler, David Z. (1918–): describes meeting of Eisenhower, IIR, and SAC, 249

Bell, 16

Bell Telephone Laboratories: magnetron demonstrated at, 130; knew microwave technology, 164

Berkner, Lloyd V. (1905–1967), 266

Bernard, Chester I. (1886–1962), 197*n*

Bernardini, Gilberto, 182

Bethe, Hans (1906–), 56, 166, 174, 203, 252, 258, 266; appraised Cornell faculty, 9; calculated rotational magnetic moment, 101; identified three important events in nuclear physics, 113; immigrated from Nazi Germany, 124; visited Germany (1937), 125; on Oppenheimer and IIR, 149, 154, 219; Oppenheimer wanted for Manhattan Project, 153, 217; IIR wanted for Columbia University, 182; visiting professor at Columbia University, 182; opposed hydrogen bomb, 204; quoted, 217; supported Oppenheimer at hearing, 222; on meeting between IIR and Eisenhower, 238; on meeting of SAC after Sputnik, 248, 249

Bhabba, Homi (1909–1966), 242*n;* made president of Conference on Peaceful Uses of Atomic Energy, 243

Bitter, Francis (1902–1967), 15, 52, 65; member of quantum mechanics study group, 42

Bleaney, B., 14

Bloch, Felix (1905–1983), 8, 9, 11, 14; cited in IIR's 1936 paper, 94; immigrated from Nazi Germany, 124; worked at Manhattan Project briefly, 152–153; quit Manhattan Project, 153; song at IIR's Nobel Party, 170; on IIR-Oppenheimer relationship, 218–219

Bloembergen, N., 14, 16

Bloom, 16

Bohr, Aage (1922–), 218

Bohr, Niels (1885–1962), *ix,* 15, 50, 62, 63, 67, 166, 237; applied quantum ideas to question of atomic structure (1913), 46; met IIR in Copenhagen, 58; dismissed IIR to Hamburg, 58–59; senior advisor to Oppenheimer, *x,* 155; announced discovery of nuclear fission, 147; discussed nuclear fission with IIR and Fermi, 147; warned Roosevelt about atomic arms race (1945), 194; opinion of Oppenheimer, 215; met Feynman, 218

Bohr's Institute, *see* Institute for Theoretical Studies

Bohr's model, *see* hydrogen atom

Bomb, atomic: IIR opposed to, 152, 166–67; development of, 154–55; exploded in test, 156; prediction about Russian development of, 201; Russians explode, 201

Bomb, hydrogen: supported by Teller, 200–201, 202; GAC called to consider, 202, 204–5; supported by Lawrence, 202; majority addendum against development of, 204–5; minority addendum by IIR and Fermi against development of, 205–6; Truman overruled GAC recommendation to abort development of, 208; unworkable as first conceived, 209; issue at Oppenheimer hearing, 223–24; IIR on, at hearing, 224

Boot, Henry: developed cavity magnetron with Randall, 130

Born, Max (1882–1970), *ix,* 55, 62, 67; interpreted Schröedinger's wave equation, 53; IIR and Stern visited, 73; declared physics to be over, 73

Bowen, Edward "Taffy": generated radiowaves 1.5m long, 130

Bragg, William Lawrence (1890–1971): measurement of electric susceptibility of Tutton salts interested IIR, 40

Brahe, Tycho de (1546–1601), 245

Breit, Gregory (1899–1981), 3, 6, 11, 175; published paper with IIR on determining nuclear magnetic properties by means of molecular beams, 80; proposed scientific censorship committee during Second World War, 127

Breit-Rabi Theory, 10, 11, 84, 89, 103; exemplified IIR's theoretical expertise, 7; foundation of experimental molecular-beam work, 80

Breslin, Jimmy (1930–), 260

Index

Millman *(continued)*
  magnetic resonance method, 97; worked
  at Columbia Radiation Laboratory, 143
Mitchell, Dana (1899–1966), 149, 149n
Mitscher, Marc, Admiral, 163
Modern Electrics, 26; IIR's first scientific
  paper published in, 27
Molecular beam experiments: Stern-Gerlach, 49, 60, 74; Stern's Hamburg work,
  60, 60–61; IIR in Stern's lab, 61–62; IIR
  enticed by, 71, 74; IIR's Columbia work,
  74–76, 85–122; IIR began lab (1931), 80;
  Breit-Rabi Theory foundation for experimental work in, 80; zero-moment
  method, 88–89; 94; deflecting field
  method, 89–90, 105; refocusing method,
  91–92, 94; reorientation process (Stern
  group), 92; T-field, 92–94, 107; magnetic
  resonance method, 95–98; Stern-Frisch
  experiment, 100–102; Stern-Estermann
  experiment, 102; hydrogen experiments,
  105–9, 110–13; Stern and Rabi results at
  odds, 105–9; dynamical vs. spectroscopic
  modes of conceptualization, 119; radiofrequency spectroscopy method, 121–
  22
Montgomery, Bernard L., General (1887–),
  160
Morris Loeb Lecture, 256–57
Morrison, Philip (1915–): on Oppenheimer, 214, 215, 229–30; on IIR-Oppenheimer relationship, 218
Morse, Philip (1903–1969): needled by IIR to
  make Brookhaven the biggest, 186
Mott, Sir Neville (1905–), 241
Mottelson, Benjamin, 15
Moyers, Bill (1934–): hosted CBS reenact-
  ment of Alamogordo test, 195n; featured
  IIR on television show, 260
Mullikan, Robert (1896–), 3, 7
Murphy, G. M. (1903–1969): discovered deu-
  terium with Urey and Brickwedde, 8

Nafe, John (1914–), 14; discovered intrin-
  sic moment of the electron with IIR and
  Nelson, 171
Nafe-Nelson experiment, 173; described
  173–74; response to, 174–75
National Academy of Sciences, 178
National Aeronautic and Space Adminis-

tration (NASA): created by President's
  Science Advisory Committee, 250
National Defense Research Committee
  (NDRC): established by Roosevelt (1940),
  127
National Research Council: set up scientific
  censorship committee in Second World
  War, 127; proposed by Breit, 127
Nature: IIR published first molecular beam
  paper in, 62
Neddermeyer, Seth (1907–): on Oppen-
  heimer, 221
Nelson, Edward (1916–), 14; discovered
  intrinsic moment of the electron with IIR
  and Nafe, 171
Neumann, John von (1903–1957), 66; de-
  scribed conditions for Jews in Nazi Germany, 124; supported Oppenheimer at
  hearing, 220
Neutron, discovery of, 8, 84
Neutron, magnetic moment of, 106, 108
Newmark, Alexander: worked with Norman Thomas, 70; Helen and IIR stayed
  with, 70
Newmark, Helen, *see* Rabi, Helen Newmark
New York State Regents Scholarship: IIR
  won, 31
New York Times, 170–71, 198
Nierenberg, William (1919–), 14; quoted,
  71
Nishina, Yoshio (1890–1951): sent to Hamburg with IIR, 59; did theoretical work
  with Pauli, 60; colleague of IIR at Hamburg, 62; directed Japanese cyclotrons,
  196
Nixon, Richard (1913–): eliminated
  White House science advisory structure,
  251
Nobel Prize in physics: IIR won, x, 167, 168,
  169–70
Nordheim, L., 15
Nordsieck, A. (1911–), 182
Nuclear fission: discovered (1939), 146; announced by Bohr, 147; discussed by
  Fermi and IIR with regard to bombs, 147;
  isotopes accumulated from Oak Ridge
  and Hanford, 154; *see also* Chain reaction
Nuclear reactors: necessary for modern
  physics, 183; not available at Columbia
  University, 183

Nuclear Test Ban Treaty: groundwork laid by PSAC, 250
Nucleus: discovered by Rutherford, 84

Oersted Medal: IIR won, 72
Office of Naval Research (ONR): commissioned "Rabi Tree," 9–10; worked closely with university physicists after Second World War, 187
Office of Science and Technology Policy, 251
Office of Scientific Research and Development (OSRD), 150; discouraged by technical difficulties on Manhattan Project, 154
Office of Special Assistant to the President for Science and Technology, 250
Operation Overlord: radar used during, 161
Oppenheimer, Frank (1912–1985): Groves sent for, 155; on J. Robert Oppenheimer, 215, 231
Oppenheimer, J. Robert (1904–1967), x, 3, 6, 166, 195n; quoted, 4; discussed with IIR need to make American physics best, 6; European study added depth to physics, 6; combined experimental data with theoretical knowledge, 7; met IIR in Leipzig, 65; led study at University of California, Berkeley, on feasibility of atom bomb, 148; director of Los Alamos laboratory, 148; sought IIR's advice, 148, 154, 216, 255; wanted militarized lab, 149–50, 216; outlined Manhattan Project in letter to Conant, 150–51; persuaded to keep lab civilian, 151; recruited staff, 151; offered IIR position of associate director, 152; wanted Bethe and Bacher, 153; discouraged by technical difficulties, 154; tense as detonation approached, 155; style as director of Manhattan Project, 159; celebrity after Second World War, 164; IIR wanted at Columbia, 181–82; had trouble conveying nature of basic research to Fulbright, 188; projected stages of nuclear bomb development, 195; suggested international control of atomic energy, 195; supported May-Johnson bill, 196; met with IIR to discuss international control of atomic energy, 196–97; presented idea of international control to

Lilienthal group, 197; served on GAC of AEC, 200; wrote Conant about GAC response to Russian atomic bomb, 202–3; discussed upcoming GAC meeting with IIR, 204; opposed development of hydrogen bomb, 204; angered by Truman's decision to build hydrogen bomb, 208; life parallels IIR's, 211–13; as cult figure, 213; contributed to development of theoretical physics, 214; asked to direct studies on nuclear physics, 216; dropped communist connections, 216; wrote IIR on Manhattan Project, 217; wanted IIR at California Institute of Technology, 219–20; director of Institute for Advanced Study, 220; chairman of GAC of AEC, 220; AEC brought twenty-four charges against, 220; angered many people, 221; humiliated Strauss, 221–22; hearing against, 220–28, 240; lied about conversation with Chevalier, 222; accused of subverting hydrogen bomb development, 223; so-called member of ZORC, 223; presented himself poorly at hearing, 227–28; sense of self, 228–29; eschewed Jewishness, 228–29; martyrdom of, 230; obvious president of international conference, 243
Orthodox Hebrew, *see* Religion
Overhauser, A. W., 15

Packard, Martin, 14
Pais, Abraham (1918–): told IIR that Einstein nominated him for Nobel Prize, 177; on Oppenheimer, 215
Pake, George, 14, 15
Particle accelerator: necessary for modern physics, 183; not available at Columbia University, 183
Paul, W., 15
Pauli, Wolfgang (1900–1958), ix, 39, 59, 62, 63, 67, 154; 1925 paper on exclusion principle, 51; reaction to Uncertainty Principle, 55; encounter with Ehrenfest, 59; IIR got better of, 59; became professor at Zurich, 66; postulated nuclear magnetic properties, 78; spoke at Rad Lab seminar series, 165
Pauling, Linus (1901–), 3–4, 6, 7, 56
Pearl Harbor, 139
Pegram, George B. (1876–1958), 58; offered

Index

Index

Rabi *(continued)*

periment, 50; worked with Kronig extending Schröedinger's quantum mechanics, 51–52; discovered answer in Jacobi's work, 52; published paper on symmetric top with Kronig, 52; appointed Barnard Fellow, 55; resigned from CCNY, 55; left for Zurich, 56; left for Munich, 56; calculated magnetic susceptibility of hydrogen molecules, 57; with Sommerfeld group, 57; to BAAS meeting, 57; Helen joined, 57; went to Copenhagen, 58; sent to Hamburg, 58–59; Kronig snubbed, 59; got better of Pauli, 59; worked with Fraser and Taylor, 60; did theoretical work with Pauli, 60; performed first molecular beam experiment in Stern's lab, 61–62; published paper in *Nature* and *Zeitschrift fur Physik*, 62; compared American and European physics, 63; rediscovered America, 64; introduced liveliness to lab, 64; put Dirac's equation into magnetic field, 65; went to Leipzig, 65; met Oppenheimer and Teller, 65; applied quantum mechanics to solids, 65; went to Zurich, 66; offered job at Columbia University at Heisenberg's suggestion, 66, 104, 168; went to New York, 67; introduced quantum mechanics to Columbia curriculum, 68; taught quantum mechanics and statistical mechanics, 69; bored by solid state theory, 70, 72; promoted to assistant professor, 70–72; research overwhelmed teaching, 71–72; won Oersted medal, 72; visited Born with Stern, 73; merged theory and experiment, 74, 83; corresponded with Fraser on molecular beams, 74; believed fundamental physics brings one "nearer to God," 79–80; started seminar group, 80; published paper on determing nuclear magnetic properties with Breit, 80; presented paper on nuclear spin of cesium at APS meeting, 80; conducted deflection experiments with Cohen, 81; tested quantum mechanics, 84–85, 86; relied on intuition, 86, 94; proposed zero-moment method to Millman, 88–89; devised deflecting magnetic field method, 89–90; got support from Pegram, 90; Urey split grant with, 90, 168; developed refocussing method, 91; ran T-field experiments, 92–93; pre-

sented "flopping method" in 1936 paper, 94; 1936 paper cited by Purcell and Bloch independently, 94; 1937 paper theoretical basis for magnetic resonance method, 95; discussed magnetic resonance method with Zacharias, 95; delayed magnetic resonance method, 95–96; visited by Gorter, 96, 120; tested magnetic resonance method with Kusch, Zacharias, Kellogg, Millman, 97; threw party to celebrate success of magentic resonance method, 98; remeasured proton's magnetic moment, 103; began work on hydrogens with Kellogg and Zacharias, 104–9, 110–13; whittled and supplied ideas, 105, 116–17; first experimental result on magnetic moment of proton, 106; second experimental result on magnetic moment of proton, 108; first experimental result on magnetic moment of deuteron, 106; second experimental result on magnetic moment of deuteron, 108; results at odds with Stern's, 105–9; third experiment (using molecular hydrogen) on magnetic moment of proton, 111; third experiment (using molecular hydrogen) on magnetic moment of deuteron, 112; opinion of women physicists, 116; approach to physics, 116–18; played tricks with nuclear spins, 118; preferred resonance method to spectroscopy, 118–19; visiting professor at Institute of Advanced Study, 121; argued over title of paper, 122; conducted spectroscopic studies on lithium and potassium, 122–23; presented paper at AAAS meeting, 123; awarded prize for paper, 123; received news and letters about German Nazification, 124–25; discussed European war with Zacharias, 126, 132; attended MIT Conference on Applied Nuclear Physics, 131–32; attended radar meetings at Algonquin Club, 132; left Columbia for MIT Radiation Laboratory, 132, 134; toured for Sigma Psi, 133; recuited for MIT Rad Lab, 133; volunteered for Rad Lab, 134; began work on magnetron at Rad Lab, 134; pushed for shorter wavelengths, 137–38; head of Research Division, 140; worked closely with military, 141; kept work dedicated to winning war, 143; nonresident director of Columbia Radiation Lab-

Index